Animal Cognition

COGNITION Special Issues

The titles in this series are paperback, readily accessible special issues of *COGNITION: An International Journal of Cognitive Science*, edited by Jacques Mehler and produced by special agreement with Elsevier Science Publishers B.V.

VISUAL COGNITION, Steven Pinker, guest editor

THE ONSET OF LITERACY: Cognitive Processes in Reading Acquisition, Paul Bertelson, guest editor

SPOKEN WORD RECOGNITION, Uli H. Frauenfelder and Lorraine Komisarjevsky Tyler, guest editors

CONNECTIONS AND SYMBOLS, Steven Pinker and Jacques Mehler, guest editors

NEUROBIOLOGY OF COGNITION, Peter D. Eimas and Albert M. Galaburda, guest editors

ANIMAL COGNITION, C. R. Gallistel, guest editor

Animal Cognition

edited by

C. R. GALLISTEL

A Bradford Book
The MIT Press
Cambridge, Massachusetts
London, England

First MIT Press edition, 1992

Reprinted from *Cognition: International Journal of Cognitive Science,* Volume 37, Numbers 1–2, 1990. The MIT Press has exclusive license to sell this English-language book edition throughout the world.

Printed and bound in the Netherlands. This book is printed on acid-free paper.

Library of Congress Cataloging-in-Publication Data

Animal cognition / edited by C.R. Gallistel. — 1st MIT Press ed.
   p.   cm. — (Cognition special issues)
"A Bradford book."
Includes bibliographical references and index.
ISBN 0-262-57089-0
  1. Cognition in animals. I. Gallistel, C. R., 1941–   . II. Series.
QL785.A7 1992
591.5'1—dc20   91-19890
                                             CIP

Contents

Animal Cognition

Cognition, 37 (1990) 1–22   **1**

Representations in animal cognition: An introduction

C.R. GALLISTEL*

UCLA

Gallistel, C.R., 1990. Representations in animal cognition: An introduction. Cognition, 37:1–22.

Representations

Over the last decade, questions about representations have come to the fore in the literature on animal learning and cognition. The papers in this special issue show the central role this concept now plays. They review contemporary experimental findings regarding animal representations of space (Gould); time, number, and rate (Church & Gibbon); the properties of experienced stimuli and experienced relations between stimuli (Holland); the categorization of natural and artificial stimuli (Herrnstein); and social relations among conspecifics (Cheney & Seyfarth). In each case, the central problem is to derive from behavioral data the nature of the representations that underlie behavior.

The concept of a representation

The concept of representation, what representations are, whether they exist, and what role the concept of a representation should play in theories of animal and human behavior are controversial topics. I have argued (Gallistel, 1989, 1990) that representation should have the same meaning in psychology as it has in mathematics, where it means a functioning isomorphism between systems. The isomorphism (formal correspondence) between the two systems makes it possible to use operations in one system to draw conclusions about the other, as when algebraic operations are used to draw geometric conclusions in analytic geometry.

By analogy, a representation in psychology is a functioning isomorphism between processes within the brain or mind (depending on the level of

---

*Reprint requests should be sent to C.R. Gallistel, Psychology Department, UCLA, 405 Hilgard Avenue, Los Angeles, CA 90024, U.S.A.

0010-0277/90/$6.80

analysis) and an aspect of the environment to which those processes adapt the animal's behavior. More formally, a representation exists if:

(1) There is a mapping from external entities or events (temporal intervals, numerosities of sets, rates of food occurrence, shapes of patterns, chemical characteristics of foods, members of a matrilineal family within a monkey group, and so on) to mental or neural variables that serve as representatives of those entities.

(2) There is a formal correspondence between relational and combinatorial operations involving these neural or mental variables and relations and combinatorial processes involving the things denoted by them. An example would be a correspondence between the brain's processing of neural signals denoting two different observed rates of food occurrence and the concurrent operation in the world of the two processes. If the rate of food occurrence when the two processes operate concurrently is the sum of the rates generated by each process operating alone and if the brain combines the two rate-representing signals additively in computing the rate expected during concurrent operation, then there is a formal correspondence between the process of concurrent functioning (a combinatorial process in the represented system) and the additive combination of the relevant variables within the nervous system (a combinatorial process within the representing system).

(3) The mapping processes and the combinatorial processes are together such that the combinatorial processes in the representing system generate valid anticipations of events and relations in the represented system. The outcomes of operations in a brain module predict or anticipate the outcome or state of processes and relations in a system external to that module.

(4) The capacity of the neural or mental operations to generate generally correct anticipations of external events and relations is exploited by the mechanisms that generate behavior adapted to those events and relations. In other words, the formal correspondence between mind or brain processes and world processes serves a biological purpose.

Those familiar with the theory of measurement, as developed initially by Stevens (1946) and more recently by Krantz, Luce, Suppes, and Tversky (1971), will recognize the parallel between this use of representation and its use in measurement theory, where the principal task is to establish the necessary and sufficient empirical conditions for the existence of an isomorphism between a to-be-measured psychological variable (e.g., loudness) and some or all of the number field. The isomorphism depends on finding a suitable measurement procedure (scale), which maps from the psychological variable to numerical representatives thereof, and on the existence of a formal correspondence between combinatorial operations on the psychological variables (as manifest in, for example, "louder than" judgments) and numerical operations such as ">", "+", and "=". This correspondence permits one to draw valid inferences about the psychological variables from mathematical operations on their suitably determined numerical representatives.

It is inherent in this definition of representation that representations come in varying degrees of richness or power, as do scales of measurement. The richness or power of a representation is determined by the variety of the combinatorial operations that may be employed to draw valid conclusions about the represented system. In a maximally impoverished representation, such as a nominal scale, only one operation may be validly employed. In the case of a nominal scale, this is the identity operator (=). When one uses a nominal scale (for example, the numbers on athletic jerseys), represented entities (players) are one and the same if and only if they have the same representative (same number). In more powerful representations, interrelated combinatorial operations may be employed. If one has attained a ratio scale representation of some psychological variable such as perceived heaviness, then the entire number field may be employed ($\geq$, $+$, $*$) to draw valid conclusions about the numerically represented variable, as when one concludes that a given weight will be perceived as more than twice as heavy as two other given weights combined.

The combinatorial operations in the representing system need not be isomorphic to the arithmetic operations of the number field. The combinatorial operations may apply to, for example, tree structures or nested categories, rather than to numbers.

It is important to distinguish between a representative and a representation. A representative is a symbol in the representing system denoting an entity, or the value of a variable, or a relation between variables in the represented system. Mental or neural representatives exist when there is a stable mapping from world variables to mental or neural variables. Roughly speaking, the study of sensory processes is the study of the mapping of low-order physical variables to their low-level psychophysical or neural representatives – for example, the study of the mapping of spectral composition to activity in the transducer channels (psychophysical level of analysis) or to cone activities (neural level). The study of perception is the study of the mapping of high-order stimulus variables – for example, object shape – to high-level mental or neural representatives, such as the locus of activity in a cortical field thought to code for shape.

The existence of neural representatives does not establish the existence of a neural representation. To show, for example, that the activity in some cortical region varies in an orderly way with the numerosities of sets does not establish that the brain represents numerosity. A representation is a relation between systems, not between variables. Both the represented system and the representing system are composed of variables, relations between variables, and processes or operations involving the variables. In order for a representation to exist, the neural or mental representatives of environmental variables must enter into combinatorial neural or mental processes that generate valid inferences about the represented variables.

Making the concept of a mental or neural representation depend on the demonstration of a mapping from world variables to mental or neural variables and on a formal correspondence between operations in the two domains may seem unduly restrictive. It means that the concept does not apply, at least not strictly, in cases where one cannot give a suitable formal characterization of the aspect of reality that is thought to be represented psychologically. There is, for example, no characterization of spectral composition – the physical variable in color vision – that corresponds to the formal characterization of our hue perceptions (the color circle). Relations between perceived hues have no counterpart in the stimuli that generate them. Metameric color matches are lights of different spectral composition that produce identical mental representatives. Metameric matches are ubiquitous; color television and color printing depend on them because neither of these media reproduces the correct spectra of the surfaces shown; they routinely "fool the eye". Thus, even the identity operator cannot validly be employed with our hue percepts. Color is in the mind not in the world, and, conversely, spectral composition, which is in the world, is not represented in the mind.

I would argue, however, that the mathematical definition of representation is conceptually useful even when applied in the many domains where we cannot yet formally characterize what it is about the world that we believe is captured by some mental model. The elaboration of the mental model (the psychological theory) and the formal characterization of what is modeled are interdependent enterprises, as is evident to anyone who has followed the interaction between the theory of syntax in linguistics – the formal characterization of the structure of language – and theories of language production and comprehension in psychology.

Comments on the papers

The papers in this issue are instructive from the standpoint of the proposed definition of representations because some of them deal with domains where the relevant physical reality has a well-established formal characterization (the domains of time and space) while others deal with domains where we are far from having such a characterization (the domains of natural kinds and social interactions).

Gibbon and Church

The proposed definition of representation applies straightforwardly to the work of John Gibbon, Russell Church and their collaborators, most notably Warren Meck and Seth Roberts, on the representation of temporal intervals and the variety of roles that this representation plays in animal behavior. This work began with the seminal paper of Gibbon (1977), building on earlier work by Killeen (1975). It has been extensively reviewed by several chapters in Gibbon and Allan (1984) and by Gallistel (1990). Few stories in experimental psychology equal this one in the rigor and thoroughness with which a formal model of the underlying psychological processes has been elaborated and in the precision and completeness with which the model accounts for an extensive body of data from a variety of experimental paradigms.

Gibbon and Church begin with a brief discussion of the many roles that the representation of temporal intervals may be expected to play in the foraging behavior of animals. (For more in this line, see a recent paper by Gill (1988) on the complex role that the memory for temporal intervals plays in the foraging behavior of the humming bird.) They go on to review a new experimental paradigm, inspired by foraging considerations, and to develop a trenchant analysis of trial to trial covariations in the onset and offset of responding and the implications of these variations for models of the underlying decision process. This work is illustrative of the many insights that they have derived from their careful attention to sources of variance in the decision processes underlying behavior that depends on remembered temporal intervals.

It is hard to see how one could account for the data on temporal discrimination in animals with a theory in which there were no variables in the animal nervous system whose values were related in a systematic way to the experienced duration of temporal intervals. Thus, the data on temporal discriminations in animals are evidence for a mapping from temporal intervals to mental/neural representatives thereof. More importantly, Gibbon and Church's careful theoretical and experimental attention to the decision processes in timing behavior has provided about as compelling evidence as it is within the power of behavioral data to provide that common laboratory birds and mammals have representations of temporal intervals in the sense here advocated. They perform with representatives of temporal intervals operations isomorphic to subtraction, division and comparison ($\geq$), in order to draw valid inferences about the current state of the world.

For example, in the experiment by Brunner reviewed in Gibbon and Church's paper, as in several of their previous experiments (e.g., Gibbon & Church, 1981), the experimental data are fit by a model in which the decision process computes the difference between an elapsing interval and a remembered standard, divides this difference by the value of the standard, and tests whether the quotient exceeds the decision threshold. The model with this decision rule accounts for these and other data with impressive precision, while other models do not. Unless someone can produce an equally successful account of the experimental findings that does not involve the subtraction, division and comparison of variables that are representatives of temporal intervals, these findings are evidence that the animals possess a representation of temporal intervals in the mathematical sense of representation. The system of psychological operations on psychological variables is isomorphic to the temporal system.

Church and Broadbent

This paper compares and contrasts a new connectionist model of an animal's temporal representation with the earlier nonconnectionist model of Gibbon (1977). It is a valuable contribution to the controversy regarding the merits of connectionist versus nonconnectionist models of mental and neural processing, in part because the predictions of the model are matched against real experimental data instead of against the schematic "data" that many connectionist models have sought to account for.

Advocates of the connectionist approach to psychological theory building have championed conflicting views about representations. One school of thought – the "subsymbolic" school – maintains that connectionist approaches reveal the intellectual bankruptcy of the long-standing, but always controversial view that the mind or brain represents reality in any meaningful sense (Churchland, 1989; Smolensky, 1986). According to the subsymbolic view, there are no identifiable representatives (symbols) of real-world entities or variables in the associative network that mediates mental function. A fortiori, there are no combinatorial or relational operations performed on these nonexistent mental entities (no symbol processing). It is not clear how the anti-representational version of connectionism might apply to the analysis of timing behavior. It would seem to require that we dispense with the idea that there are representatives of temporal duration in the brains of these animals despite their success at matching their behavior to the varying intervals they experience (in, for example, the peak procedure).

On the other hand, many adherents of connectionism are committed to exploring how parallel distributed networks might represent and process symbolic variables. This school does believe in mappings from real-world variables to identifiable, albeit physically distributed representatives of those variables, and it does believe that network processes involving these distributed representations are isomorphic to (model) corresponding processes in the represented domain. Church and Broadbent fall in with this latter, representationist school of connectionist thought. Their paper provides an illustration of what a temporal representation might look like if the brain operates in the manner envisioned by connectionists.

The connectionist model they propose differs computationally from the information-processing model in the comparison operation. In their model, the similarity between the currently elapsing interval and the remembered reference interval is represented by the cosine of the angle between the two vectors that represent these two intervals, while in the information-processing model the similarity (actually the dissimilarity) is represented by the arithmetic difference between the two quantities that represent the two intervals. These two measures of similarity/dissimilarity are not isomorphic; hence it ought to be possible to decide between the models on the basis of a careful comparison of their quantitative predictions.

Connectionist models will need to stand or fall on their relative success or lack of success at accounting for the behavioral data, since the often-made claim that they have greater neurobiological plausibility will not withstand serious examination. The relation of connectionist assumptions to the well-established, clearly understood aspects of neurophysiological functioning is at the level of a cartoon or metaphor. The conceptual gap between our understanding of neurophysiological processes and our understanding of the mental operations underlying learned behavior is so great that it is a delusion to imagine that the neurophysiological understanding places interesting constraints on psychological theories.

In general, the components required by any well-specified psychological theory can be realized by some speculative neurophysiological model just as plausibly or implausibly as the components required by any other. In their ingenious derivation of binary time vectors from biological oscillators, Church and Broadbent willy-nilly show how to create the neurobiological analog of the chain of flip-flops used to represent number and time in computers and modern watches. A binary counter is the sort of component that one expects to find in an information-processing model, the kind of model that is supposedly not neurobiologically plausible.

We do not yet understand how the nervous system implements elementary computational operations, such as the multiplication of two variables. Nonetheless, an operation isomorphic to multiplication is assumed in every formally specified psychological theory with which I am familiar. The weighting operation in connectionist modelling is an instance of the multiplication of variables. When we do not understand how simple multiplication is implemented at the neurophysiological level, it is hard to see how we can imagine that what we understand about the nervous system constrains computational theories of behavior.

Our increasing understanding of how the entities and processes postulated in classical genetics are realized by molecular entities and processes has promoted a radical change in our conception of the sophistication and complexity of chemical processes at the molecular level. The concept of chemical processes that "read" the message encoded in the structure of a single molecule was foreign to conventional chemical thinking in the early 1950s on the eve of the revolution triggered by Watson and Crick, as was the concept of a machine-like single-protein molecule with many functionally distinct components whose conformation changed repeatedly in order to carry out some complex function such as the uptake and release of oxygen, the pumping of ions across membranes, or the transduction of photon absorptions into changes in membrane polarization. When we celebrate the progress of molecular biology over the last four decades we should be thankful that the classical geneticists who elaborated the basic concepts on which this progress rested did not allow themselves to be constrained by what was plausible within the context of the conventional chemical thinking of their time.

It is true that there is at present no known neurobiological process with the properties required of the accumulator in Gibbon and Church's information-processing model of the timing process, but the existence of a neural mechanism with the capacity to integrate a signal with respect to time over long intervals is implied by behavioral data on phenomena as diverse as timing behavior, the vestibulo-ocular reflex (Robinson, 1989), and dead reckoning (Müller & Wehner, 1988). The neural realization of the temporal integration process implied by these diverse behavioral data is neither more nor less mysterious at present than was the chemical realization of the gene in 1940. The physical characteristics required for the long-term temporal integration that underlies dead reckoning (or path integration) in animal navigation are those of an ideal information storage element; hence, solving the neurobiological mystery posed by the evidence for long-term temporal integration may reveal the secret of information storage in the nervous system, revealing the physical basis of memory (see Gallistel, 1990, Chapter 16).

Gould

Gould's paper reviews his work on two closely related questions about the ability of bees to represent the geometry of two-dimensional visual patterns and three-dimensional spaces. His work and the work of others (e.g., Beusekom, 1948; Cartwright & Collett, 1983, 1981; Cheng, Collett, Pickhard, & Wehner, 1987; Collett & Land, 1975; Tinbergen & Kruyt, 1938; Wehner, 1981) establish that insects use the geometric relations between a goal and the landmarks surrounding it to direct their movements toward the goal.

They recognize the landmarks from widely different angles of view, and they recognize similarities in two- and three-dimensional shape in a manner that seems to rule out any kind of simple template matching. Bees and ants (Cosens & Toussaint, 1985), at least, also have some kind of record of the large-scale structure of the environment within which they forage and this "map" enables them to orient toward diverse goals from diverse positions in their foraging territory.

Geometry is the formal characterization of spatial relations. The existence of this formal characterization of the represented system makes possible the straightforward application of the definition of spatial representation here advocated. To say that an insect represents the spatial structure of its environment or some aspect thereof is to say that there is a mapping from elements of this structure to representatives thereof in the nervous system of the insect and that the insect nervous system performs operations on these representatives that are isomorphic to operations on the spatial configurations they represent. The fact that bees readily learn to discriminate two-dimensional patterns would seem to imply a mapping from these patterns to representatives in the nervous system and the use of at least an identity operator.

The question whether these representatives are pictorial (images) or not can be formulated as a question about what classes of geometric relations in the pattern are preserved by the mapping, that is, by the process of pattern perception and pattern memory. The claim that the mapping is pictorial is, I believe, equivalent to the claim that the neural representative of the pattern preserves the metric geometric relations that determine the shape of an object in the Euclidean plane. Implicit in most feature-list models of pattern perception is the assumption that the feature list does not preserve all the Euclidean relations. The mental or neural representative of the pattern is impoverished in that some of the geometric relations between elements of the pattern are not represented (cannot be recovered from the code).

It is tempting to imagine that the record of a two-dimensional pattern in a "simple" creature like a bee does not preserve the metric relations among the pattern elements, the distances and angles that define the shape of the pattern in the ordinary sense of the term shape, because these relations are not preserved in the projection of the pattern onto the retina. If they are coded in the mental representative of the pattern, then they must be recovered from the initial receptor-level representative of the visual image by an operation equivalent to the inversion of the projection from the plane of the pattern onto the roughly spherical surface of the retina.

The question whether an animal has a cognitive map of its environment can also be reformulated within a geometric framework (Cheng, 1986; Cheng & Gallistel, 1984). Many insects, in common with many other animals, find goals by means of remembered geométric relations between the goal and surrounding landmarks (for review, see Gallistel, 1990). The question is, what kinds of geometric relations are represented and what kinds of operations can be performed to infer other relations from the primary (directly encoded) relations?

A map represents the shape of an environment. Shape, as it is ordinarily understood, is defined by the relative metric positions of the surfaces that compose the environment. Relative metric positions determine the angles formed by surfaces and the distances along and between surfaces – and vice versa. Thus, one way to pose the question whether an animal has a map is to ask whether it represents metric relations between a goal and the surrounding landmarks. If it does not, then it does not represent the shape of the environment in the ordinary sense of shape. However, Cartwright and Collett (1983) have shown that bees record the compass bearings of the landmarks near a food source (an angular relation) and Cheng, et al. (1987) have shown that, given landmarks at different distances from a food source but of the same shape and apparent size, bees rely more on the nearer landmark, implying that they also record the distance between the landmarks and the source. In short, bees record metric relations between goals and surrounding landmarks, which is what they must do if they are to have a map of the environment and the positions of their goals within that environment.

The distances of the landmarks from the source may be estimated by parallax – by the change in the visual angle for a given lateral displacement of the bee (Cartwright & Collett, 1979; Kirchner & Srinivasan, 1989; Srinivasan, Lehrer, Zhang, & Horridge, 1989). The importance of parallax in estimating distances may explain the zig-zag flight pattern that a bee or a wasp makes on approaching and leaving a food source or its nest (Wehner, 1981). The zig-zag flight pattern may be similar in function to the side-to-side peering motion that a locust makes before jumping to a target (Collett, 1978; Wallace, 1959) and to the vertical head-bobs that a gerbil makes before jumping across a gap (Ellard, Goodale, & Timney, 1984). Sobel (1989) used artificially induced variations in parallax to show that the locust's take-off velocity is a function of the parallax motion of the target during its pre-jump peering. The monotonic function relating horizontal take-off velocity to the distance to be jumped was reproduced using a target at a fixed distance moved laterally during the locust's peering to produce the requisite parallax.

The estimation of distance from parallax may play a central role in the construction of maps at all scales because this mechanism is suited to the quantitative determination of arbitrarily large distances in any mobile animal capable of monitoring the distance through which it has moved. The greater the distance to be estimated, the greater the lateral displacement required to estimate it with a given degree of accuracy by parallax. The construction of a map also requires that one combine distance and angle estimates made from different points of observation. To do this, the moving animal must record the metric relation between different points along its course.

There is a substantial literature showing that a variety of animals from ants to bats keep track of their current position by dead-reckoning or path integration, that is, by neural operations at least crudely analogous to the integration of their velocity with respect to time (e.g., Wehner & Srinivasan, 1981). Dead-reckoning may provide the estimate of displacement distance (or velocity) required in the parallax estimation of long distances and it may provide the information about the relative metric positions of different points of observation required in the construction of a geocentric map. Gallistel (1990) spells out the computations required to combine position and heading information from the dead-reckoning module with object distance and angle information from perceptual modules (like the module for computing distance from parallax) to generate a geocentric metric map.

The displacement experiments reviewed by Gould are the most sophisticated in a sequence dating back to Romanes (1885), showing that displaced bees can set a fairly direct ("beeline") course for the hive, provided they are released within familiar territory. Janzen (1971) showed that the wide-ranging orchid bees in Costa Rica come home from an experimenter-chosen release site as much as 20 km from the hive. Gould's experiments are noteworthy for their elaborate controls and for the fact that in some conditions the displaced bees departed for goals other than the hive. His results suggest that bees can compute the compass course they should follow from their estimate of their current position on their map and their estimate of the position of their goal – an instance of a combinatorial operation involving two representatives of metric position.

Perhaps the most intriguing experiments that Gould reports are those showing that bees being recruited by the dance of a returning forager tend to ignore foragers that signal nectar in an "impossible" place like the middle of a lake. This suggests that bees integrate representatives of radically different stimulus properties acquired at different times and by different modes (direct observation vs. the dance of a returning forager) by means of spatial addresses, that is, by means of the position assigned to the distal source – its putative location on the cognitive map. Gallistel (1990) has speculated that the use of the spatiotemporal addresses of recorded stimulus properties is the key to the general problem of integrating the diversely experienced and analyzed properties of one and the same stimulus (the problem of feature integration, cf. Treisman, 1986; Treisman & Gelade, 1980).

As this issue was going to press, a review by Wehner and Menzel (1990) appeared in which they report displacement experiments somewhat like Gould's. In these experiments, the bees did not depart on appropriately corrected courses after they were displaced, rather they departed on the course they would have taken had they not been displaced. This leads Wehner and Menzel to question Gould's conclusion that the bee uses a map.

Obviously, further experimentation is required to determine the conditions that yield Gould's result and the conditions that yield the Wehner and Menzel result. However, some features of the Wehner and Menzel results suggest the use of a map. In particular, they found that on overcast days when the sun could not be used to determine a compass course, their bees oriented by reference to the terrain, so that the results on overcast days were similar to the results on sunny days. They suggest that this finding is analogous to Dyer and Gould's (1981) finding that bee's learn the course of the sun's azimuth relative to the landmark panorama surrounding the hive so that on overcast days the dance of a returning forager indicates the momentary solar heading of a source even when neither the dancer nor the interpreters of the dance have seen the sun all day. Gallistel (1990) has argued that the Dyer and Gould result is strong evidence that the bees have a large-scale geocentric Euclidean map of their foraging terrain. Wehner and Menzel's (1990) finding that bees can orient by reference to their foraging terrain even after displacement strengthens this conclusion.

Wehner and Menzel suggest that bees locate themselves by means of dead-reckoning and by reference to images of the terrain. They favor a model of the kind proposed by Collett and Cartwright (1983) and Cartwright and Collett (1983) in which bees and ants store "something akin to a two-dimensional snapshot of the landmarks [around the goal] ... [and they] continuously compare this remembered snapshot with their current retinal image and move so as to reduce the discrepancy between the two" (Wehner & Menzel, 1990: 404). When Cartwright and Collett (1983) conducted computer simulations of models of this kind, they found that it was not easy to make them work, nor were they computationally simple. To make their final model work they had to assume "that the bee is equipped with a mechanism that [maintains the retinal snapshot in the correct orientation], but no attempt has been made to enlarge upon how the mechanism might work" (Cartwright & Collett, 1983). In other words, it has yet to be convincingly shown that this kind of model can be made to work.

Cartwright and Collett (1983) apparently did not deal with the case in which the goal lay within the array of landmarks, although one of their experiments used a goal located in the center of a 50-cm square array of four landmarks (4 × 40 cm black cylinders). The difficulty of pairing the retinal

Figure 1.   *Illustration of the difficulties that confront navigational schemes that rely on two-dimensional retinal "snapshots" (or eidetic images) of the landmark configuration surrounding a goal. The diagram at top is a plan of the four-cylinder array (a,b,c,d) used by Cartwright and Collett (1983) in one of their experiments with bees. The cylinders are 4 cm in diameter and 40 cm tall. (A) The retinal image of the array when the bee is on the ground at G headed north (straight up on the plan). This snapshot could equally as well result from the array a',b',c',d' in the diagram at top (with cylinders 8 × 80 cm) and from an infinity of other arrays. (B) The retinal image of the a,b,c,d array when the bee is on the ground headed north at p. (C) The retinal image of the a',b',c',d' array from the same vantage point. The image comparison process must be able to match both B and C (and an infinity of other wildly differing images) to A. How this is to be accomplished is far from clear. On the other hand, if the bee computes the three-dimensional Euclidean shapes of the arrays from both vantage points (using parallax mechanisms to get the distances), the comparison of the resulting uniquely determined three-dimensional arrays is straightforward.*

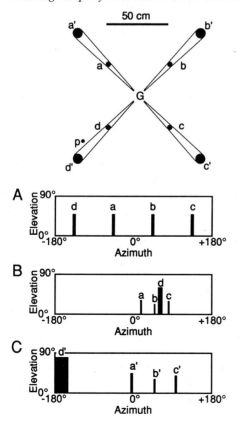

image when the array is seen from a point outside an array of landmarks with a snapshot taken when the bee is at the goal inside the array is shown in Figure 1. Figure 1 is meant to suggest that the intuition that algorithms based on the matching of two-dimensional images are computationally simpler than algorithms based on the computation of three-dimensional structure is probably not well founded. The computationally simplest way to recognize that the landmarks seen from a remote vantage point are the landmarks seen from the goal may be to compute the three-dimensional shape of the landmark array and compare this to the previously computed shape residing in memory. The computation of the three-dimensional shape of the environment is, of course, synonymous with the computation of a cognitive map. It must be emphasized that the experiments of Cartwright and Collett (1983) and Cheng et al. (1987) have shown that bees record the compass bearings of landmarks and the distances to them, which are the essential data in a record of the Euclidean relation between the goal and the shape defined by the landmarks. It must further be emphasized that the dead-reckoning process provides the required data on the geocentric relations between the animal's positions and headings at different vantage points. Thus, it has been experimentally demonstrated that the perceptual and dead-reckoning systems of the bee between them provide the data required to construct a geocentric Euclidean cognitive map. Computing such a map is the hard part. Using it is computationally straightforward, at least as straightforward as using two-dimensional images.

Holland

Representational questions have also become central in the study of classical conditioning, as experimental findings have steadily eroded the simple temporal-pairing models of classical conditioning that dominate textbook presentations of the subject and research on the cellular basis of learning. It has been shown that temporal pairing is neither necessary nor sufficient for the formation of an association in classical conditioning (Rescorla, 1988), so contemporary research focuses not so much on establishing the laws of association as on the question of what kinds of relations between stimulus events can be learned. To a first approximation, it has been shown that when there is any nonrandom temporal relation between conditioned stimulus (CS) occurrence and unconditioned stimulus (US) occurrence that would enable the animal to predict US occurrence or nonoccurrence from information about the time of CS occurrence, then the rat and the pigeon learn this predictive relation (Kaplan, 1984), provided that US occurrence is not better predicted by some other variable (Kamin, 1969; Wagner, Logan, Haberlandt, & Price, 1968). This suggests that the proper formal characterization of the represented system in classical conditioning is in terms of the statistics of multivariate time series analysis. Gallistel (1990) develops a model of the conditioning process based on these assumptions.

Recently, Matzel, Held, and Miller (1988) did an interesting experiment along these lines. They first taught rats that the onset of a tone was followed 5 s later by the onset of a light. Note that, historically, this has been called sensory preconditioning, because both stimuli have traditionally been regarded as CSs, not USs. In fact, it is impossible to say which is the CS and which the US. However we label this phase, the authors then taught the rats that the onset of shock occurred 5 s before the onset of light. (This usually is called backward conditioning, because the CS (the light) comes after the US (the shock).) When the authors tested whether the rat reacted fearfully to the backwardly conditioned light, they observed no reaction (no conditioned emotional response), which is what traditional models of the conditioning process would lead one to expect (no backward conditioning). When, however, they tested the rat's reaction to the tone, they did observe a fearful reaction. From their experience that the tone leads the light by 5 s and their experience that the light lags the shock by 5 s, the rats apparently deduced the approximate coincidence of tone and shock.

The Matzel et al. result is evidence that in classical conditioning rats learn the temporal intervals separating stimuli, a conclusion that is not surprising in the light of the work of Gibbon, Church and their collaborators. It is also evidence for combinatorial operations in the brain. The rats can combine representatives of two such intervals to get a representative of a third interval that they have not experienced. Their anticipatory behavior is based on this computationally derived third representative, the representative of the expected interval between tone and shock. This is consistent with the evidence from the experimental paradigms of Church and Gibbon and their collaborators that the brains of rats and pigeons add, subtract and divide the representatives of temporal intervals. It takes us a long way from the traditional conception of an association.

In order to represent relations between stimuli, the brain must have representatives of those stimuli themselves. Holland's work addresses itself primarily to the question, what properties of the stimuli experienced in classical conditioning are preserved in the record of these experiences and can these representatives of stimulus properties enter into combinatorial operations? His experiments make a strong case that a representative for the US is generated in the course of conditioning and that this representative includes a specification of the US flavor. The subsequent activation (or accessing) of the representative of the US's flavor also activates (accesses) an experience-dependent hedonic evaluation of that flavor.

The application of the mathematical definition of representation in this domain is seriously impeded by the absence of a formal characterization of the structural-chemical property of a substance that corresponds to or determines its experienced flavor. Given the diversity of chemicals that produce the same taste, it seems likely that flavor will prove to be analogous to color in that it will not correspond to any readily specifiable physical attribute of a substance. Hence, the formal correspondence between the mental processing of flavors and chemical combinatorics is apt to be very limited.

Nonetheless Holland's experiments give surprising evidence of some combinatorial processing of flavors. His experiments 2 and 3 show the compounding of the different flavor tokens evoked by two different CSs and a response to the compound that is opposite in character from the response to the constituents. This result is reminiscent of the results of an experiment by Church and Meck (1984). Rats were taught to press the left lever when they either heard two sounds or saw two flashes of light and to press the right lever when they heard or saw four sounds or flashes. When they were tested with the simultaneous presentation of two sounds and two flashes, they chose the right ("four") lever. The compound produced a different choice of lever from either of its constituents. When the rats were presented with one flash and one sound, they chose the right ("two") lever, so simultaneous presentation per se did not favor a choice of either lever. In short, the response to the combined presentations of two separately trained CSs was based on the additive combination of their representatives, not on the additive combination of the learned responses to these inputs. Similarly, the responses in Holland's experiments are based on the flavor representative generated by combining the representatives of the training flavors, not on the responses to the training flavors.

Herrnstein

In Herrnstein's review, an issue that surfaced briefly in the Gould and Holland papers becomes the center of focus – the categories of representatives for a complex stimulus and how these categories may be organized. Here, it is extremely unclear what the appropriate formal description of the external reality might be. Nonetheless, I believe the mathematical notion of a representation can help clarify some central issues.

In discussions of categories and concepts, it helps to keep clearly in mind the distinction between the mappings from the represented entity to its representatives and operations on those representatives. A category is a representative of a number of distinguishable entities that are treated as equivalent in some context (for some set of operations). Numbers are prototypic instances of categories; the number three represents all those otherwise wildly divergent sets whose numerosity is three. It may be used in operations designed to draw inferences about those sets only in a context where their numerosity is the relevant variable. There are two radically different ways to define a category. One is to give a rule (intensive definition) or list (extensive definition) that identifies all the things the representative of that category validly denotes. For example, the number three validly refers to all sets that may be placed in one–one correspondence with an abstract reference set constructed for the purpose of testing for threeness. This way of defining three focuses on the mapping process from numerosities to their representatives. It says nothing about the roles those representatives play in any inferential system. The other way to define a category is to specify the role it plays in a system. Three is the integer that comes immediately after two and immediately before four, the first prime greater than one, the sum of the first two integers, the difference between five and two, and so on. This approach to defining a category (or concept) makes no reference to what the representative validly denotes. The truths of arithmetic are inherent in the system of arithmetic, not in the domains that system may be used to represent. When a category is defined in this way, we are more apt to speak of it as a concept.

Experiments reviewed by Herrnstein show that when a pigeon is reinforced for responding to a few exemplars of some natural kind, such as trees, it treats novel exemplars of that category as predictive of reinforcement, even though it can be shown by reinforcing only some of the tree photos and not others that the pigeon readily distinguishes between the exemplars. (Thus, photos of trees are not like metameric color stimuli that have identical, hence indistinguishable mental representatives.) The analyses he reviews indicate that the conditioning occurs at the category level rather than at the level of the individual exemplars in that novel exemplars are responded to at all stages of conditioning as readily as exemplars used previously to instantiate the category that is reinforced.

It would seem that pigeons already have or readily form a category for many of these natural kinds. We might think of categories as the volumes enclosed by a bounding surface in a multidimensional descriptive space. A mental or neural descriptive space is a space whose dimensions correspond to dimensions that describe objects. It appears that the cortex is composed of such spaces in that foci of activity in different cortical fields define the values of a stimulus along various descriptive dimensions. If the pigeon has innate categories for some or all of these natural kinds, then these bounding surfaces are pre-existent and what the pigeon does in the course of conditioning is identify the volume into which the predictors of reinforcement reliably map. Alternatively, the pigeon may have interpolative algorithms for generating surfaces that enclose constellations of experienced points, in which case it constructs a category (a volume enclosed by a bounding surface, such as a cortical region) on the basis of the points it experiences. In either case, it does not follow that the pigeon has any nontrivial concept of tree, by which I mean a system of inferential operations in which a representative of the category tree (a tree symbol) plays a role. The kinds of experiments Herrnstein reviews do not test for the existence of a system that makes inferences about these natural categories; they only test the mapping process. They do, however, reveal a mapping process of remarkable subtlety. They call attention to how little we understand about how the brain generates representatives of complex stimuli such as trees, and water, and landscapes, or, to use Pavlov's terminology, how little we understand about the cortical "analyzers" that the brain applies to natural stimuli.

Cheney and Seyfarth

The observations and experiments reviewed by Cheney and Seyfarth suggest that the brain of the vervet monkey maps from conspecifics into categories of conspecifics (member of my troop, relative, close associate, etc.) and that the representatives of these categories enter into an inferential processing system that takes consanguinity and dominance into account. Here again, the central question has to do with the richness of the representation underlying the monkey's social behavior. In order to address this question, one must first have a formal description of the reality that the monkeys may represent: what are the rules of the game of monkey social life? An interesting portion of the Cheney and Seyfarth paper deals with the objectively confirmable facts, such as that relatives or close associates of one party to a quarrel often pursue the quarrel later by attacking relatives or close associates of the other party. They then turn to their ingenious experiments designed to test to what extent this behavior is controlled by a representation of the rules of the game and the different categories of players to which those rules apply.

In their introduction, they give an interesting example of a very limited representation and its behavioral consequences – the ant's representation of a conspecific corpse. It appears that the only property of a corpse that is preserved in the ant's representative of a conspecific corpse is its odor, the odor of oleic acid. It also appears that the behavior-generating processes that are triggered by this input do not test for any other properties of the object: if it smells of oleic acid, they remove it, period. Thus, we have strong reasons for believing that an ant's concept of a corpse does not correspond at all to our own. The mapping from stimulus to its mental representative is greatly impoverished and there is no combinatorial processing remotely resembling those that we engage in when reacting to death. By contrast, the representations that underlie monkey social behavior appear to be considerably richer. This does not, of course, mean that these representations are isomorphic to the representations that underlie our own social behavior, which is why we must be cautious in applying rich labels like "son of" or "cousin of" to the representations we impute to monkeys.

While, on the one hand, we must be cautious in imposing our own social categories and our own conception of the principles that govern social intercourse on our analyses of the social behavior of other species, we must, on the other hand, also be wary of our tendency to ignore the complexity and subtlety of these social interactions, the central role that social life plays in the biology of some group-living primates, canids, and birds, and the likely demands that this aspect of their biology makes on their representational capacities. The complexity and fluidity of the categorization and inference structures that may underlie the ability of a vervet monkey to find its niche in the group and pass its genes on to a significant fraction of the next generation tends to defeat our own capacity for formal analysis and to enhance the appeal of simple-minded explanations of what are in fact complex phenomena. Part of the importance of sustained observation of free-living monkey groups is that it has revealed predictable regularities in their social interactions, particularly in the patterns of behavior associated with kinship and dominance rank. These regularities are reviewed briefly in the contribution by Cheney and Seyfarth and more extensively in several chapters in the volume on *Primate societies* edited by Smuts, Cheney, Seyfarth, Wrangham, & Struhsaker (1987).

Central to the Cheney and Seyfarth paper is their analysis of the extent to which these interactions can be explained by schemes that rely only on associative bonds between the mental representatives of individuals in the troops. The strength of these associations would be expected to be a function of how frequently the individuals were observed together, hence one is tempted to explain the various manifestations of alliance-like behavior as based simply on relative strengths of associations rather than on some more elaborate categorization process (just as the associative tradition has generally tried to treat categories as associative clusters). Cheney and Seyfarth give reasons to think that the categorization of individuals as relatives or close associates rests on many features of the individuals involved (sex, age, birth history) other than the simple frequency with which they are seen together and that the subtlety of the behavioral use made of these categories indicates a kind of internal computation that transcends what is ordinarily thought of as the reflex-like translation of associative bonds into stereotyped reactions.

The interest that the representation of social relations holds for the more general study of mental reputations is that the computational structure of a social representation would seem to be very different from the arithmetic structure that is appropriate in the analysis of time, space, number, and rate. One is led to ask, what are the computational primitives appropriate to the representation of social structure? In a recent thought-provoking analysis of what he claims are the four basic modes for organizing human social inter-changes, Fiske (in press) has argued that these modes in fact correspond to the different scale types, which in turn are distinguished by the extent to which the different arithmetic operators may be validly applied. Thus, oper-ations isomorphic to arithmetic operations may be important even in the social domain.

References

Beusekom, G.v. (1948). Some experiments on the optical orientation in *Philanthus triangulum* Fabr. *Be-haviour, 1*, 195–225.

Cartwright, B.A., & Collett, T.S. (1979). How honey bees know their distance from a nearby visual landmark. *Journal of Experimental Biology, 82*, 367–372.

Cartwright, B.A., & Collett, T.S. (1983). Landmark learning in bees: Experiments and models. *Journal of Comparative Physiology, 151*, 521–543.

Cartwright, B.A., & Collett, T.S. (1987). Landmark maps for honey bees. *Biological Cybernetics, 57*, 85–93.

Cheng, K. (1986). A purely geometric module in the rat's spatial representation. *Cognition, 23*, 149–178.

Cheng, K., Collett, T.S., Pickhard, A., & Wehner, R. (1987). The use of visual landmarks by honey bees: Bees weight landmarks according to their distance from the goal. *Journal of Comparative Physiology, 161*, 469–475.

Cheng, K., & Gallistel, C.R. (1984). Testing the geometric power of an animal's spatial representation. In H.L. Roitblatt, T.G. Bever, & H.S. Terrace (Eds.), *Animal cognition* (pp. 409–423). Hillsdale, NJ: Lawrence Erlbaum Associates.

Church, R.M., & Meck, W.H. (1984). The numerical attribute of stimuli. In H.L. Roitblatt, T.G. Bever, & H.S. Terrace (Eds.), *Animal cognition* (pp. 445–464). Hillsdale, NJ: Lawrence Erlbaum Associates.

Churchland, P. (1989). A neurocomputational perspective: The nature of mind and the structure of science. Cambridge, MA: MIT Press.

Collett, T.S. (1978). Peering: A locust behavior for obtaining motion parallax information. *Journal of Experi-mental Biology, 76*, 237–241.

Collett, T.S., & Cartwright, B.A. (1983). Eidetic images in insects: Their role in navigation. *Trends in Neuroscience, 6*, 101–105.

Collett, T.S., & Land, M.F. (1975). Visual spatial memory in a hoverfly. *Journal of Comparative Physiology, 100*, 59–84.

Cosens, D., & Toussaint, N. (1985). An experimental study of the foraging strategy of the wood ant *Formica aquilonia*. *Animal Behaviour, 33*, 541–552.

Dyer, F.C., & Gould, J.L. (1981). Honey bee orientation: A backup system for cloudy days. *Science, 214*, 1041–1042.

Ellard, C.G., Goodale, M.A., & Timney, B. (1984). Distance estimation in the Mongolian gerbil: The role of dynamic depth cues. *Behavioural Brain Research, 14*, 29–39.

Fiske, A. (in press). Structures of social life: The four elementary forms of human relations. New York: Free Press (Macmillan).

Gallistel, C.R. (1989). Animal cognition: The representation of space, time and number. *Annual Review of Psychology, 40*, 155–189.

Gallistel, C.R. (1990). *The organization of learning.* Cambridge, MA: Bradford Books/MIT Press.

Gibbon, J. (1977). Scalar expectancy theory and Weber's law in animal timing. *Psychological Review, 84*, 279–335.

Gibbon, J., & Allan, L. (1984). *Timing and time perception* (p. 654). New York: New York Academy of Sciences.

Gibbon, J., & Church, R.M. (1981). Time left: Linear versus logarithmic subjective time. *Journal of Experimental Psychology: Animal Behavior Processes, 7*, 87–107.

Gill, F.B. (1988). Trapline foraging by hermit hummingbirds: Competition for an undefended renewable resource. *Ecology, 69*, 1933–1942.

Janzen, D.H. (1971). Euglossine bees as long-distance pollinators of tropical plants. *Science, 171*, 203–205.

Kamin, L.J. (1969). Predictability, surprise, attention, and conditioning. In B.A. Campbell & R.M. Church (Eds.), *Punishment and aversive behavior* (pp. 276–296). New York: Appleton-Century-Crofts.

Kaplan, P. (1984). Importance of relative temporal parameters in trace autoshaping: From excitation to inhibition. *Journal of Experimental Psychology: Animal Behavior Processes, 10*, 113–126.

Killeen, P. (1975). On the temporal control of behavior. *Psychological Review, 82*, 89–115.

Kirchner, W.H., & Srinivasan, M.V. (1989). Freely flying honey bees use image motion to estimate object distance. *Die Naturwissenschaften, 76*, 281–282.

Krantz, D., Luce, R.D., Suppes, P., & Tversky, A. (1971). *The foundations of measurement.* New York: Academic Press.

Matzel, L.D., Held, F.P., & Miller, R.R. (1988). Information and expression of simultaneous and backward associations: Implications for contiguity theory. *Learning and Motivation, 19*, 317–344.

Meck, W.H., & Church, R.M. (1984). Simultaneous temporal processing. *Journal of Experimental Psychology: Animal Behavior Processes, 10*, 1–29.

Müller, M., & Wehner, R. (1988). Path integration in desert ants, *Cataglyphis fortis, 85*, 5287–5290.

Smuts, B., Cheney, D.L., Seyfarth, R.M., Wrangham, T.T., & Struhsaker, T.T. (1987). *Primate societies.* Chicago: University of Chicago Press.

Rescorla, R.A. (1988). Pavlovian conditioning: It's not what you think it is. *American Psychologist, 43*, 151–160.

Robinson, D.A. (1989). Integrating with neurons. *Annual Review of Neuroscience, 12*, 33–46.

Romanes, G.J. (1885). Homing faculty of Hymenoptera. *Nature, 32*, 630.

Smolensky, P. (1986). Information processing in dynamical systems: Foundations of harmony theory. In D.E. Rumelhart, & J.L. McClelland (Eds.), *Parallel distributed processing: Foundations* (pp. 194–281). Cambridge, MA: MIT Press.

Sobel, E. (1990). Depth perception by motion parallax and paradoxical parallax in the locust. *Die Naturwissenschaften, 77*, 241–243.

Srinivasan, M.V., Lehrer, M., Zhang, S.W., & Horridge, G.A. (1989). How honey bees measure their distance from objects of unknown size. *Journal of Comparative Physiology A., 165*, 605–613.

Stevens, S.S. (1946). On the theory of scales of measurement. *Science, 103*, 677–680.

Tinbergen, N., & Kruyt, W. (1938). Über die Orientierung des Bienenwolfes (*Philanthus triangulum* Fabr.). III. Die Bevorzugung bestimmter Wegmarken. *Zeitschrift für vergleichende Physiologie, 25*, 292–334.

Treisman, A. (1986). Properties, parts, and objects. In K. Boff, L. Kaufman, & J. Thomas (Eds.), *Handbook of perception and human performance* (Vol. II). New York: Wiley.

Treisman, A., & Gelade, G. (1980). A feature integration theory of attention. *Cognitive Psychology, 12*, 97–136.

Wagner, A.R., Logan, F.A., Haberlandt, K., & Price, T. (1968). Stimulus selection in animal discrimination learning. *Journal of Experimental Psychology, 76*, 171–180.

Wallace, G.K. (1959). Visual scanning in the desert locust *Schistocera gregaria* Foskål. *Journal of Experimental Biology, 36*, 512–525.

Wehner, R. (1981). Spatial vision in arthropods. In H. Autrum (Ed.), *Comparative physiology and evolution of vision in invertebrates* (pp. 287–617). New York: Springer.

Wehner, R., & Menzel, R. (1990). Do insects have cognitive maps? *Annual Review of Neuroscience, 13*, 403–414.

Wehner, R., & Srinivasan, M.V. (1981). Searching behavior of desert ants, genus *Cataglyphis* (Formicidae, Hymenoptera). *Journal of Comparative Physiology, 142*, 315–338.

Cognition, 37 (1990) 23–54

Representation of time

JOHN GIBBON*

New York State Psychiatric Institute and Columbia University

RUSSELL M. CHURCH

Brown University

Abstract

Gibbon, J., and Church, R.M., 1990. Representation of time. Cognition, 37: 23–54.

Memory representation for time was studied in two settings. First, an analysis of timing in a laboratory analog of a foraging situation revealed that departure times from a patchy resource followed a Weber Law-like property implied by scalar timing. A trial-by-trial analysis was then pursued in a similar but more structured experimental paradigm, the Peak procedure. Study of covariance structures in the data implicated scalar variance in the memory for time as well as in the decision process, but the correlation pattern ruled out multiple access to memory within a trial.

> Time present and time past
> Are both perhaps present in time future,
> And time future contained in time past.
> T.S. Eliot, *Burnt Norton.*

Introduction

Eliot's words remind us that our current position on the arrow of time, fixed on the present instant, has been prefigured in the past, and in turn foreshadows what is to come. There is a sense in which the life of any living thing is continuously timed, from its genetically prescribed beginning into its programmed senescence.

On a smaller, one might say fractal, scale all movement is timed, some-

---

Reprint requests should be sent to John Gibbon, Department of Biopsychology, New York State Psychiatric Institute, 722 West 168th Street, New York, NY 10032, U.S.A.

times with exquisite precision, as when the batter starts his swing, the musician his downstroke, or the peregrine folds its wings and dives. These are but some more dramatic examples of prefiguring a future event with precisions that are extraordinary. In a broader sense, however, we continuously prefigure future events. Any movement entails a representation of a future event, its anticipated outcome, and of course no system of the body is ever entirely at rest.

Much temporal anticipation is rhythmic: activity/rest cycles, respiration cycles, heartbeats, even our speech patterns, reflect rhythms that may repeat endlessly, or sometimes at will. Once initiated, each shows a characteristic period and variability. Periodicity of this sort may be represented in our nervous system in the time constants of a collection of oscillating neurons. Most such rhythmic timing systems exhibit remarkable precision, but little flexibility in the range of times represented. Evolution has built them for essentially one time value, and they often execute this value with precisions of 1–2% or less. Several circadian rhythms, for example, are in this class, with low variability and an entrainment range of a few hours around 24 (cf. Aschoff, 1984).

Some rhythmic timing systems, however, can synchronize with a variety of temporal values in the environment, for example when a musician changes tempo, or when a horse adjusts its gait. Timing functions of this sort usually are in the seconds, or possibly minutes, range, and they may be begun at any arbitrary point in time, and reset arbitrarily. Such rhythms have received some study in humans (e.g., Wing, 1980; Wing & Kristofferson, 1973), and almost none in animals. These timing systems share features with the more rigid and precise biological oscillators mentioned above, as well as with the more arbitrary interval timers, described below.

This, most flexible, kind of timing allows arbitrary onsets for beginning of a timed interval, arbitrary records for the time of important events in the interval, and discriminations among past and present time intervals. Such a system is exemplified by the one that allows foragers, including human hunter-gatherers, to adjust their food-search strategies to changing, usually depleting, resources. The representation of times like these – intervals that may take on a variety of values requiring different sorts of behavioral adjustments, are the topic of this paper. These timing functions are wonderfully flexible: they may begin virtually at will, reset virtually at will, and time a broad range of target values, from seconds to minutes or perhaps even hours. Interval timing functions pay for their flexibility with imprecision. Evolution cannot tune them for a given target value, but must build in record-keeping systems and temporal readout systems, which can assume a range of values and forms.

Representation is going to mean for us here a rather abstract conception of some semi-permanent feature of these timing functions. We will not be so concrete as to specify neural mechanisms, nor so abstract as to specify complete and rigorous mathematical development. Rather, our representations will be memories lying somewhere between the cell and the theorem. We will ask what kind of mnemonic variability and subjective scale are implied by memory for arbitrary time intervals.

Perhaps unfortunately, we must approach these questions through still another construct, harboring its own vagaries, namely the performance, including especially a decision structure, that reveals properties of temporal memory. It will be a major aim, then, to partition variance we see in performance into components reflecting differing features of temporal processing. In particular, our interest centers on three sets of processes: (1) the mechanism whereby animals perceive the passage of time – the clock system; (2) processes whereby a given time value is marked, distinguished and recorded in memory; and finally (3) the way in which decisions based on these temporal memories are made. We will identify features of temporally organized performances which differentially reflect imprecision in these three basic components of timing – clock, memory, and decision.

An example: Foragers' giving-up times

Let us be concrete. A starling in the springtime forages for food in fields round about its nest ("central place" foraging). The pressure to forage efficiently, and thereby collect the greatest yield per unit time, is extreme when birds are feeding their young. Evolution has tuned their timing system so that they can recognize productive as opposed to unproductive fields ("patches"), and also to recognize when such patches are depleted – when to search for richer pickings. The optimal time for such a new search may be shown to depend critically on how long it took to travel to the patch in the first place, as well as on the initial prey density, and the depletion rate (e.g., Krebs & Kacelnik, 1984).

A performance like this requires at least two different kinds of time records, that is, two representations. First, birds must know how long it takes to get to a given area from the nest site. To forage optimally, they should stop foraging in a given patch at different overall residence times, depending on how far away the path is from the nest. When the patch is distant, persistence in the patch pays better than when the patch is close. Intuitively, the investment in a longer travel must be made up by a greater yield. Second, they must have an appreciation of when a patch is no longer productive. The decision to leave may depend on variability in the perception of prey density. If the patch is initially rich, and depletes fast, detection of depletion may be easier. Subjects may stay a shorter time after finding the last prey item in a rapidly depleting patch, than if the initial prey density was lean, and capture rates low.

Our example will examine an extreme case, the appreciation of a given prey density which has abruptly soured. We ask when birds "think" an expected prey item is no longer forthcoming. If rate of food capture is represented as a typical interval between feedings, at what point after that interval has been exceeded do subjects no longer expect food? We will attempt first to understand the mechanism for the simplest of these cases, strict periodicity, in which there is no variability in interfood delivery times.

The data we present are from the dissertation research of Danielle Brunner in collaboration with Alex Kacelnik and John Gibbon (Brunner, Kacelnik, & Gibbon, 1989; Kacelnik, Brunner, & Gibbon, 1988).

Brunner simplified the foraging problem to study it in the laboratory in the following manner: Starlings were required to fly a certain distance (comprising the "travel" or "search" time) by completing a number of flights between two perches in a large chamber. When the ratio was completed, a "patch key" was illuminated above a third perch, at which they could earn food on a given schedule. The schedule is the analog of the "patch". It is a repeating, periodic fixed-interval schedule, which at some point "dies". After arrival at the perch, the next feeding was scheduled a standard time (FI = S s), with probability p. After food occurred, the next feeding was scheduled at the same standard, S s later, again with probability p. If a feeding was missed, with probability $q = 1 - p$, then all subsequent feedings for that visit to the patch were cancelled. Thus a string of 0, 1, 2, 3, ..., n feedings occurred with a geometrically declining probability in any one patch visit.

The patch could be reset only by leaving and again flying between the two travel perches. As soon as subjects left the patch perch, its key darkened. Interest centered on the properties of the giving-up time, defined as the time between the last feeding (or arrival at the patch) and departure to resume travel. Brunner studied these giving-up times for several weeks at six different fixed-interval values, ranging in log steps from $S = 0.86$ s to $S = 25.6$ s between feedings.

If subjects appreciated the size of the fixed-interval with perfect accuracy, then an optimal forager would leave the patch the moment it is clear that no more food is coming. And this should happen just after S s from the last feeding. Of course, a little variability in the representation of the time interval, and a tight criterion for leaving would result in occasional missed feedings when subjects in fact left before the next delivery time. Hence a conservative strategy would be to wait somewhat longer than the expected feeding time to avoid missing a programmed feeding. And when the fixed-interval schedule is long, and memory for it is correspondingly more variable, one might expect the margin of safety, the duration of the overshoot experienced before leaving, also to be long.

Figure 1. *Relative frequency distributions of giving-up times at six different standard values. Inset shows mean and standard deviation of giving-up times as a function of the standard. The straight lines are regression fits to each data set.*

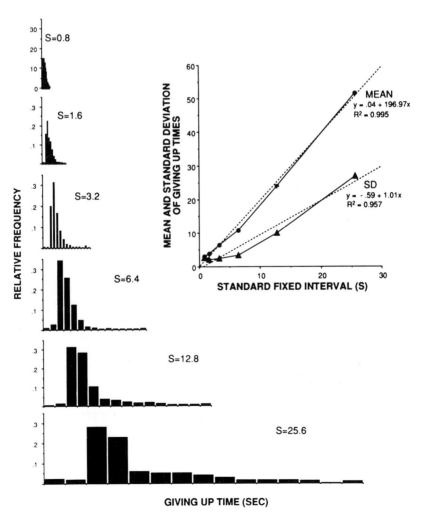

This is indeed what occurred. Figure 1 presents distributions of giving-up times pooled over 6 subjects at each of the 6 fixed-interval values. The scheduled feedings occur at the beginning of the third time bin, so that times to the left of this value (two left-most bars) are departures before subjects could "know" whether the next feeding was scheduled or not. The distributions have some skew, and are rather peaked with a modal giving-up time which moves further to the right of S as S grows. The distributions also flatten somewhat at the longer fixed-interval values. In the inset we plot the mean and standard deviation of these distributions as a function of the standard FI value. Both are relatively linear, especially at the longer time values. The very small intercept in the mean function makes it nearly proportional to real time. This means, most importantly, that birds are, on average, leaving the patch when a given proportion of time beyond the standard has been passed: they leave at about twice the standard time after the last feeding. The standard deviation function appears to level off as the FI value becomes smaller and smaller, perhaps approaching some minimum variance level for this timing system.

Scalar timing: Giving-up times

The distributions for the longer FI values, like many others in the literature, exhibit a property we have called the scalar property: they are approximately scale transforms, one of another. This property may be revealed by replotting these distributions as a function of the giving-up time divided by the fixed-interval standard. This is done in Figure 2. The three longest S values are shown with histogram bars, while the three shorter S values are indicated with connected points. Notice first that the proportion of "missed" opportunities, represented by the leftmost two categories, are low and roughly constant for the three long standards. The modal category for these distributions is the third, in which reinforcement is obtained. The decline on the right shows some skew, and is roughly comparable for these three standards. In contrast, the connected point distributions show a mode in the category to the right of reinforcement, and an increased spread with *decreasing* FI value. This is the reflection, noted above, of some minimal variance in temporal processing shown in the flat portion of the standard deviation curve in Figure 1. This irreducible component of variance has greater relative impact as scalar variance grows small.

Figure 2.   *Distributions of giving-up times (Figure 1) plotted in time relative to the standard.*

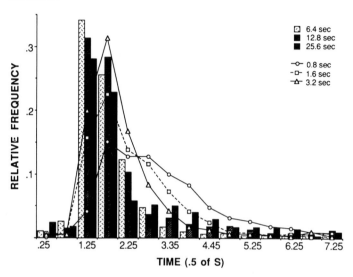

Memory variance

We have argued that these data reflect the scalar property, but it is not obvious just how giving-up times are tied to a scalar representation of the reinforcement interval. The simplest proposal for variance in subjective representation is shown in Figure 3. In the top panel, two distributions associated with two different standards are shown, with mean and standard deviation function below. The distributions may be thought of as errors in the representation that possess the scalar property in its simplest form: the proportion of errors below a given proportion of the interval is constant for any size interval – the result of scalar multiplication of the entire distribution. The standard deviation is proportional to the mean, so the coefficient of variation, the sensitivity of the system (usually represented by $\gamma = \sigma/\mu$) is constant. These assumptions are discussed in considerable quantitative detail elsewhere (Church & Gibbon, 1982; Gibbon, 1981; Gibbon & Church, 1981).

Brunner has adapted this memory representation to a threshold model for giving-up times. In Figure 4 the left-hand ordinate shows subjective time increasing as a linear function of real time, and a memory distribution around the subjective representation of the standard is indicated there. The decision to give up is based on the relative discrepancy between the perceived subjective duration of the currently elapsing interval, and the memory for the rein-

Figure 3.   *Hypothetical distributions of subjective time associated with one and two units of real time. The distributions possess the scalar property with mean and standard deviation proportional to real time.*

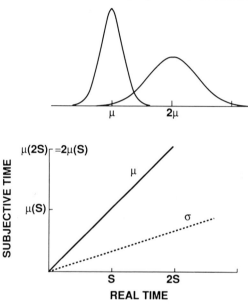

Figure 4.   *Threshold model for giving up time distributions associated with variable memory and fixed threshold (adapted from Brunner et al., 1989).*

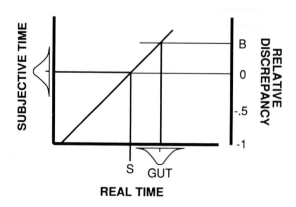

forced standard duration. This is the difference between the current and remembered times, divided by the remembered time. Subjects leave the patch when the elapsed time since the last feeding exceeds some fraction beyond the expected time to the next feeding. Formally, the giving up time rule is:

$$(t - s)/s \geq b, \tag{1}$$

where t is the current time since the last feeding, s is the remembered time to the next feeding, the subjective value corresponding to S in real time, and b is the threshold. (We adopt the convention that lower-case letters represent random variables and upper-case letters fixed values. For example, in the figure the threshold is represented at the fixed value, B.)

The relative discrepancy between the expected delivery time and the perceived current time is shown on the right-hand ordinate of the figure. This measure begins at -1, when the time since the last feeding is zero, and increases through zero when the time since the last feeding equals the remembered time to the next feeding. A departure decision occurs when the relative discrepancy crosses some positive threshold level beyond the expected time of food.

It is readily shown that a giving-up rule based on relative discrepancy will generate superposition of the giving-up time distributions as long as memory variance for the standard is scalar. It is also true, however, that a scalar memory representation alone is not sufficient to produce superposition. The rule for generating giving-up times must be based on relative rather than absolute discrepancy. If the proximity between current and remembered time is not normed by remembered time, the scalar property is violated. For a larger standard, an absolute discrepancy rule would result in a mean giving-up time relatively closer to S, but with a concomitant increase in variance so that a larger proportion of giving-up times would occur before S had elapsed. That is, such a system would produce a great many underestimates or "too short" errors as S is increased. In fact, subjects keep the proportion of these errors about the same, and lengthen the mean giving-up time linearly with the size of the standard.

An absolute discrepancy rule would be unlikely in any case, since it would have to entail an extremely small margin of error above S to accommodate the range of standards used here, and not involve missing more than one reinforcer. An alternative way to say this is that if subjects are guided by the amount of potential reinforcement missed, then the way to keep this at a minimum is to use a relative rule. Such a rule ensures that missing only one feeding when the standard is large does not result in missing many when the standard is small.

Comparator variance

We argue, then, here as previously, that a relative comparator rule (equation (1)) is required for performance of this sort. Subjects must remember what the appropriate food delivery time is, and compare that memory with the current elapsed time in a manner that permits a given proportional, rather than absolute, discrepancy to be detected. Equivalently,

$$t \geq (1 + b)s. \tag{2}$$

In this form it is clear that when there is no variance in the appreciation of the current time ($t \equiv T$), scalar variance in memory for S would directly translate (via the proportional constant, $1 + b$) into scalar variance in the giving-up time distribution. This is illustrated in Figure 4. Varying the memory shifts the relative discrepancy (right ordinate) zero point, and thus also the time at which the threshold is met.

In the above form (2), however, it is clear that variable giving-up times might be produced by another source as well. Variance in the threshold, b, since it multiplies S, also would generate scalar giving-up time variance. This is illustrated in Figure 5, which depicts no variance in the memory for the target time, but variance in the threshold, b, around a mean, B.

Figure 5.   *Distribution of giving-up times associated with threshold variance, but no memory variance.*

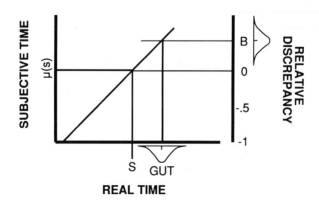

Current time variance

It is equally clear from equation (2) that one might ascribe all variability in giving-up time to the percept of the current time, t, rather than memory or threshold. For such a mechanism to be realistic, one would require that the translation of a reinforced current time into memory for the standard include an averaging mechanism, so that the noisy percept would vary from trial to trial, while the remembered (mean) value would not.

Figure 6 shows a system in which the accumulation of subjective time as a function of real time drifts from trial to trial. The representation of the remembered reinforced time, S, is now fixed on the subjective scale $[\mu(S)]$ and the threshold is fixed on the discrepancy scale (B). Variability in the giving-up time distribution on the abscissa is induced solely by changes in the rate of accumulation of subjective time. Examples in which the current time appreciates faster than usual (higher slope line), or slower than usual (lower slope line), are indicated in the figure, and would correspond to early or late giving-up times in the abscissa distribution.

Skew

This process translates symmetry in variability in the appreciation of current time (in this example normality in the rate of the clock) into asymmetry in the giving-up time distributions represented on the abscissa (an inverse Gaussian form). It is imported to recognize that the scalar property is pre-

Figure 6. *Distribution of giving-up times associated with accumulator rate variance. Note the induced skew.*

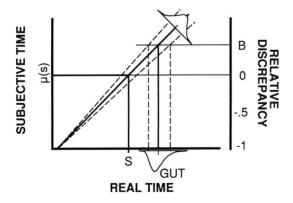

served in a system like this, even though skew is introduced into the performance measure. When rate varies as shown in Figure 6, more variation occurs for long times than for short times, but the scalar property evident in Figure 2 is still satisfied.

Since the data show some skew, there is a question whether they are better described by clock rate variance than memory or threshold variance. In general, we will argue that discriminations based on distribution shape alone are not strong inferences. There are at least three ways in which skew may be induced. First, rate may indeed vary symmetrically, inducing skew as in Figure 6. Second, as is evident from Figures 4 and 5, the shape of a memory-variance-only or threshold-variance-only distribution is translated directly into giving-up times, hence skew in the memory or in the threshold distributions also would translate into skew in the giving-up time distribution.

While it is often attractive to assume the action of many factors contributing to variability in laying down memories or in establishing a threshold, and hence normality at some level in these processes, it is equally likely that sub-components of these systems multiply rather than add, which brings us to a third reason for the weakness of inferences based on skew.

The third reason is that it is also readily demonstrated that symmetric normals acting multiplicatively generate a skewed product random variable (cf. Gibbon, Church, & Meck, 1984). Therefore, were *both* memory and decision variance operating in the giving-up time performance, the right side of equation (2) requires that these act multiplicatively, thus inducing some skew in the resultant giving-up time distribution. To compound this problem, note that multiplicative variance with right skew in either or both of the variates alone is enhanced in the product. For all of these reasons skew in a performance variable such as that seen in Figure 2, and indeed in many latency phenomena from a variety of literatures, is not yet diagnostic of an identifiable source.

Psychophysical problem

We arrive then at a classical psychophysical conundrum: which of several sources of influence contribute to performance, and to what extent? We have identified three such sources. We have noted that they produce somewhat differently shaped performance distributions, but we are unable to discriminate on that basis alone how each contributes.

We develop below a technique which discriminates much more powerfully the components of variance in performance based on remembered time. The technique follows in spirit the advance in classical psychophysics provided by obtaining latency as well as probability correct measures. In our context we will provide two measures quite different from latency and probability, but which share the feature that different patterns of these measures implicate different sources of control. The technique requires a trial-by-trial analysis of an alternative timing procedure, the peak procedure. This procedure has received considerable attention in other contexts, and models for peak performance provided the basis of Brunner's adaptation to giving-up times.

We will see that, just as in the analog of foraging, we can identify a giving-up time. We can also identify a "start" time based on expectation of food in the same trial. We will develop tests of trial-by-trial patterns expected when the primary components of variance are either response (comparator) based, or clock or memory based.

The peak procedure: Individual trial analysis

The peak procedure is an extension of an operant fixed-interval schedule to discrete trial, partial reinforcement. It was devised by Catania (1970), and has since been used by Roberts (1981) and others to identify temporal expectation on both sides of a remembered time for food. The technique is simple and elegant. Discrete trials begin with the onset of a cue and terminate sometimes with response-produced food at a given criterion, standard time, S. On other trials, no food is given (peak trials), and the trial signal simply remains present for a long time beyond the food time. This is our reference procedure, and some typical data pooled over four pigeons is shown in Figure 7. The trial signal was the onset of a white key light, food was the delivery of a few seconds of grain, and the peak trials, when no food was given, lasted a minimum of $3S$, plus a random time averaging an additional S s. The data shown here were collected from peak trials from the last 4 days of two 3-week determinations at different standards, $S = 30$ and $S = 50$. Responding rises to a peak near the criterion time for both functions, and declines in a roughly symmetric manner beyond this time. There is a small rise in both peak functions toward the end of the trial which probably reflects anticipation of its termination and the onset of the next trial (Church, Miller, Meck, & Gibbon, submitted). In the bottom panel the scalar property is shown for these data, with superposition of the peak functions when plotted as proportions of the mean. Again, the scalar property (a form of Weber's law in this setting) will be seen to force strong constraints on the kind of variance in percept and memory, and the kind of response rule used to generate performances of this sort.

Figure 7.   *Pooled peak functions for four subjects studied at 30 s and 50 s peak re-*
inforcement times. The upper panel shows absolute rate functions, the lower
panel shows the same functions as proportions of the reinforcement time,
T/S. The lower ordinate has been scaled min. to max.

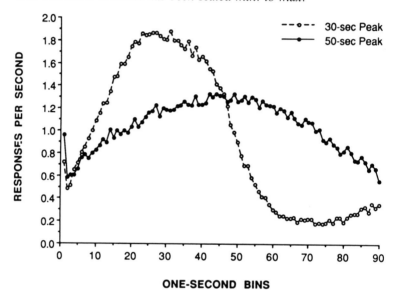

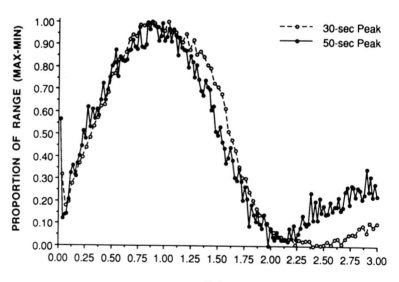

Two states: Break–run–break

The smooth, bell-shaped peak functions we see in this procedure might be achieved in at least two different ways: either with a smooth acceleration and deceleration on every trial, or with a discrete, two-state process, in which responding abruptly changes from a low rate to a high constant rate for a period of time around the time of reinforcement, and then abruptly falls to a low rate again. With variable locations for the high rate on different trials, averaging these discrete, two-state, individual trial functions would produce a smooth curve. This idea is an extension of Schneider's early seminal "break–run" analysis of fixed-interval performance (Schneider, 1969) to a break–run–break pattern appropriate to the peak procedure.

The two possibilities are sketched in Figure 8. Scalar timing theory, from

Figure 8.   *Diagram of two possible alternatives generating smooth peak functions. In the left column the peak function is an average of smooth functions on individual trials. In the right-hand column it is an average of step functions on individual trials that vary in location and spread.*

NUMBER OF RESPONSE STATES

INFINITE   **TWO**

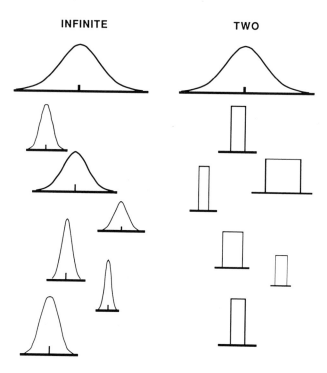

its earliest analysis of this situation (Gibbon, 1977), assumed that the system worked in the two-state manner, but until now we had not tested the implications of this idea.

The smooth curves at the top of the figure might result from smaller, variably located, smooth rate functions as shown on the left, or from variations in start and stop times for a middle portion of the trial, representing a high, constant rate, as shown on the right. The two-state assumption is precisely the kind of assumption embodied in the giving-up time models (Figures 4–6) in that a discrete threshold crossing is associated with a "stop," or giving-up time in the patch, when food is no longer expected. What is added for the peak procedure is that prior to each stop time there is a "start" time as well, when proximity is close enough to the expected time of food to warrant increased responding.

We present below a break–run–break analysis which distinguishes between these two kinds of mechanisms.[1] The analysis is applied to our illustrative data set from the four birds shown in Figure 7.

A least-squares regression program was developed to fit three horizontal line segments to the data from each trial, an extension of Schneider's (1969) "break–run" analysis. It permits us to average rate functions from individual trials when they are lined up so that either the start or stop break points coincide. Rates averaged forward and backward from the break point, both for the transition from low to high (start) and again from high to low (stop), are shown in the top panels of Figure 9. In the upper left panel the start times were lined up before taking the average; in the upper right, the stop times were lined up. The overall peak function is shown for reference in both panels.

The position of the break points were set at their average position across trials. They may be seen to lie near the middle of the rising and falling wings of the average peak function. (The program tends to identify a large difference between adjacent time bins as a break point, and this accounts for the especially low and especially high values just before and just after the high state is entered, and vice versa when it is left.) Once responding has begun at a good clip, however, it remains roughly constant for a period of time.[2] The stop break function in the right-hand panel shows the reverse pattern.

These data in the upper two panels of Figure 9 are to be contrasted with

---

[1]A more complete analysis, including idiosyncratic subject differences and more quantitative detail, is in preparation.

[2]The start break function on the left becomes ragged at the right edge since very few high states last this long, and so the number of observations entering into the average is low for long times. The reverse is true for the stop break function on the right.

Figure 9. *Mean break functions for the start of a two-state process (upper left), and the end, or stop, of the two-state process (upper right). They are positioned at the mean break position for these data. The lower two panels show continuous function simulations of these break patterns using Gaussian curve fits for individual trials. See text for details.*

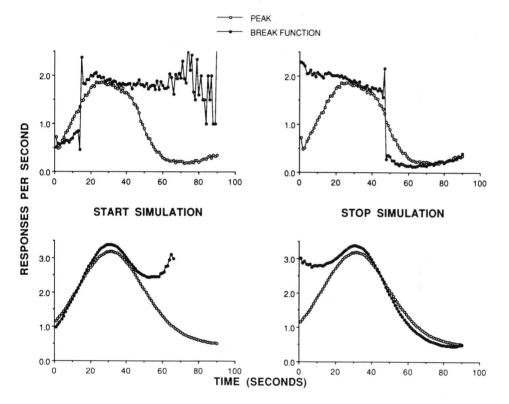

an extreme control analysis shown below. The control simulates smooth trial-by-trial curves like those on the left of Figure 8. The break functions in the lower panels were obtained using the fitting program on artificial "data" curves, which themselves were smooth, bell-shaped functions fit to the real trial-by-trial data. For each real data trial, we first fit a three-parameter bell-shaped curve to the data: a Gaussian error curve with mean, variance, and level as free parameters. We then subjected the Gaussian, not the data, to our break–run–break regression program. Thus this analysis asks whether the break point fitting program, when operating upon smooth continuous functions, produces a different form from that seen in the data.

The results are shown below the real data. The forward and backward average break functions are those with the rising right and left tails. The smooth bell-shaped functions are the overall averages of the Gaussian curves, comparable to the peak functions that would have been obtained if the data themselves were smooth Gaussian curves.

The simulation break functions share some features with the real data, but are clearly different in shape. The start break function shows a smooth rise with no abrupt break, to a peaked middle portion of the curve, unlike the real data. On the other hand, like the real data, beyond the peak the break function falls less steeply than the underlying average peak function. The late rise in the tail is due to the fact that the real data, upon which the Gaussian curves were based, showed considerable variability in location and spread of the high rate portion of each trial. Gaussians with very broad spread contribute predominantly in the right tail of the start break functions. The stop break functions show these same features in mirror image.

To a first approximation, we argue that the break–run–break pattern in the real data shows a two-state character not matched by our continuous simulation. A question currently under study is the degree to which the continuous alternative might approach the flat character of the data as noise is added to the instantaneous levels around a smooth, bell-shaped function.[3]

For our present purposes we will regard Figure 9 as justifying the following examination of patterns in start and stop times obtained through this analysis. We will see that the constraints these patterns place on several different models permit strong inferences about sources of variability contributing to the data.

Scalar timing: Break–run–break

As with giving-up, or stop times, we may define a start time for the peak procedure as that time in the trial at which the (positive) discrepancy crosses threshold before the target time is reached. The stop time is the analogous value, defined just as for giving-up times on the far side of the standard. This defines an absolute value discrepancy rule,

$$|(t - s)/s| \geq b \tag{3}$$

as a generalization of equation (1). The absolute value of the relative discrepancy function has the value 1.0 at the beginning of the trial, decreases linearly

---

[3]In an extreme case, in which the added noise swamps any underlying form in the bell-shaped curves, the break–run–break regression should fit horizontal line segments which do not differ in height, since the break points should then be a random sample from the time continuum.

to zero as time in the trial approaches the reinforced time, and increases linearly beyond this time. The subject starts responding at a high rate when the discrepancy function falls below the threshold, and stops when it rises above the threshold on the far side of the reinforced time. That is, the high rate continues as long as the proximity of the current percept, t, to the target, remembered time, s, is less than the threshold fraction, b, of the target time.

No variance
The absolute value rule is illustrated in Figure 10, which shows the start and stop times associated with fixed values of memory and threshold, and no variance in the accumulation of clock time. The threshold crossing for the start time is shown both for the positive discrepancy, B, on the positive relative discrepancy function at the top, and for a negative threshold, $-B$, on the linear accumulator function for current time. No variance in the timing process results in a step function for response rate beginning at the same start time and ending at the same stop time on every trial (shown on the abscissa).

The smooth, bell-shaped peak functions we observe, of course, require variance in start and stop times, resulting in a variety of step functions which,

Figure 10. *Threshold model for peak functions indicating start and stop times associated with the same threshold, B, and no variance.*

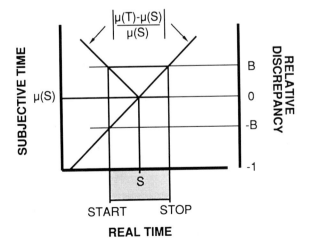

when averaged, produce a smooth curve. However, we have seen that almost any source of variance is compatible with the average data. We will show below that this is not true for covariance patterns of trial-by-trial start and stop times.

The variance sources to be analyzed are just those already considered: memory or clock, and threshold. However, we now analyze cases in which different sources contribute variability simultaneously, and also successively, for the start and stop decision separately. For example, variability might be present in the representation of the target time over successive trials, but remain constant, though in error, within a trial (one sample case). Alternatively, memory might be accessed separately for the start and again for the stop decision within a trial (two-sample case). But the same is true for var-

Table 1. *Nine models*

			Threshold		
			No variance	Variance	
		Number of samples	0	1	2
Memory or clock	No variance	0	1 (0,0)	3 (0,1)	7 (0,2)
	Variance	1	2 (1,0)	4 (1,1)	8 (1,2)
		2	5 (2,0)	6 (2,1)	9 (2,2)

iance in threshold, so that combined with the fixed, no variance (zero sample) case, there are nine combinations, shown in Table 1. While the evaluation of nine different models may seem at first blush a formidable task, we will see that the strength of the correlational analysis is such as to render most of the inferences transparent.

The nine cells are numbered in the order in which the models will be considered. The first, with no variance from either source, $1(0,0)$, is the trivial case just considered (Figure 10), disqualified on the basis of the bell-shaped peak function. The other cases all involve one or more samples of random variables and hence all pass the simple test of the form of the peak function. We begin with memory or clock variance.

$2(1,0)$. Memory or clock variance, no threshold variance

In Figure 11, we reproduce the schematic of Figure 10, but now indicate the kind of peak function produced by introduction of variability in either the memory (left ordinate), or the rate of accumulation of current time (slope). Trials in which memory overestimates the target time result in broader step functions than for underestimates, with the result that peak functions for memory variance show some right skew. But skew is induced by current time (slope) variance also, just as with giving-up times in our earlier analysis. In the figure the two functions lying nearly on top of each other on the lower ordinate represent the predicted shape of the peak func-

Figure 11. *Hypothetical peak functions. The two functions indicated on the abscissa reflect the predictions associated with normal variance in either the memory system (ordinate) or the rate of accumulation (diagonal function). Note the similarity between the functions.*

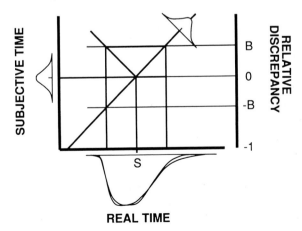

tion implied by variance of equal magnitude operating in either memory or current clock time alone. They have roughly the character of the data (Figure 7), with some skew, and again we will not attempt a discrimination based on shape.

It will be convenient in what follows to assume that the perceived accumulation of subjective time is veridical, proportional to real time, and examine the consequences of memory variance in the trial-by-trial pattern. It should be remembered that while we will speak of memory variance, we mean memory or clock variance, since these have the same trial-by-trial pattern. However, we will be able to draw a strong distinction between variance of any stripe in the memory (or clock) versus variance in threshold or decision processes. The distinctions will be forged by examining the trial-by-trial covariance pattern implicated by these two sources of variability. These patterns are independent of distribution shape.

Over a set of trials, then, start and stop times distribute, with means, variances, and covariances. It is useful to look at the variance/covariance patterns between start and stop, and also two derived measures, the "spread", the duration of the high state between start and stop, and the "middle", the arithmetic center of the high state. Covariance patterns amongst these four descriptors are quantitatively, and, we hope to illustrate intuitively, diagnostic for relative contribution to performance.

If noise in memory for the target reinforced time were the only contributor to variability, a pair of trials might look like those shown in the discrepancy diagram in Figure 12. (Recall that we are assuming proportionality in the clock, and hence variability in remembered time results in variance in the target value at which the discrepancy on the ordinate in Figure 12 is zero.) In this example, trial 1 has a somewhat shorter target time than trial two. Notice that this results in an earlier start time, and earlier stop time, and hence a shorter duration of responding on this trial as well.

This is shown graphically by the vertical and horizontal hatching for these two trials below the discrepancy diagram. The correlation pattern is immediately obvious. Start and stop times should be positively correlated, as should start time and spread. Since the relative discrepancy crosses threshold later for long target times than for short times, the system acts just as though there were in fact two different target times, and scalar timing theory requires that spread be proportional to target time. This is the scalar property that we see so dramatically when studying different target times experimentally across different conditions (e.g., Figure 7). Now we are in a position to ask whether this property holds *within* trials. When subjects overestimate the reinforced time, do they show a broader duration of the high state than when they underestimate? Below the diagram a qualitative schematic of correlations between the start, stop, spread, and middle are shown. If memory is the only source of variance, all of these correlations should be positive. In particular, the start and the spread should be positively correlated as described above.

Correlations computed from the bird data (Figures 7 and 9) are presented next to this pattern, and we see that the correlations between all measures except start and spread are positive, as memory variance would imply. However, the start and spread measures are negatively correlated. (The box for

Figure 12. *Example of two trials associated with two different samples from a variable memory. The spread is greater in trial two with a larger memory sample. The lower left panel shows linear diagrams for the predicted correlations between start, stop, spread, and middle. The corresponding real correlations from the data set of Figure 9 are shown on the right. Note the discrepancy between the start, spread prediction (positive) and the data (−0.337).*

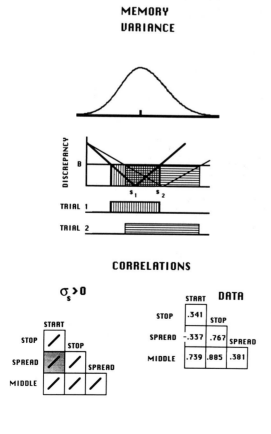

this prediction is shaded, to indicate the discrepancy with the data pattern.) This means, intuitively, that subjects compensate for a late start by an early stop. It is as if they "knew" that they were closer than usual to the target time when they started their high state and used a strict criterion to stop. This is in fact the correlation expected for these two measures from threshold variance, studied next.

Figure 13. *Example of two trials associated with two different samples from a variable threshold. The lower left panel shows linear diagrams for the predicted correlations. The data pattern is schematized on the right with three levels of slope, indicating high, moderate, or zero correlations. Note that without memory variance there is no correlation predicted between the middle and the other variables, and that the start and spread correlation is negative, as required by the data. However, the start and stop correlation is also negative, contrary to the data.*

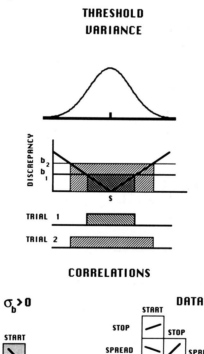

3(0,1). No memory variance, threshold variance

The pattern for threshold variance is shown in Figure 13. Again, two trials are indicated, produced by two different threshold levels on the relative discrepancy axis. Here the discrepancy function does not change location from trial to trial, and is shown decreasing toward zero at the mean remembered time, *S*, and increasing proportionally on the other side. Variance in threshold produces a pattern in which the center on all trials is located at the mean, but start and stop times are perfectly *negatively* correlated, with a late start inducing an early stop, and vice versa. Thus on trial 1, a tight threshold is adopted, and the response state is correspondingly short, while on trial 2, the threshold is more conservative, and responding begins earlier and ends later. The correlation pattern shown in diagram form below has zero correlation between the middle (constant) and the other measures, while start and stop, and start and spread, are negatively correlated. Spread and stop are the only positively correlated measures.

The data pattern is shown schematically next to the predicted pattern diagram. It reveals discrepancies in most of the measures (shaded boxes in the predicted pattern), with the important exception of the key negative correlation found in the data between start and spread. This correlation is an important, and new, index of timing patterns in the peak procedure, and we see that it implies some contribution from variation in the decision process to respond. The negative correlation at some level has been found for nearly every subject analyzed with our break–run–break program (more than 40) to date. The ubiquity of this negative correlation is important not only for its contribution to our thinking about threshold variance, but also because it helps to rule out some alternative timing processes considered later.

On the other hand, while a negative correlation between start and spread is implied by threshold variance – a late start predicts a short period of responding – one should also expect a negative correlation between start and stop – a late start predicts an early stop. The data we have analyzed are equally clear in showing a positive correlation between start and stop – a late start predicts a *late* stop – which is the pattern expected from memory variance.

We are then faced with the question of the relative control of the correlation pattern by two sources of variation, memory or clock on the one hand, and decision strategy on the other. The relative contribution of both variance sources dictates the degree to which the quantitative features of the actual data pattern may be accommodated. In fact, for some subjects there may be some strain between the data pattern and the theoretical account, even when both sources of variation are allowed, but with one sample per trial for each.

4(1,1). Memory and threshold variance

The data requires *both* the strong negative correlation between start and spread, and the positive correlation between start and stop. It may be shown that if subjects make but one decision (sample) about the proximity required for responding, and another decision about what the target time is on each trial, then the positive correlation between start and stop and negative correlation between start and spread directly trade. That is, if there is large variation in memory the correlation between start and stop is high positive and that between start and spread is at best low positive. Whereas if there is a large contribution of variance from threshold, the correlation between start and spread is high negative, and that between start and stop is at best low negative. Thus while group correlation patterns may be consonant with the pattern expected from one-sample variance from memory and threshold, individual subject's patterns may occasionally show some strain for this model, with unusually high positive correlations between start and stop, and start and middle – the pattern expected from memory variance – and unusually high negative correlations between start and spread – the pattern expected from threshold variance.

The models considered thus far assume but one random sample per trial, from memory or threshold or both, so that variation is at the level of successive trials. We consider now models assuming different samples associated with each response decision, to start and to stop responding fast.

5(2,0). Two memory samples, threshold constant

Consider first the pattern generated by two independent samples from memory, one for starting and another for stopping. The situation is shown schematically in Figure 14. The start decision is based on sample one, and the stop decision on sample two. With independent samples, any correlation between the two decisions is abolished. However, a negative correlation between start and spread *is* induced. In the figure, the target time associated with starting is shorter than usual, and it is clear that sample two, via regression to the mean, induces a longer spread than would be produced by sample one (and vice versa for a late start) so that this model fits the moderate negative correlation seen in the data between these two measures. The predicted correlation patterns are contrasted with the data pattern below, and it is clear that they are similar, except for the disqualifying exception of the zero correlation between start and stop.

Figure 14. *Correlation pattern expected with two memory samples, one for start, and one for stop. The data pattern is reproduced on the lower right, and the predicted correlation patterns are shown in diagram form on the left. Note the zero correlation between start and stop in the predicted pattern, contrary to the data.*

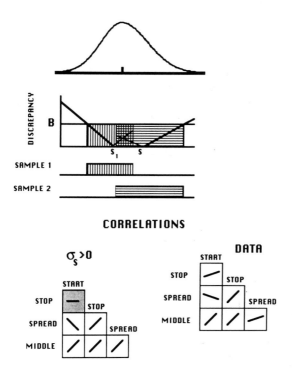

6(2,1). Two memory samples, one threshold sample

Adding variation in threshold level from trial to trial does not make the start, stop correlation positive. In fact, adding threshold variance turns that correlation somewhat negative. The threshold pattern in Figure 13, when added to two memory samples, exacerbates rather than alleviates the discrepancy with the positive start, stop correlation. Thus this modification does not accommodate the data pattern, and must be rejected.

7(0,2). Memory constant, two threshold samples

The alternative multiple sampling possibility, multiple thresholds, is schematized in Figure 15. Independence between a start and stop threshold results, as in the memory case, in a zero correlation between start and stop. However, the correlation between start and spread remains negative for the two-threshold model, for much the same reason that it is negative in the two-memory sample model. Regression toward the mean for the second sample ensures that unusually early (or late) starts are associated with stops closer to the average, hence with long (or short) spreads.

Figure 15. *Correlation pattern associated with two threshold samples, one for start, and one for stop. The data pattern, as in previous figures, is on the right, and the predicted, two-sample pattern on the left. Note that, again, start and stop become uncorrelated with two samples.*

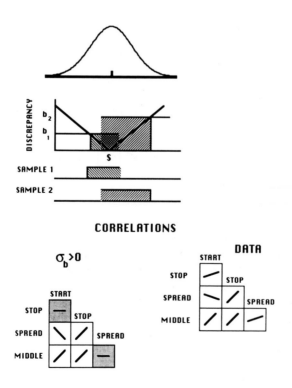

This model must be rejected for the same reason as the two-memory sample model. It renders the start, stop correlation zero, while in the data this correlation is consistently positive. Another less critical feature perhaps of this correlation pattern is that the middle and spread become uncorrelated as well, and in the data these measures also remain somewhat positively correlated.

8(1,2). One memory sample, two threshold samples

A modification that is not disqualified, and indeed fits all of the data we have collected, is one in which two thresholds are assumed, one for starting and one for stopping, but only one memory sample is used per trial. Variation in this memory induces a positive coupling between start and stop, as expected from the memory pattern in Figure 12, and yet the negative correlation between start and spread is maintained, although, under some parameter choices, attenuated. This model suggests that the level of proximity which is good enough to start responding may not be the same level as that associated with stopping, and this accords with other qualitative features of the data. For example, it is usually the case that a sharp start onset time for the high state is learned earlier than a sharp stop time. The result is that early in training subjects show considerably more skew in their peak functions than late in training.

A second feature that this model accommodates is the fact that the start time is often closer to the target-reinforced time than is the stop. While two thresholds are not required to accommodate this kind of a finding, they do so quite naturally, and they may accord with differential costs for late starts versus late stops. Starting late simply means that reinforcement sometimes does not occur quite as soon as it might otherwise have done. Stopping early, however, might be more costly in that reinforcement could be missed altogether if no more responding occurs on a to-be-reinforced trial.

9(2,2). Two memory samples, two threshold samples

For completeness, we note that a model in which there are start and stop memory samples, and start and stop threshold samples, is also ruled out by our data. It is clear from the above analysis that a system in which the task is completely redefined for starting and again for stopping eliminates the correlation between start and stop, as do the two memory (5) or two-threshold (7) sample models.

Conclusion

This completes our conceptual analysis of covariance patterns associated with memory and decision variables underlying timing performance. We have shown that strong inferences eliminating several kinds of models may be made by examining the correlation pattern between start and stop in a two-state analysis of performance in the peak procedure. The key features of the data pattern that discriminate amongst several models are:

(1) a positive correlation between start and stop times;
(2) a negative correlation between start and spread times, that is, between the time that the high state begins and its duration; and
(3) a positive correlation between the middle of the high state and its duration.

Of the nine possible scalar timing models, this data pattern disqualifies all but two: those with one memory sample and either one- or two-threshold samples.

Our analysis is summarized in Table 2. Successive rows correspond to the numbering in the cells of Table 1, in order of increasing number of random variables per trial. Models 4 and 8, with one memory sample, are the only survivors of the stringent test imposed by the three key data correlations listed above. The positive correlation between start and stop requires some

Table 2.

		Models		Data	
No. of independent random samples	Model no. (Table 1)	Memory/ clock	Threshold	Disqualified (X), or not $(\sqrt{})$	Start, stop, spread disqualification
0, no variance	1(0,0)	Fixed; $\mu(S)$	Fixed: B	X	σ^2 (start) > 0 σ^2 (stop) > 0
1 sample	2(1,0)	Variable: s	Fixed: B	X	ρ(start, spread) < 0
	3(0,1)	Fixed: $\mu(S)$	Variable: b	X	ρ(start, stop) > 0
2 samples	**4(1,1)**	**Variable: s**	**Variable: b**	$\sqrt{}$**(?)**	**ρ(start, stop) $\rightarrow$ +1,** **ρ(start, spread) $\rightarrow$ −1**
	5(2,0)	Variable: s_1, s_2	Fixed: B	X	ρ(start, stop) > 0
	6(0,2)	Fixed: $\mu(S)$	Variable: b_1, b_2	X	ρ(start, stop) > 0
3 samples	7(2,1)	Variable: $s_1 s_2$	Variable: b	X	ρ(start, stop) > 0
	8(1,2)	**Variable: s**	**Variable: b_1, b_2**	$\sqrt{}$	**NONE**
4 samples	9(2,2)	Variable: s_1, s_2	Variable: b_1, b_2	X	ρ(start, stop) > 0

variance in memory for the target time, but this memory cannot be assessed independently for the start and stop decision.

Threshold variance is required as well, to accommodate the negative correlation between start and spread. This finding is new, and especially noteworthy as it is in direct opposition to the scalar property seen across different reinforcement time conditions. When reinforcement time is changed, the scalar increase in memory variance dominates the spread of the average peak function. But within a single reinforcement time condition, memory and threshold variance act in opposition: sufficient threshold variability induces a negative correlation between start and spread, while still permitting a positive correlation between start and stop.

The flexibility of the surviving models is of course bought at some cost, since additional assumptions ineluctably lead to additional parameters. In the three-sample case (model 8), we require different mean start thresholds and stop thresholds, although not different variances necessarily. On the other hand, such flexibility we believe is cheap enough considering the power with which the account excludes some otherwise reasonable alternatives, such as the two memory sample models. Indeed, it suggests to us that a considerable advance in our thinking about temporal memory will be effected by procedures which experimentally explore changing correlation patterns associated with changing task demands that differentially manipulate memory and decision variables.

References

Aschof, J. (1984). Circadian timing. In J. Gibbon & L.G. Allan (Eds.), *Timing and time perception* (*423*, pp. 442–468). New York Academy of Sciences.

Brunner, D., Kacelnik, A., & Gibbon, J. (1989). Psychophysical constraints on optimal foraging. *Proceedings of the 21st Conference of Ethology*, Utrecht.

Catania, A.C. (1970). Reinforcement schedules and psychophysical judgements: A study of some temporal properties of behavior. In W.N. Schoenfeld (Ed.), *The theory of reinforcement schedules* (pp. 1–42). New York: Appleton-Century-Crofts.

Church, R.M., & Gibbon, J. (1982). Temporal generalization. *Journal of Experimental Psychology: Animal Behavior Processes, 8*, 165–186.

Church, R.M., Miller, K.D., Meck, W.H., & Gibbon, J. (submitted). Symmetric and asymmetric sources of variance in temporal generalization.

Gibbon, J. (1977). Scalar expectancy theory and Weber's law in animal timing. *Psychological Review, 84*, 279–325.

Gibbon, J. (1981). On the form and location of the psychometric bisection function for time. *Journal of Mathematical Psychology, 24*, 58–87.

Gibbon, J., & Church, R.M. (1981). Time-left: Linear vs. logarithmic subjective time. *Journal of Experimental Psychology: Animal Behavior Processes, 7*, 87–108.

Gibbon, J., Church, R., & Meck, W. (1984). Scalar timing in memory. In J. Gibbon & L.G. Allan (Eds.), *Timing and time perception* (*423*, pp. 52–77). New York Academy of Sciences.

Kacelnik, A., Brunner, D., & Gibbon, J. (1988). Psychophysical constraints in optimal foraging: Starlings and Weber's law. *Proceedings of the Conference on Behavioral Ecology*, Vancouver.

Krebs, J.R., & Kacelnik, A. (1984). Time horizons of foraging animals. In J. Gibbon & L.G. Allen (Eds.), *Timing and time perception* (*423*, 278–291). New York Academy of Sciences.

Roberts, S. (1981). Isolation of an internal clock. *Journal of Experimental Psychology: Animal Behavior Processes, 7*, 242–268.

Schneider, B.A. (1969). A two-state analysis of fixed interval responding in the pigeon. *Journal of the Experimental Analysis of Behavior, 12*, 677–687.

Wing, A.M. (1980). The long and short of timing in response sequences. In G.E. Stelmach & J. Requin (Eds.), *Tutorials in motor behavior*. North-Holland: Amsterdam.

Wing, A.M., & Kristofferson, A.B. (1973). Response delays and the timing of discrete motor responses. *Perception and Psychophysics, 14*, 5–12.

Cognition, 37 (1990) 55–81

3

Alternative representations of time, number, and rate*

RUSSELL M. CHURCH
HILARY A. BROADBENT

Brown University

Abstract

Church, R.M., and Broadbent, H.A., 1990. Alternative representations of time, number, and rate. Cognition, 37: 55–81.

Three facts of time perception are described based upon a temporal generalization task for rats (the peak procedure) in which food reinforcement is delivered on half the trials following the first lever-press response after some fixed interval after signal onset. (1) The mean response rate as a function of time is a smooth, slightly asymmetric, function with a maximum near the time of reinforcement; (2) the response rate on individual trials is characterized by an abrupt change from a state of low responding to a state of high responding and finally another state of low responding (break–run–break pattern); and (3) the mean response rate in 12-s and 20-s peak procedures is similar when plotted against time relative to the time of reinforcement (superposition). An information-processing version of scalar timing theory is described and compared to an alternative connectionist version of scalar timing theory that involves multiple oscillators and an autoassociation network. Psychological, mathematical and biological descriptions of the two versions are described and some possible extensions of the connectionist version are proposed to deal with perception of number, rate, and spatial orientation.

*The authors express appreciation to James Anderson, John Gibbon and Daniel Kersten for comments and assistance in the development of ideas expressed in this article, and to many others for helpful comments following descriptions of a connectionist model of timing at the Columbia University Seminar on the Psychobiology of Animal Cognition (December 8, 1988), a symposium at the meeting of the American Association for the Advancement of Science (January 19, 1989), at a symposium on neural network models of conditioning and action at Harvard University (June 3, 1989), at a symposium on cognitive aspects of stimulus control at Dalhousie University (June 13, 1989), and at the meeting of the Psychonomic Society (November 19, 1989). This research was supported by a grant from the National Institute of Mental Health (RO1-MH44234). Reprint requests should be sent to: Russell M. Church, Psychology Department, Brown University, Providence, RI 02912, U.S.A.

Introduction

Animals can estimate the duration of an interval, count a number of discrete events, and estimate the rate of occurrence of events. These cognitive capacities are closely related (Gallistel, 1990) so the same explanation that accounts for animal timing should be able to be extended gracefully to account for the abilities to discriminate between stimuli based upon number and rate. Primarily due to the efforts of John Gibbon, a quantitative explanation of animal timing has been developed (Gibbon, 1977). It is usually referred to as scalar timing theory, and it provides a mathematical description of performance under a wide variety of timing tasks. An information-processing version of scalar timing theory has been useful in explaining animal timing, and it has been extended to account for number and rate discrimination by animals. A connectionist version of scalar timing theory is now under development which also may be extended to account for discrimination between stimuli based upon number, rate, and possibly spatial orientation.

This article reviews some facts about animal time discrimination. It describes both an information-processing version of scalar timing theory and an alternative connectionist model of scalar timing theory and it applies both of these models to the same facts about animal time discrimination. Somewhat more briefly, the article describes how information-processing and connectionist models might account for some facts about animal number and rate discrimination and about orientation in space. The major purpose of this article is to describe a connectionist representation of time and to compare it to an information-processing representation.

Time

Three facts about time perception

Figure 1 shows results from one subject tested in a temporal generalization procedure that has been called the peak procedure (Church, Miller, Gibbon, & Meck, 1988). In this example, the subject was a rat, and the experiment was conducted in a lever box. There were two types of trials: food trials and nonfood trials. On food trials a white-noise signal began, and the first lever response after 20 s was followed by food and termination of the signal; on nonfood trials a signal began and lasted for 120 s and there was no food. The time of each response since stimulus onset was recorded throughout the session. The procedure was originally described by Catania (1970), and it was first used to make inferences about timing mechanisms by Roberts (1981).

Figure 1.   *Performance of a single rat in a temporal generalization task. The top panel shows the probability of a response in each 1-s interval since the signal began on nonfood trials averaged over five 2-h sessions of a 20-s peak procedure; the center panel shows the probability of a response in each 1-s interval since the signal began on a single nonfood trial of a 20-s peak procedure; the bottom panel shows the probability of a response as a function of time relative to the time of reinforcement on five sessions in which food was available at 20 s (closed circles) and on five sessions in which food was available at 12 s (open circles).*

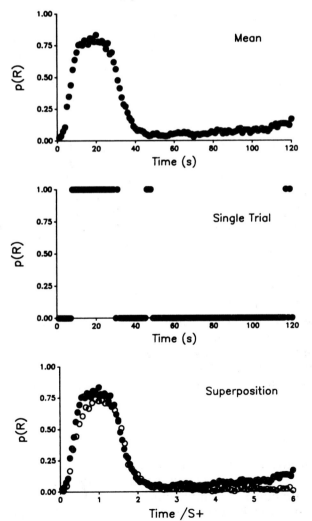

The mean probability of a response in each 1-s interval as a function of the time since signal onset is shown in the top panel of Figure 1 for one rat during five 2.5-h sessions. The mean probability of a response increased to a maximum near the time that food was sometimes received and then it decreased in a fairly symmetrical, but slightly asymmetrical fashion. The first fact that any theory of temporal generalization must account for is the smooth peak function in which the mean probability of a response gradually increases to a maximum near the time of reinforcement and then decreases in a slightly asymmetrical fashion.

The probability of a response in each 1-s interval as a function of the time since signal onset is shown in the middle panel of Figure 1 for the same rat during single trial. The second fact that any theory of temporal generalization must account for is that performance on individual trials, unlike the mean function, is characterized by an abrupt change from a state of low responding to a state of high responding and finally another state of low responding (Schneider, 1969). This is called the break–run–break pattern of responding on single trials.

The time that food was available was changed from 20 s to 12 s for 15 2.5-h sessions, and the mean probability of a response as a function of time since signal onset was calculated for the last five sessions. The bottom panel of Figure 1 shows the probability of a response as a function of the time relative to the time of reinforcement (20 s). (This is a replot of the data shown in the top panel.) In addition, it also shows the probability of a response as a function of time relative to the time of reinforcement when food was sometimes available at 12 s. The function for 12 s and 20 s were very similar when time was plotted in proportional units. The third fact that any theory of temporal generalization must account for is that the mean functions are very similar with time shown as a proportion of the time of reinforcement. (The functions are generally even more similar with time shown as proportion of the time of maximum responding; Gibbon, Church, & Meck, 1984.) This superposition result is a central consequence of Gibbon's scalar timing theory and it is an example of Weber's law.

Other examples of these three facts are described by Gibbon and Church (this volume).

An information-processing explanation

Following the influential analyses of Broadbent (1958), it has become conventional to consider a person as an information-processing machine. The machine consists of modules and interconnections among modules, and the analytical task of the investigators is reverse engineering. The input consists of sensory stimuli; the output consists of motor responses. On the basis of observations of the relationship between the input and the output, inferences are made about the nature of the machine. Broadbent's analysis consisted of a selective filter, a limited channel, and a long-term store. The parts were connected in a serial manner such that information moved from the sensory apparatus to central processing to motor output.

Sternberg's (1966) analysis of memory search as a serial and exhaustive process appeared to provide support for both specific and general conclusions. The specific conclusion was that (at least, some) memory search was conducted in a serial fashion with comparison only at the end of the search. The general conclusion was that analysis of the input–output functions (in this case, the number of items in memory and the mean reaction time) provides information regarding the nature of the information-processing machine. Subsequent analyses have qualified these conclusions. A parallel information-processing machine can also generate the input–output functions of the memory search task (Ratcliff, 1978). This has led to the view that the choice among representations must be made on the basis of a thorough comparison of the theories, and that one cannot reject a representation on the basis of a single critical experiment.

The same approach that has been used extensively in the study of human cognition has also been used in the study of animal cognition more generally. For process explanations of timing, three types of concepts have been used: psychological, mathematical and biological.

Psychological description
A general information-processing model contains a sensory register, some selective mechanisms, perceptual store, working memory, reference memory and decision processes. An example is shown in the top panel of Figure 2. This type of flow diagram was applied to time perception by Treisman (1963) and it has been further developed by others (Gibbon et al., 1984). The Gibbon et al. version contains a pacemaker, switch, accumulator, working memory, reference memory, and comparator (see bottom panel of Figure 2). The number of pulses in the accumulator (a) is the pacemaker rate of pulses per second (λ) times the number of seconds (t) that the switch from the pacemaker to the accumulator has been closed. The number of pulses stored in reference memory on a single trial is the number of pulses in the accumulator at the time of reinforcement multiplied by a memory constant (k^*). Reference memory consists of distributions of such values. Decisions are based on the similarity of the value in the accumulator with a random sample of a single value from reference memory. The similarity measure is a ratio of the difference between the number of pulses in reference memory

Figure 2.   *A general template for an information-processing model (top), and an application of this general template for timing (bottom).*

A General Information–Processing Model

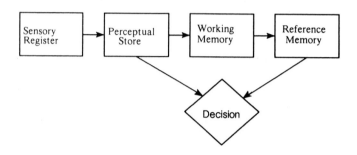

An Information–Processing Model for Timing

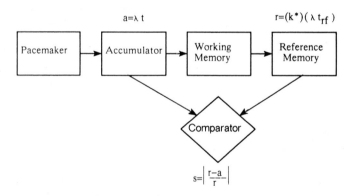

and the accumulator, relative to the number of pulses in reference memory. On some trials, the animal may attend to the stimulus and this information-processing model will apply, and on other trials the animal may not attend to the stimulus and the animal will respond at some fixed level (Church & Gibbon, 1982; Heinemann, Avin, Sullivan, & Chase, 1969).

The modular design of an information-processing model makes it possible to identify the selective effects of various independent variables on stages of the timing process. For example, the operation of the hypothetical switch can be changed by differential reinforcement: during a gap in a signal it can be made to remain closed or to open (Church, 1978; Roberts & Church, 1978). These have been called the "run" and "stop" mode, respectively, since the value in the accumulator either continues to increase or not during the gap. In addition, there is an "event" mode in which a relatively fixed value is added to the accumulator when a signal of variable duration is begun (Meck & Church, 1983), and a "reset" mode in which the value in the accumulator is initialized to zero at signal onset (Church, 1980).

Mathematical description

The information-processing model is formulated with psychological variables (clock, memory, and decision processes) and the scalar timing theory is described in terms of formal variables (symbols, distribution forms, and combination rules). The two representations have been developed in coordination so there is a one-to-one correspondence between each of the terms in the information-processing model and in the formal representation. The psychological representation has contributed to the development of the formal representation by providing content facilitating intuitions about the consequences of changes in parameter values; the formal representation has contributed to the development of the psychological representation by providing logical and quantitative precision.

The formal analysis of an information-processing model of scalar timing theory has involved the identification of sources of variance, and this model has provided excellent quantitative explanations of many facts of animal timing. Two approaches have been used: analysis based upon single trials, and upon distribution forms from multiple trials. As described by Gibbon and Church (this volume), the range of possible accounts of the timing processes is greatly restricted by analyses based upon single trials.

Since the information-processing representation provides psychological concepts and processes that map simply and clearly onto the formal concepts and processes, and since scalar timing theory provides an excellent quantitative description of time perception and timed responding of animals, the information-processing representation of time perception has become standard and generally accepted.

Biological description

The information-processing model has also been mapped onto biological processes. There is considerable support for the biological basis of some of the parameters. For example, primarily due to the efforts of Warren Meck, there is considerable evidence that drugs and other manipulations that affect the action of the neurotransmitter dopamine change the speed of the clock (λ), and that drugs and other manipulations that affect the action of the neurotransmitter acetylcholine alter the storage of the clock reading into memory (k^*) (Meck, 1983).

The biological analysis has also provided some information about the general location of some modules. A lesion of the fimbria fornix, a major extrinsic connection of the hippocampus, and an excitotoxin lesion of the septal area which has cell bodies that project to terminal fields in the hippocampus, have similar effects (Meck, Church, & Olton, 1984; Meck, Church, Wenk, & Olton, 1987). In both cases, they decrease the memory constant (k^*) and interfere with retention of the duration of a signal during a gap without interfering with the timing of a single continuous signal. A lesion of the frontal cortex, and an excitotoxin lesion of the nucleus basalis magnocellularis which has cell bodies that project to terminal fields in the cerebral cortex, have effects that are similar to each other (Olton, Wenk, Church, & Meck, 1988). In both cases, they increase the memory storage constant (k^*) and interfere with divided attention without interfering with the timing of a single continuous signal.

A fundamental problem with the development of a biological explanation in parallel with a psychological one is that the terms of the two may or may not map onto each other neatly. This is not to deny that there is a biological concomitant of any particular psychological process, but that the natural categories of the one and the other may be entirely different. This is an empirical problem. Some philosophers believe that the attempt to map biological and psychological processes will be successful (Churchland, 1986), and this is the assumption of many investigators who are attempting to provide a biological analysis of central psychological processes (such as perception, memory, and decision) that is as convincing as the biological analysis of peripheral processes (such as sensory and motor).

Of course, general laws of cognitive processing of time might be realized in many different ways (Fodor, 1975). It is possible that the same information-processing analysis of timing may apply to many different species, such as bees, rats, and people, but the biological implementation methods may be radically different. This "multiple realizability" argument against biological analysis has also been applied more generally since the same cognitive model can be duplicated in many different types of hardware. The generality of psychological principles and of biological principles is an empirical question, but most investigators assume that there is sufficient similarity in the biological implementation of a given psychological process in related species to make the analyses of the biological basis worthwhile.

An information-processing representation of scalar timing theory has been useful for explaining the ability of animals to estimate the duration of an interval. Unfortunately, this version contains some cognitive activities that are difficult to implement with known biological mechanisms. One problem with an information-processing version of scalar timing theory is that there is no known biological correlate for the accumulation of time, for the retention of a distribution of values, or for random sampling from memory.

Another problem involves the capacity of the system. Storing the information learned on successive trials, according to the information-processing model, requires storing an increasingly large number of values. The hardware used to store each value must therefore be replicated as more values are stored, or else previous values must be forgotten as new ones are added. Furthermore, for such a system to remember different times, multiple distributions of values must be maintained and kept separate. Yet animals do not exhibit any obvious difficulty in handling many trials or different times of reinforcement, nor do they appear to lose all vestiges of past training (Meck & Church, 1984).

A connectionist explanation

A connectionist version of scalar timing theory is now under development that requires only standard assumptions about the operations of neural networks. It deals with many of the facts of duration discrimination, it may also deal with the closely related cognitive capacities of rate and number discrimination, and it avoids some of the problems of the information-processing model.

Parallel distributed processing models have been developed as an alternative to serial information-processing models (Rumelhart, Hinton, & McClelland, 1986). Various terms have been used for this class of models, such as connectionist, parallel distributed processing (PDP), and neural network. The model described in this article is not strictly parallel because it has some serial features. It is not strictly a neural network because no assumptions are made about the biological implementation. But it has a matrix of connection strengths so the term "connectionist" will be used as a relatively neutral term. As in the case of the serial models, the subject is considered to be an information-processing machine and characteristics of the machine are normally inferred from the input–output relationships. The major difference is that many processes occur at the same time (parallel) and representations are not dependent upon the state of any particular element (distributed). Among the virtues of such representations are the fact that they are characteristic of the nervous system of animals, that the same system of elements can contain information about different events, and that performance is less likely to be disrupted by modification of internal components.

Figure 3. *A diagram of a connectionist model for timing. See text for details.*

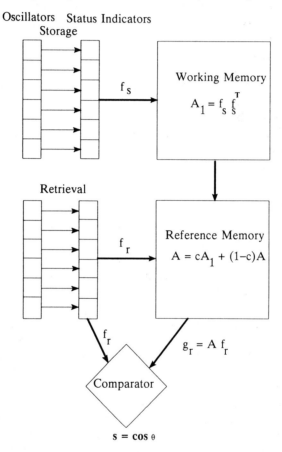

Oscillators   Status Indicators
    Storage

f_s

Working Memory

$$A_1 = f_s f_s^T$$

Retrieval

f_r

Reference Memory

$$A = cA_1 + (1-c)A$$

f_r

$$g_r = A f_r$$

Comparator

$$s = \cos \theta$$

Psychological description

The connectionist model of timing shown in Figure 3 is similar to the information-processing model in having a clock, working memory, reference memory, and a comparator, but it differs in three essential ways.

First, the pacemaker of the information-processing model is expanded in the connectionist model into a set of pacemakers (oscillators) with different periods. This expansion into multiple oscillators is intended to provide a single mechanism for both periodic timing and interval timing in nearly all time ranges. For example, it may be used for the discrimination between intervals in the range of seconds and minutes and for circadian rhythms.

Second, the accumulator of the information-processing model is replaced in the connectionist model by a set of status indicators, one for each oscillator. This is not a simple expansion from one accumulator to many, since each status indicator records not the number of cycles of its oscillator, as does the accumulator, but rather information about the phase of the oscillator.

Third, the sample distributions that compose working and reference memory in the information-processing model are replaced in the connectionist model by matrices of connection weights, so any given time is stored throughout the matrix rather than being held as a scalar (one-dimensional) number. A distributed memory matrix of fixed size can store information about an infinite number of samples of a value, whereas a distribution of values must necessarily increase in size to accommodate additional samples. Furthermore, the same matrix can be used to store multiple values, whereas new distributions must be created to store new values in the information-processing model. Of course, the distributions contain full information about each sample (except its order) but the matrix does not, which could be a source of both systematic and random errors.

Mathematical description

As an overview, in the connectionist model, times are represented as vectors, and memories are represented as matrices of connection strengths between the units of the time vectors. During storage, information from oscillators is recorded in status indicators (a storage vector, f_s), transferred into working memory (A_1) and, from there, into reference memory (A). During retrieval, information from oscillators is recorded in status indicators (a retrieval vector, f_r) which provides input to reference memory. The output from reference memory (g_r) is compared to the retrieval vector (f_r), and this results in a measure of similarity of the two vectors (s).

Oscillators for storage.   Gallistel (1990) provided the essential insight into the representation of time that is used in this model. He noted that time can be recorded as the phase of a single oscillator but that the information from an oscillator with a period shorter than the interval would be ambiguous, and the information from an oscillator with a period much longer than the interval would lack precision. A rapid oscillator would lack resolution since an animal could not distinguish between time intervals that are multiples of the fundamental oscillation; a slow oscillator would lack precision since a small error in the phase (or the reading of the phase) would produce a large error in perceived time. He proposed that animals do not record the phase of a single oscillator but record the phases of a set of oscillators. One of them would be the well-known circadian oscillator that cycles approximately once a day and which can be entrained to the length of the day. Others would cycle more rapidly or more slowly. Some of them would have periods in the range of milliseconds, others in the range of seconds, minutes, hours, days, weeks, months, or years (Aschoff, 1981). They might include oscillations in central nervous systems, respiratory systems, circulatory systems, hormonal systems, and behavioral systems. Since animals have many endogenous oscillatory processes ranging from fractions of a second to multiples of years, and since many physiological systems oscillate at fairly regular intervals, use of these processes for timing would permit measurement of time intervals from fractions of a second to years. If the fastest oscillator had a period of 200 ms and each successive oscillator had a period double the previous one (200, 400, 800 ms, etc.), 30 oscillators would be sufficient for the lifetime of a rat – the slowest of these oscillators would not cycle in the $3\frac{1}{2}$-year lifetime of the animal.

For quantitative predictions it is necessary to specify the periods of the oscillators, the type of coupling between oscillators, any sequential dependencies, and the type of random variation. For simplicity, in the simulations we have used 11 oscillators with the periods of adjacent oscillators in a ratio of 2:1 (200 ms, 400 ms, etc.). We assumed that the oscillators were tightly coupled: on each trial the period of each oscillator was its mean period multiplied by a single random normal variable with a mean of 1.0 and some standard deviation (γ).

Status indicators for storage. Gallistel (1990) notes that a record of the phases of a series of oscillators provides a representation of current time, but animals also need to represent durations of time. The duration between two events can be computed from the times of the two events and he proposes that animals are capable of making such computations.

In the simulations, we did not assume that animals could read the phase of an oscillator (for example, to the nearest degree), but merely could record the half-phase (+ or −). The reading of the time consists of recording the half-phase of each oscillator into its status indicator. Thus, the value of a given status indicator toggles back and forth between two values rather than increasing steadily as time progresses. The set of status indicators is the storage vector (f_s). In the simulations, the representation of time is a series of +1 and −1s; the vector also has one additional element that is +1 or −1 depending upon whether food was known to be available or not (or 0 if the status of food is unknown) at the time represented by the vector.

The oscillators were reset to zero (i.e., −1 in each bit of the vector) at the start of each trial. This captures the idea that oscillators should, like the circadian oscillator, be able to be reset or entrained by a stimulus. Of course,

Figure 4. *A storage vector (f_s) used in the simulations.*

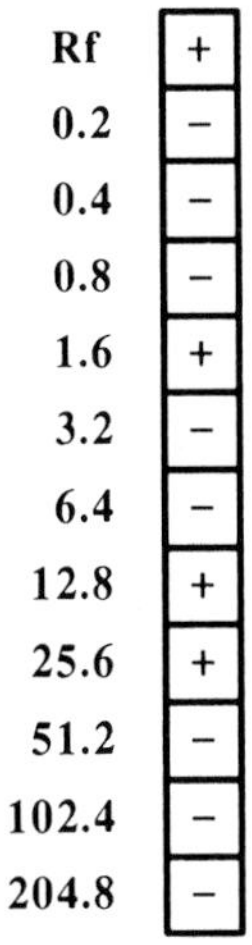

Rf	+
0.2	−
0.4	−
0.8	−
1.6	+
3.2	−
6.4	−
12.8	+
25.6	+
51.2	−
102.4	−
204.8	−

it is not reasonable to suppose that all oscillators are reset by all stimuli. For example, a circadian oscillator should not be reset at the start of a signal that lasts only a few seconds or minutes, but relaxing the assumption that the oscillators are tightly coupled should permit resetting or entrainment of nearby oscillators at the start of a signal, while leaving alone the oscillators whose periods are very different from the duration of the signal. The storage vector for 40 s (without random variability) is shown in Figure 4. As in a binary counter, the elements representing the time are set to $+1$ ($25.6 + 12.8 + 1.6 = 40$), as is the reinforcement element.

Working memory. James Anderson, in his treatments of connectionist models for concept formation, such as his brain-state-in-a-box model, has provided the essential insight into the representation of memory by an autoassociation (Anderson, Silverstein, Ritz, & Jones, 1977). If each of the n elements of a storage vector is connected to each of the other elements in this vector, each of the $n(n - 1)$ connections can be represented as having a weight. (Since elements were assumed not to be connected to themselves, the weight of the connection of an element with itself was set to zero.) This weight is a connection strength that is calculated as a product of the value of the corresponding elements. Thus, the matrix of weights is the outer product of the storage vector with its transpose. Following David Olton's use of the term, we refer to this matrix of weights as "working memory" (Olton & Samuelson, 1976). These weights provide a record of the elements that are

Figure 5.   *A working memory matrix (A1) used in the simulations calculated from the storage vector shown in Figure 4 (f_s) and its transpose (f_s^T).*

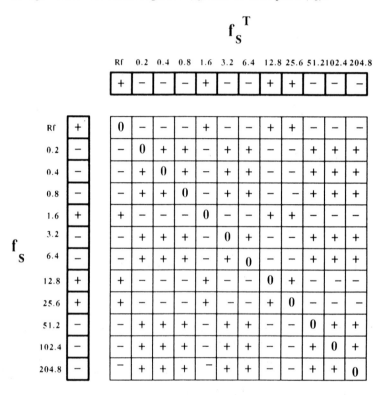

set in the storage register at the time of reinforcement and of the association of pairs of elements. (The weights are +1 if both elements are the same and −1 if they are different.) The working memory matrix for the 40 s storage vector is shown in Figure 5.

Reference memory.   At the time of reinforcement, the contents of working memory are combined with the contents of reference memory according to a linear rule. The working memory matrix is combined with a longer-term reference memory matrix by a linear combination rule applied to each of the corresponding elements – in most of the simulations it consists of 1% working memory plus 99% reference memory. This linear operator rule is familiar from its use by Bush and Mosteller (1955), Rescorla and Wagner (1972), and others. A simulation was done with reinforcement at 40 s, a standard deviation of the random oscillator period of .2, 1000 trials and a 1% working

Figure 6. *A reference memory matrix (A) used in the simulations with values based on a simulation in which reinforcement was available at 40 s, standard deviation of the clock (γ) of .2, learning rate parameter (c) of .01, and 1000 trials of storage.*

Rf	0.2	0.4	0.8	1.6	3.2	6.4	12.8	25.6	51.2	102.4	204.8
Rf	.00	.02	.00	-.04	.03	-.08	-.02	.12	.80	-.85	-1.0	-1.0
0.2	.02	.00	-.01	-.13	.03	.05	-.04	.05	.02	-.04	-.02	-.02
0.4	.00	-.01	.00	.17	-.03	-.13	.15	-.09	.01	-.01	.00	.00
0.8	-.04	-.13	.17	.00	.00	-.11	.06	-.04	.02	-.01	.04	.04
1.6	.03	.03	-.03	.00	.00	-.05	-.10	-.08	-.03	.00	-.03	-.03
3.2	-.08	.05	-.13	-.11	-.05	.00	-.09	-.01	-.08	.07	.08	.08
6.4	-.02	-.04	.15	.06	-.10	-.09	.00	-.19	.04	-.09	.02	.02
12.8	.12	.05	-.09	-.04	-.08	-.01	-.19	.00	.23	-.28	-.12	-.12
25.6	.80	.02	.01	.02	-.03	-.08	.04	.23	.00	-.95	-.80	-.80
51.2	-.85	-.04	-.01	-.01	.00	.07	-.09	-.28	-.95	.00	.85	.85
102.4	-1.0	-.02	.00	.04	-.03	.08	.02	-.12	-.80	.85	.00	1.0
204.8	-1.0	-.02	.00	.04	-.03	.08	.02	-.12	-.80	.85	1.0	.00

memory plus 99% reference memory combination rule. The reference memory matrix is shown in Figure 6. An inspection of the matrix shows the covariation of the storage vector elements at the time of reinforcement. The large positive values connect elements that are strongly positively related; the large negative values connect elements that are strongly negatively related; the values near zero connect elements that are not closely related. Information regarding the time of reinforcement is contained in both the positive and negative values. For example, in the reference memory matrix for 40 s there was a positive association of .23 between the element for 12.8 and the element for 25.6 s, and there was a negative association of −.95 between the element for 25.6 and 51.2 s. This indicates that, when reinforcement occurred at 40 s, the 12.8 and 25.6-s elements were typically the same and the 25.6-s and 51.2-s elements were typically different.

The oscillators, status indicators, working memory, and reference memory complete the storage system. This is the assumed process for the storage of the time of reinforcement but, for behavior, the value represented in memory must be retrieved.

Oscillators for retrieval.   The characteristics of the oscillators used for retrieval are identical to those used for storage. The purpose of using a different set of oscillators for storage and retrieval was to make it possible for independent variables to have different effects on storage and retrieval processes.

Status indicators for retrieval.   The characteristics of the status indicators used for retrieval are identical to those used for storage. The set of status indicators will be referred to as the retrieval vector (f_r). The current time is represented by a retrieval vector, just as the time to be stored is represented by a storage vector (f_s).

Output vector.   The reference memory is multiplied by the retrieval vector to compute an output vector ($g = A f_r$). The first element of this output vector is the sum of the products of each element in the first row of the matrix with each corresponding element in the retrieval vector, the second element of the output vector uses the second row of the matrix, and so on. In this fashion, the output vector contains information about the relationship of the elements in the retrieval vector with the pair-wise relationships stored in reference memory.

Another way of describing the information in the output vector is to note that the matrix acts as a filter that is tuned to the time of reinforcement. The retrieval vector is, in a sense, passed through the matrix in the process of computing the output vector; a retrieval vector that is similar to the stored time of reinforcement will be transmitted faithfully through the matrix to result in an output vector that resembles the retrieval vector, whereas a retrieval vector that is very different from the stored time of reinforcement will result in an output vector that does not resemble the retrieval vector.

Similarity measure.   The current time must be compared to the time stored in the reference memory matrix (see Figure 7). Once an output vector (g_r) has been computed it must be compared to the retrieval vector. A similarity measure is computed as the cosine of the angle between the retrieval vector and the output vector, a value that varies continuously between -1 and $+1$. This similarity measure is the inner product of the two vectors, normalized by the lengths of the vectors as described in equation (1). It may be regarded as the population correlation coefficient of the elements of the vectors.

$$s = f_r^T g_r / [(f_r^T f_r)(g_r^T g_r)]^{1/2}. \tag{1}$$

The similarity measure is compared to a threshold (set at .5 in the simula-

Figure 7. *The retrieval vector (g$_r$ = Af$_r$) obtained from the value of the reference memory (A) shown in Figure 6 and the value of f$_r$ shown in this figure. The similarity measure (s) is the cosine.*

Retrieval Vector   Output Vector

	f$_r$	g$_r$
Rf	0	3.96
0.2	−1	0.31
0.4	−1	−0.28
0.8	−1	−0.08
1.6	+1	0.16
3.2	−1	0.01
6.4	−1	−0.28
12.8	+1	1.05
25.6	+1	2.78
51.2	−1	−2.85
102.4	−1	−2.92
204.8	−1	−2.92

$$s = \frac{13}{\sqrt{(11)(49.97)}} = .55$$

Figure 8. *Probability of response as a function of time since the signal began for two simulated series. The simulations were based on two sets of 1000 storage trials and 100 retrieval trials with reinforcement at 40 s, c = .01, γ = .2.*

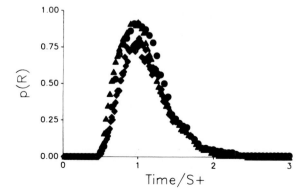

tions). If the similarity of the input and output is above threshold a response is recorded; otherwise it is not. This completes the description of the connectionist model.

There are many qualitative similarities between the results simulated by the model and the experimental results. A simulation was done of 100 trials of retrieval from a reference memory matrix formed from the storage process described with a standard deviation (γ) of the oscillator periods of .2. The mean response rate as a function of time since the signal began was a smooth function with a single maximum near the time of reinforcement, and slightly skewed to the right. Two replications are shown. Note the functions were smooth and slightly asymmetrical, the maxima were near the time of reinforcement, and the two replications were similar (Figure 8).

In contrast, a simulation based on a single retrieval trial produced a response function consisting of a series of steps that could be categorized as low, high, and low. Note that single trials had the break–run–break pattern of responding and the two replications were similar (Figure 9). Although the functions shown in Figures 8 and 9 were based upon the same storage mechanism with 1000 storage trials, the mean probability of a response as a function of time averaged over 100 retrieval trials was a smooth function (Figure 8) but the probability of a response as a function of time on a single retrieval trial was a step function (Figure 9).

Figure 9.   *Probability of response as a function of time since the signal began for two simulated series. The simulations were based on two sets of 1000 storage trials and a single retrieval trial with reinforcement at 40 s, c = .01, γ = .2. (The data from one set was slightly displaced from 0 and 1 so that the points would be visible.)*

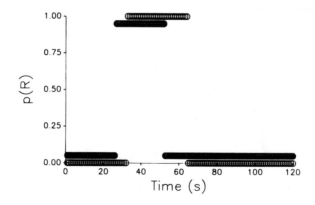

Figure 10. *Probability of response as a function of time since the signal began. The simulations were based upon three sets of 1000 storage trials and 100 retrieval trials. One series was with reinforcement at 20 s, one at 40 s, and one at 80 s; c was .01 and $\gamma = .2$ in all cases.*

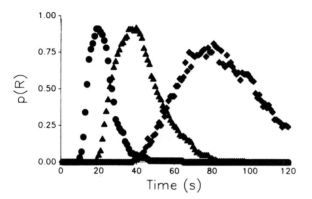

In addition to the simulation with reinforcement at 40 s, additional simulations were done with reinforcement at 20 s and 80 s. The other parameters were set to the same values used in Figure 8. Although the time of the maximum response probability was approximately at the time of reinforcement, the spread of the function increased as the time of reinforcement increased. The functions shown in Figure 10 are replotted in Figure 11 with time as a proportion of the time of reinforcement. The functions for 20, 40 and 80 s superposed when time was scaled relative to the time of reinforcement.

The simulations demonstrate that the connectionist model of scalar timing theory is adequate to reproduce the three facts about time perception shown in Figure 1. Averaged across many trials, the probability of a response gradually increased to a maximum near the time that food was sometimes received and then it decreased in a slightly asymmetrical fashion; on individual trials there was an abrupt change from a state of low responding to a state of high responding and another abrupt change from a state of high responding to a state of low responding; and the functions for different times of reinforcement were very similar when time was scaled relative to the time of reinforcement.

Biological description

In the description of an information-processing explanation, many other facts about time perception were described. For example, some variables affect clock speed and other variables affect the memory storage constant. The effects of these variables can also be accounted for in the connectionist

Figure 11. *Probability of response as a function of time since the signal began relative to the time of reinforcement (S+). These are the same data that were shown in Figure 10.*

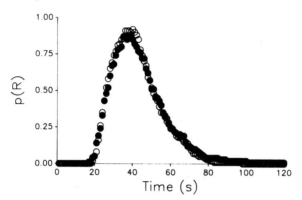

model by the separation of storage and retrieval processes. Although the same kind of oscillators used for storage are used for retrieval, they need not be identical. That is, they may be running with slightly different mean periods. Thus, after a particular physical time, the value of the elements of status indicator used for storage (the storage vector) may not be identical to the values of the elements of the status indicator used for retrieval (the retrieval vectors). Consider a treatment that affected both storage and retrieval oscillators (or, alternatively, the storage and retrieval vectors). If, for example, the treatment sped up both sets of oscillators, at the time of reinforcement the time represented in the retrieval vector would be longer than the time stored in the reference memory matrix, and the time stored on that trial would also be longer. A change in both sets of oscillators, therefore, resembles a change in clock speed. If, however, a treatment sped up only the storage oscillators, at the time of reinforcement the time represented in the retrieval vector would be similar to the time stored in the reference memory matrix, but the time stored on that trial would be longer. A change in the storage oscillators, therefore, resembles a change in the memory constant. Thus, the connectionist model can account for the results of physiological manipulations if the speed of both sets of oscillators is assumed to be regulated by dopamine and the speed of the storage oscillators is assumed in addition to be modifiable by acetylcholine. As with the information-processing model, inattention involves trials on which the model is not applied (no time is stored or retrieved) and the animal will respond at some fixed level.

A loss of a part of the storage mechanism, such as the pathway from the storage vector to working memory or the pathway from working memory to reference memory, would leave the retrieval mechanism intact, but new information could not enter reference memory. Thus, a treatment that differentially affected such a pathway should produce anterograde amnesia. In contrast, a treatment that differentially interfered with contents of reference memory should produce retrograde amnesia.

A comparison of the information-processing and connectionist explanations of timing

The two architectures are compared in Figure 12. They have corresponding modules for clock, memory and decision. They differ in the assumptions about the nature of the modules and the rules. The first difference between the information-processing and connectionist architectures is that the clock

Figure 12. *A comparison of the architecture of an information-processing model of timing (top panel) and of a connectionist model of timing (bottom panel).*

Information Processing

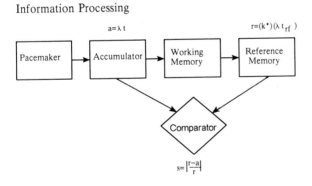

Connectionist

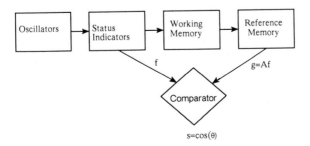

of the information-processing representation consists of a pacemaker, switch, and accumulator that represents time by an amount; the clock of the connectionist representation consists of a set of oscillators, switches, and status indicators. The alternative representations of the clock are one of the essential differences between the two architectures. Since biological oscillators are pervasive and have many functions (Gallistel, 1980), biological realization of an oscillatory system is perhaps more plausible than realization of an accumulation system. If the characteristics of oscillators used for interval timing are similar to those used for periodic timing (such as circadian rhythms) the oscillators would provide one basis for the development of a single theory for periodic and interval timing.

The second difference between the information-processing and connectionist architectures is that the memory of the information-processing representation consists of a distribution of values; the memory of the connectionist representation consists of a matrix of weights. Matrices of connection strengths may be more biologically plausible than a distribution of values. Recordings from cell populations are beginning to provide evidence that groups of neurons collectively encode information that is not contained in any single cell (Skarda & Freeman, 1987).

The third difference between the information-processing and connectionist architectures is that the decision process of the information-processing representation consists of a comparison of a sample of one element from a distribution of values with a value from the current trial; the decision process of the connectionist representation consists of a comparison of an input vector with the output vector from the memory matrix. The biological realization of a sampling process is difficult to imagine, but the biological realization of elementary matrix operations can be done with simple parallel circuits.

Rate

Animals can discriminate between rates of presentation of an auditory signal, even when the duration of the train of pulses and the number of events are unreliable indicators of the rate (Meck et al., 1984). For the information-processing version of scalar timing theory, there are several possible ways that this could be accomplished. The discrimination could be based on a duration (for some fixed number of pulses), a count of the number of pulses (for some fixed time), or a computation of the ratio of the number of pulses and the duration. Support for the idea that rate is computed from time and number is given by Gallistel (1990). Alternatively, rate could be a primitive based on the reading of an adjustable internal rate that matched an external pulse rate. None of these has been carefully examined, but the simplest cue probably is the duration between successive pulses. Thus, rate discrimination may simply be an example of duration discrimination.

For the connectionist version, the rate is directly represented in the reference memory matrix. If a stimulus is pulsed at 1-s intervals for 30 s, there would be a representation of both 1 s and 30 s in the same reference memory matrix. Of course, alternative representations of rate may be preferable, depending upon the results of further experiments. For example, methamphetamine produces an equivalent effect on time and number perception (Meck & Church, 1983). Thus, if rate is perceived as the time between pulses, then methamphetamine should have the same effect on rate perception as it does on time and number perception. But if rate is a ratio of time and number, methamphetamine should have no effect on rate perception since the numerator and denominator would be changed in the same proportion. Experiments to test these alternatives have not yet been conducted.

Number

Rats can distinguish between two auditory signals differing in number, even when all temporal cues are controlled or randomized (Fernandes & Church, 1982). There is some support for the hypothesis that the number of sequential auditory signals is coded in the same form as the duration of a signal (Meck & Church, 1983; Meck, Church, & Gibbon, 1985). Rats trained to discriminate between two continuous auditory signals of different duration (such as 2 s vs. 4 s), and then tested with discrete bursts of auditory signals, considered 10 bursts approximately equivalent to 2 s, and 20 bursts approximately equivalent to 4 s, regardless of the amount of time it took to deliver the 10 or 20 bursts, or the duration of each burst. In other words, a short versus long discrimination generalized to a few versus many discrimination. There is some evidence that the effect of drugs on time and number discrimination are the same (for a review, see Broadbent, Rakitin, Church, & Meck, in press).

In the information-processing version of scalar timing theory, the onset of each signal (regardless of the duration of the signal) permits pulses to flow from a pacemaker into an accumulator for 200 ms. In the connectionist version of scalar timing theory, number is directly represented in the reference memory matrix: some elements reflect the interval between pulses and other elements reflect the duration of a pulse train. The elements reflecting the association of the former with the latter provide information regarding number. With the connectionist representation, time and rate are both durations, but number is a relationship between durations.

Orientation

Animals can use landmarks for spatial orientation (Cheng, 1986, 1988; Gallistel, 1989, 1990). When an animal is at a goal, it can represent its location as an angle between two landmarks and the distance from the goal to the nearer landmark. When the animal is not at the goal, it can move to reduce the discrepancy between its current perceived location (represented in polar coordinates by an angle and a distance) and its remembered location of the goal. Cheng (1988) has found that the standard deviation of the error in locating the goal is linearly related to the mean distance of the goal from a landmark. This is an example of Weber's law for space which is analogous to Weber's law for time that leads to the superposition result.

Reference memory for space can be constructed in much the same way as reference memory for time, but it involves two dimensions (on a plane) rather than one. Time has been represented as a set of numbers, each of which is tuned to a different range – from fractions of a second to years. In polar coordinates, space can be represented by a set of numbers for angle and another set for a distance. An angle can also be represented as a set of numbers – each of which is tuned to a different range. If one element is $+1$ for 0 to 180 degrees and -1 for 180 to 360 degrees, the next one may be $+1$ for 0 to 90 degrees, -1 for 90 to 180 degrees, $+1$ for 180 to 270 degrees, and -1 for 270 to 360 degrees, etc. A compatible representation of distance would involve some small base distance and successive doubling of the distance.

Some tasks require only a representation of space, some require only a representation of time, and some require a representation of both space and time. The use of a sun compass for orientation (calculation of the ephemeris function), and dead-reckoning (path integration) are two examples in which a combination of space and time representations are required (Gallistel, 1989, 1990). If a vector contained information regarding both time and space, the autoassociation matrix of such a vector would contain information about time alone, space alone, and space–time. Such space–time information is required for many orientation tasks.

Conclusion

The first version of a connectionist model accounts for some results of time discrimination, and it probably can be extended to account for some results of other time discrimination tasks, number discrimination, and rate discrimination. It may also be able to be extended to spatial orientation and to tasks that require both representation of time and space. The simulations so far have been restricted to the analysis of a single timing task, the peak procedure. We now plan to apply this first version of the connectionist model to other results of time, number, and rate discrimination; to modify the assumptions of the model where necessary to account for facts that are presently known; and to conduct further experiments to test some of the unique predictions of the connectionist model of timing. Some of these experimental tests are based upon analyses of periodic timing mechanisms, such as circadian rhythms. The connectionist model of interval timing provides a way to integrate facts and ideas about periodic timing with the analysis of interval timing.

Although the connectionist model of timing has only been used for the simplest case of one signal, one response, and one time of reinforcement, animals are able to deal with multiple stimuli, multiple responses and multiple times of reinforcement (Church, 1989). One of the virtues of matrix memory representations is that they are able to hold information about many different situations without serious interference. Presumably, a connectionist model of timing can be extended to account for these more complex situations.

The application of a connectionist model to timing is not nearly as advanced as the application of an information-processing model (Gibbon & Church, this volume). Although the general forms of the distribution are promising, quantitative fits of data have shown some systematic deviations (Church & Broadbent, in press). The work would be facilitated by closed form calculations for the asymptotic levels and, especially, for the transition states. Because of the simplicity of the model, they undoubtedly can be developed. The greatest strength of the connectionist model is that it makes some testable assumptions about the biological basis of the behavior. The application of a connectionist model to data from timing experiments is particularly promising because there is a large, systematic database, and a specific alternative model for comparison.

References

Anderson, J.A., Silverstein, J.W., Ritz, S.A., & Jones, R.S. (1977). Distinctive features, categorical perception, and probability learning: Some applications of a neural model. *Psychological Review, 84,* 413–451.

Aschoff, J. (1981). A survey on biological rhythms. In J. Aschoff (Ed.), *Handbook of behavioral neurobiology, Vol. 4, Biological rhythms.* New York: Plenum Press.

Broadbent, D.E. (1958). *Perception and communication.* New York: Pergamon Press.

Broadbent, H.A., Rakitin, B., Church, R.M., & Meck, W.H. (in press). The relationship between timing and counting. In S. Boysen & J. Capaldi (Eds.), *The development of numerical ability: Animal and human models.* Hillsdale, NJ: Erlbaum.

Bush, R.R., & Mosteller, F. (1955). *Stochastic models for learning.* New York: Wiley.

Catania, A.C. (1970). Reinforcement schedules and psychophysical judgments: A study of some temporal properties of behavior. In W.N. Schoenfeld (Ed.), *The theory of reinforcement schedules* (pp. 1–42). New York: Appleton-Century-Crofts.

Cheng, K. (1986). A purely geometric module in the rat's spatial representation. *Cognition, 23*, 149–178.

Cheng, K. (1988). Some psychophysics of the pigeons's use of landmarks. *Journal of Comparative Physiology A, 162*, 815–826.

Church, R.M. (1978). The internal clock. In S. Hulse, H. Fowler, & W.K. Honig (Eds.), *Cognitive processes in animal behavior* (pp. 277–310). Hillsdale, NJ: Erlbaum.

Church, R.M. (1989). Theories of timing behavior. In S.B. Klein & R.R. Mowrer (Eds.), *Contemporary learning theories: Instrumental conditioning theory and the impact of biological constraints on learning* (pp. 41–71). Hillsdale, NJ: Erlbaum.

Church, R.M. (1980). Short-term memory for time intervals. *Learning and Motivation, 11*, 208–219.

Church, R.M., & Broadbent, H.A. (in press). A connectionist model of timing. In M.L. Commons, S. Grossberg, & J.E.R. Staddon (Eds.), *Models of behavior: Neural networks and conditioning* (p. 13). Hillsdale, NJ: Erlbaum.

Church, R.M., & Gibbon, J. (1982). Temporal generalization. *Journal of Experimental Psychology: Animal Behavior Processes, 8*, 165–186.

Church, R.M., Miller, K.D., Gibbon, J., & Meck, W.H. (1988). Symmetrical and asymmetrical sources of variance in temporal generalization. Paper at Meeting of The Psychonomic Society, Chicago, November, 1988.

Churchland, P. (1986). *Neurophilosophy*. Cambridge, MA: MIT Press.

Fernandes, D.M., & Church, R.M. (1982). Discrimination of the number of sequential events by rats. *Animal Learning and Behavior, 10*, 171–176.

Fodor, J.A. (1975). *The language of thought*. New York: Crowell.

Gallistel, C.R. (1980). *The organization of action: A new synthesis*. Hillsdale, NJ: Erlbaum.

Gallistel, C.R. (1989). Animal cognition: The representation of space, time and number. *Annual Review of Psychology, 40*, 155–189.

Gallistel, C.R. (1990). *The organization of learning*. Cambridge, MA: MIT Press.

Gibbon, J. (1977). Scalar expectancy theory and Weber's law in animal timing. *Psychological Review, 84*, 279–325.

Gibbon, J., Church, R.M., & Meck, W.H. (1984). Scalar timing in memory. In J. Gibbon & L. Allan (Eds.), *Timing and time perception* (*423*, pp. 52–77). New York Academy of Sciences.

Heinemann, E.G., Avin, E., Sullivan, M.A., & Chase, S. (1969). Analysis of stimulus generalization with a psychophysical method. *Journal of Experimental Psychology, 80*, 215–224.

Meck, W.H. (1983). Selective adjustment of the speed of internal clock and memory processes. *Journal of Experimental Psychology: Animal Behavior Processes, 9*, 171–201.

Meck, W.H., & Church, R.M. (1983). A mode control model of counting and timing processes. *Journal of Experimental Psychology: Animal Behavior Processes, 9*, 320–334.

Meck, W.H., & Church, R.M. (1984). Simultaneous temporal processing. *Journal of Experimental Psychology: Animal Behavior Processes, 10*, 1–29.

Meck, W.H., Church, R.M., & Gibbon, J. (1985). Temporal integration in duration and number discrimination. *Journal of Experimental Psychology: Animal Behavior Processes, 11*, 591–597.

Meck, W.H., Church, R.M., & Olton, D.S. (1984). Hippocampus, time, and memory. *Behavioral Neuroscience, 98*, 3–22.

Meck, W.H., Church, R.M., Wenk, G.L., & Olton, D.S. (1987). Nucleus basalis magnocellularis and medial septal area lesions differentially impair temporal memory. *Journal of Neuroscience, 7*, 3505–3511.

Olton, D.S., & Samuelson, R.J. (1976). Remembrance of places passed: Spatial memory in rats. *Journal of Experimental Psychology: Animal Behavior Processes, 2*, 97–116.

Olton, D.S., Wenk, G.L., Church, R.M., & Meck, W.H. (1988). Attention and the frontal cortex as examined by simultaneous temporal processing. *Neuropsychologia, 26,* 307–318.

Ratcliff, R. (1978). A theory of memory retrieval. *Psychological Review, 85,* 59–108.

Rescorla, R.A., & Wagner, A.R. (1972). A theory of Pavlovian conditioning: Variations in the effectiveness of reinforcement and nonreinforcement. In A.H. Black & W.F. Prokasy (Eds.), *Classical conditioning II.* New York: Appleton-Century-Crofts.

Roberts, S. (1981). Isolation of an internal clock. *Journal of Experimental Psychology: Animal Behavior Processes, 7,* 242–268.

Roberts, S., & Church, R.M. (1978). Control of an internal clock. *Journal of Experimental Psychology: Animal Behavior Processes, 4,* 318–337.

Rumelhart, D.E., Hinton, G.E., & McClelland, J.L. (1986). A general framework for parallel distributed processing. In D.E. Rumelhart & J.L. McClelland (Eds.), *Parallel distributed processing* (Vol. 1). Cambridge, MA: MIT Press.

Schneider, B.A. (1969). A two-state analysis of fixed-interval responding in the pigeon. *Journal of the Experimental Analysis of Behavior, 12,* 677–687.

Skarda, C.A., & Freeman, W.J. (1987). How brains make chaos in order to make sense of the world. *Behavioral and Brain Sciences, 10,* 161–195.

Sternberg, S. (1966). High-speed scanning in human memory. *Science, 153,* 652–654.

Treisman, M. (1963). Temporal discrimination and the indifference interval: Implications for a model of the "internal clock". *Psychological Monographs, 77,* 1–31 (whole no. 576).

Cognition, 37 (1990) 83–103

4

Honey bee cognition

JAMES L. GOULD*

Princeton University

Abstract

Gould, J.L., 1990. Honey bee cognition. Cognition, 37: 83–103.

The visual memory of honey bees is stored pictorially. Bees will accept a mirror-image reversal of a familiar pattern in the absence of the original, but prefer the original over the reversal; the matching system of bees, therefore, does not incorporate a mirror-image ambiguity. Bees will not accept a rotation of a familiar vertical pattern, but readily recognize any rotation of a horizontal pattern; the context-specific ability to make a mental transformation seems justified by natural contingencies. Bees are able to construct and use cognitive maps of their home area, though it is possible to create conditions under which they lack useful cues. Other experiments suggest that recruits, having attended a dance in the hive specifying the distance and direction of a food source, can evaluate the "plausibility" of the location without leaving the hive; this suggests a kind of imagination.

Introduction

Early in this century, von Frisch (rev. 1967) upset the prevailing view that humans were the sensory benchmarks of the animal world. His discovery that mere honey bees could sense ultraviolet light (and later, that these insects see polarized light and detect magnetic fields) led to the realization that species (including our own) live in sensory worlds that suit their niche and color their perspective. The discovery a decade later of sign stimuli by Lorenz and Tinbergen (rev. Gould, 1982) revealed that even when individuals of two species have the same sensory range, their nervous systems may operate on the information in very different ways, exaggerating one cue in the brain of one animal but emphasizing quite another in another species. These early ethological insights invite and require us to attempt to see the world from the

*Requests for reprints should be sent to James L. Gould, Department of Biology, Princeton University, Princeton, NJ 08544, U.S.A.

0010-0277/90/$6.80 © 1990—Elsevier Science Publishers B.V.

point of view of the animals we study, rather than in terms of familiar human sensory and neural-processing biases.

A similar problem arises when we consider the higher-level processing going on in the minds of animals. In order to understand how nervous systems manipulate information, we must try to infer from behavioral tests what must be going on, imagine the consequences, and use these guesses to guide hypothesis formation and testing. The mind by its nature is a private organ, and so experiments on how it works are often difficult to design and interpret clearly. Models based on the operation of simpler nervous systems in experimentally convenient creatures have the potential for helping, always assuming that there are similarities that span phyla. The general assumption until relatively recently has been that animals as distantly related as insects, with their compound eyes, crunchy exoskeletons, frenetic movements, supernumerary legs, and miniscule, distributed nervous systems have little to tell us about the cognitive processes of mammals. This picture has changed over the past decade; honey bees, at least, turn out to be more like birds and mammals, and mammals and birds more like bees (rev. Gould, 1986c) than had previously been thought. Since the lines leading to arthropods and chordates probably diverged before the emergence of well-organized nervous systems, the similarities are the result of evolutionary convergence, and suggest that there may be one set of generally optimal processing strategies which work across a wide range of brain sizes.

The aim of this paper is to look at what is going on in the honey bee mind that might be relevant to thinking about cognition. Defining cognition, either formally or operationally, is fraught with difficulty (Gould & Gould, 1982), but I am going to take it to mean "planning" or "turning things over in the mind", a process I call "cognitive trial and error" (Gould & Marler, 1984). I will touch on two classes of behavior – visual matching and landmark-based navigation.

Honey bees

One of the most enduring legacies of classical ethology is the realization that behavior can be highly species specific. Even learning can be innately guided, so that a creature "knows" in advance how to recognize when it should learn something, what object or individual it needs to focus on, which cues should be remembered, how the information ought to be stored, and when the data should be retrieved in future (Gould & Marler, 1984, 1987). This programming of learning has doubtless evolved because animals with appropriate biases in situations sufficiently predictable have learned faster and more reliably than naive competitors, and so left more offspring. Hence, much of behavior and learning best serves an animal when it is tuned to the requirements and contingencies of a species' niche, and the same could be true – indeed, is likely to be true – for cognitive processing. For this reason, it makes sense to begin with a few words about the lifestyle of honey bees (rev. Gould & Gould, 1988).

Like most bees, honey bees make their living gathering pollen (their protein source) and nectar (which supplies carbohydrates) from flowers. Honey bees differ from other temperate-zone bees in two dramatic ways: their colonies are perennial, and they have a dance language. These two oddities give honey bees a clear advantage under certain crucial circumstances. Because they survive the winter as a self-warming group (in colonies of ten to fifty thousand), they are able to begin foraging earlier in the spring and in far greater numbers. The dance language allows foraging bees to share information about the location of food sources in their home range (which is typically 1–2 km, but can extend to 14 km in periods of dearth). As a result, honey bees have an edge in exploiting new or transient food sources: a scout reporting the discovery of an outstanding supply of pollen or nectar can set off a chain reaction which results in the eventual recruitment of hundreds or even thousands of foragers within a matter of hours.

Visual matching

The simplest kind of mental transformation I want to touch on is the sort required to determine whether an object seen from a different perspective is familiar or novel. The work described here grew out of a study (Gould, 1985a, 1986a, 1988a) originally aimed at determining whether the honey bee's memory for flower shape is pictorial or, as most workers thought, based on storing a list of abstract but potentially diagnostic parameters (like spatial frequency and relative color areas). Even Wehner, who had originally concluded that bees have pictorial memory (Wehner, 1972) later pointed out that his results could be explained in terms of parameters if the list of visual features to be registered were to be expanded slightly to include line angles and color-boundary polarities (Wehner, 1981).

The experimental technique, common to all the flower-memory experiments to be mentioned here, involves training a forager to collect sugar water from the center of an artificial flower, which may be a funnel or flat disc with the pattern painted on it, or a sheet of ground glass (with the pattern back-projected onto it); this pattern is the S^+. Except for the horizontal-pattern experiment described later, all patterns are presented vertically. An alternative artificial flower with a similar pattern is always presented at the same time, but without any food; using this S⁻ increases the quality of the memory substantially (Gould, 1986a). The relative positions of the S⁺ and S⁻ are exchanged after each forager visit so that the bee does not learn simply to go to the left or right target. In most cases this is accomplished by using a rotating box with four sides, two for training (one with each of the alternative relative positions of the patterns) and two for testing (Figure 1). During testing, fresh artificial flowers without food are used to exclude odor cues left by foragers, and landings are counted. Some tests pit the S⁺ against the S⁻; others replace the S⁻ with a novel pattern (S⁰); and some use a transformed version of the S⁺.

The first experiments included alternative patterns with the same values for all suggested parameters (using Wehner's expanded enumeration as a guide), differing only in the arrangement of the "petals"; by this criterion,

Figure 1.   *Device used for training and testing in many of the visual memory experiments. Each side of the rotating box offers two patterns. On the training sides, one (the S⁺) contains food while the other (S⁻) does not; neither has food on either of the testing faces. The left–right arrangement of the alternatives is reversed on the two sides in each pair, and the box is rotated after each forager visit.*

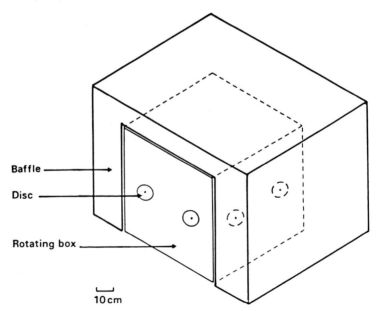

Baffle

Disc

Rotating box

10 cm

they demonstrated that the memory is indeed pictorial, with a resolution of about 8° (compared to real-time visual resolution of 1–2°; as far as I know, visual memory is always grainier than real-time resolution). Of course it is always possible that the memory *is* parameter-based, but that the list is simply much longer than had been imagined (Gould & Gould, 1988); despite our introspective opinion to the contrary, the same could even be true of human visual memory. Happily, the questions addressed in this paper do not necessarily depend on whether memory is pictorial; they are concerned with in what ways a pattern presented to a returning forager can differ from the pattern it was trained on and still be reliably identified as similar. The experiments shed some light on the nature of the mental transformations honey bees are capable of, though not as yet how these transformations are made.

The first of these follow-up tests involved mirror-image patterns. A variety of species are able to recognize a left–right reversal of a familiar pattern as similar (or identical) to the original (Bornstein, Gross, & Wolf, 1979; Corballis & Beale, 1970; Shepard & Metzler, 1971), and an oft-heard assumption posits that the recognition is automatic and unconditional – that is, the animal experiences a complete mirror-image ambiguity, and cannot without training recognize the difference between a pattern and its left–right reversal.

Previous work (Gould, 1985a) had shown that bees can learn to recognize a pattern even if the S^- is mirror image, and so in these tests (Gould, 1988c) the initial strategy was to use an S^- that was no simple transformation of the S^+, and then use the mirror image as an S^0 during testing. The patterns used each consisted of four "petals" arranged around the food well; each petal in a pattern was a different color. Bees readily chose the training pattern over its left–right reversal (Figure 2). On the other hand, when the testing offered a choice between a mirror image of the S^+ and a novel pattern, the foragers chose the reversal (Figure 2). This indicates that bees can recognize a mirror image as similar to the original pattern, but have no automatic neural ambiguity – that is, they perceive that there is a difference, but also that the two patterns have something important in common. This may not be so different from the many vertebrates that are said inevitably to confuse left and right: the tests usually offer the reversal alone and see whether the organisms respond to it at a roughly normal rate; by this criterion bees would be judged to suffer from this mirror-image confusion. Only by presenting a simultaneous choice was the lack of an actual ambiguity made obvious, and it could be that many or all vertebrates would show the same ability if tested in this way.

Analogous tests demonstrated that there is no up–down ambiguity, nor any ability to recognize such a transformation as similar to the training pattern; similarly, bees will not respond to a 90° rotation (rev. Wehner, 1981; Gould, 1988c). The inability to recognize a rotation is a bit unexpected:

Figure 2.   *Results of the mirror-image experiment. The training patterns consisted of an array of four circular "petals", each a different color; the open circle corresponds to white, solid to blue, cross-hatched to yellow, and striped to orange. (A) After training, four bees were each offered 25 independent choices (for a total of 100 in all) between the S⁺ and its mirror image, and, as the bar graphs indicate, chose the unaltered pattern about 90% of the time. The lower graph shows the results of a counterbalanced experiment to control for stimulus bias. (B) When the choice was between the mirror reversal of the S⁺ and a novel pattern, bees opted for the reversal about 85% of the time.*

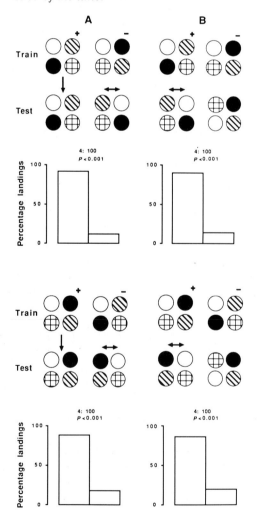

pigeons, for instance, can automatically recognize rotations while humans, though able to accommodate such transformations, require added time to perform the matching in proportion to the degree of rotation (Holland & Delius, 1983).

Since some blossoms honey bees regularly forage are "presented" to potential pollinators horizontally, the inability to recognize a rotated pattern as familiar would require a forager either to "circle" a flower to find the right perspective, or to store several alternative pictures to allow for any approach angle. Experiments to determine which strategy bees use yielded the entirely unexpected result that foragers *can* perform mental rotations of *horizontal* patterns. In these experiments the discs (again with four petals of different colors) are oriented horizontally and located in large baffles which prevent

Figure 3.   *Device for training and testing bees in the horizontal-pattern experiment. The top and sides of the device were translucent so that light could pass through but bees could not see the patterns except from the open front. The thin netting in each section prevented bees from viewing the discs from any but the front quadrant.*

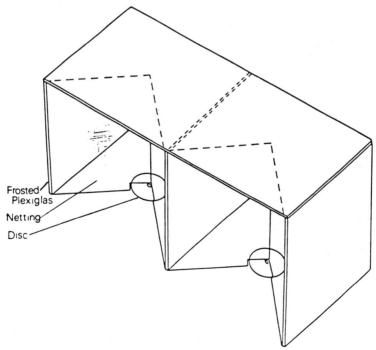

Frosted
Plexiglas

Netting

Disc

Figure 4. *Results of the horizontal-rotation experiment. In each case bees were tested with both the S⁺ and S⁻ rotated 180°; because of the netting and translucent device, the choice had to be made from a perspective at least 90° away from anything seen in training. The accuracy was about 70%, significant at the p < .01 level, but well below the 90–95% value obtained in analogous 4-petal tests pitting the S⁺ against the S⁻ using vertical, unrotated discs.*

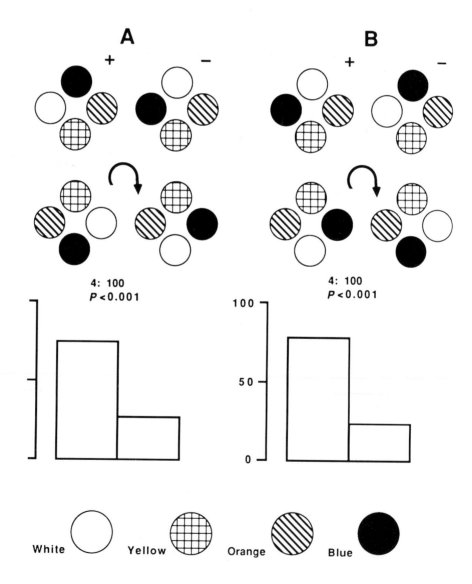

White   Yellow   Orange   Blue

the forager from approaching from above, behind, or from the sides (Figure 3). Fine netting restricts the bee's perspective to the forward quadrant; the pattern cannot be "photographed" from any position in the remaining 270° of arc. During testing, bees can be presented with the same pattern rotated up to 180°, but not visible from a familiar perspective; to choose the transformed training pattern, the forager's nervous system needs to perform some sort of mental rotation. Bees readily choose a rotated training pattern over a rotated S⁻ (Figure 4).

Each of these abilities and inabilities corresponds roughly to the realities of flower morphology: blossoms are invariably bilaterally symmetrical, but often have no up–down symmetry; vertically oriented flowers that are not rotationally symmetrical have a typical orientation that rarely varies more than 30°; horizontally oriented flowers, on the other hand, have no defined orientation since the perspective experienced by a bee depends on its angle of approach. I know of no other case in which the ability to recognize a rotation depends on the vertical/horizontal "context" of the target, though this has not been a subject of particular investigation.

Work in progress suggests that the honey bee brain processes visual information in a way that also generates size constancy and object constancy, though more data are needed to be sure (Gould, unpublished). If true, these sorts of mental transformations, obvious capacities of birds and mammals, have invertebrate counterparts.

Cognitive maps

One of the cognitive capacities that could be of considerable use to a social insect would be the ability to construct and use maps of the home range. To the extent that these maps could be used to plan novel routes, they would satisfy my intuitive definition of cognition.

The typical model for invertebrate landmark-based navigation (Weher, 1981) imagined that insects are supposed to store a set of "snapshots" taken along familiar routes which they could use to guide them in a dot-to-dot fashion to the goal, each snapshot pointing the way to the next. But looking at all the evidence (Gould, 1984), there were clear hints of map-like processing. There is no reason to think that bees might not use a snapshot system under some circumstances and a map strategy under others, just as humans do. And there is no doubt that something like a snapshot method is available to bees: when foragers are trained along an indirect path to a goal, with a prominant landmark along the route, they frequently adopt an outward flight that passes near the marker, though the return flight is generally direct (von

Frisch & Lindauer, 1954; rev. von Frisch, 1967). What is needed to determine
if bees can use a map is a situation in which the snapshot strategy would be
of no avail to foragers.

The two hypotheses were pitted against one another in an experiment that
involved training individually marked foragers to a feeding station 160 m west
of the hive (Gould, 1986b). Later these bees were captured as they left the
hive en route to the feeder (Site A, Figure 5) and transported in the dark to
a location (Site B) 160 m from both the hive and Site A. There they were
released singly and vanishing bearings recorded. The sites were chosen because the trees on an intervening ridge blocked any direct view of landmarks

Figure 5.   (A) Experimental layout used in cognitive-map experiments. In the first test,
foragers were trained from the hive to Site A and allowed to collect food
there for several days. Later they were captured on their way out of the hive
to Site A and transported in darkness to Site B, where they were released
and tracked. A second experiment involved training to Site B and transport
to A; a third used sites about 400 m distant.

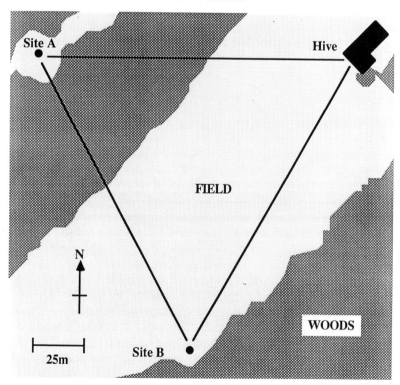

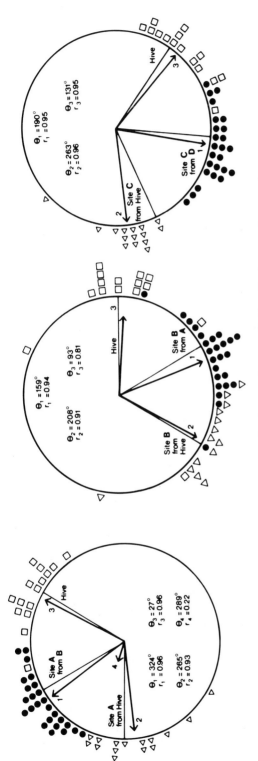

Figure 5. (B) Results for the displace-to-B test (left), displace-to-A experiment (center), and the 400-m version (right). Vanishing bearings of departing displaced foragers are indicated by black circles; directions expected based on the three alternative predictions are shown as straight lines to the periphery and labeled appropriately. Control releases to confirm the validity of the return-to-hive and ignore-displacement alternatives are shown as open squares and open triangles, respectively. (The first was obtained by capturing unmarked returning foragers and transporting them to the release site; the second by capturing marked departing foragers en route to the feeding station, transporting them half-way to the release site and then back to the hive for release.) The mean vector, which measures the average direction (θ) and degree of clustering of the vanishing bearings (r, which is 0.0 for randomly chosen angles and 1.0 for a set that are all the same), is shown for each as an arrow. (The arrow labeled "4" in the left-most diagram represents another control group: unmarked departing foragers released at the hive to check for any general directional bias.) The data indicate that displaced foragers depart directly for their original goal.

near the feeder, even from the altitude at which bees circle before departing. In addition, the precise locations were picked to insure that the flora were sufficiently different to exclude the remote possibility of a forager having visited the two locations on any single previous trip; since honey bees are temporary floral specialists, they establish regular foraging routes to patches of a single species of plant. Care was also taken to be sure that useful, unambiguous landmarks were visible at the release site.

If experienced foragers can use familiar landmarks to place themselves on a mental map, they should be able to depart directly for Site A; if they are restricted to sets of route-specific snapshots, the best they could hope to do is find Site B in their mental album and pick up the trial back to the hive, whereupon they could restart the sequence of pictures leading to Site A. Another possibility is that foragers might not realize that they had been moved at all, and so continue at the azimuth normally employed in flying from the hive to site A. Foragers, in fact, departed accurately toward Site A (Figure 5), and arrived there in about the time required for a direct flight (28.9 s from Site B vs. 25.2 s from the hive). When the experiment was replicated with a new colony and the roles of Sites A and B reversed, the results were nearly identical (Figure 5). When the distances were increased to 400 m the accuracy was at least as good, but when foragers were displaced much further, there was no consistent orientation. As Collett (1987) has pointed out, these experiments are consistent with earlier observations by Romanes (in 1885) and (even earlier) Fabre, among others. Janzen (1971), too, reported similar abilities.

I have gone into the details of this test because Dyer and Seeley (1988) have recently attacked the cognitive map interpretation, proposing instead that bees use landmarks along the (to me) rather vague lines proposed by Cartwright and Collett (1982, 1983). According to this idea, bees judge the degree of similarity between the view of things now versus a remembered

---

Figure 6.   *(A) The view from an elevated position at Site B, where displaced foragers in the first experiment chose departure bearings. (Because of practical limitations, the photographs were taken at an altitude of 7 m rather than the 9.2 m at which bees ended their circling.) The real-time and landmark-memory resolution of honey bees are indicated by the ovals; distinctive landmarks are highlighted and named in the legend. The distribution of vanishing bearings of displaced foragers is shown below the panorama. (B) The equivalent view from the hive. The barn, spruce, and distant tree are outside this panorama, but each is clearly visible to a circling bee. The distribution of vanishing bearings for departing foragers in the ignore-displacement control experiment is shown below the panorama.*

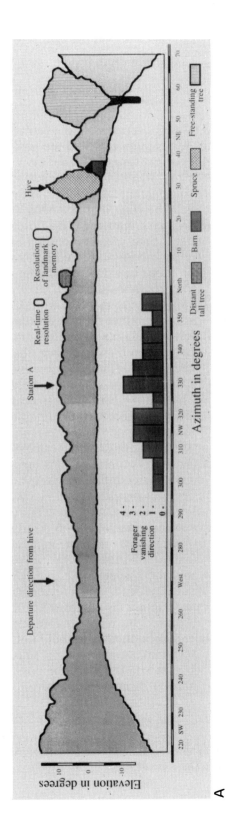

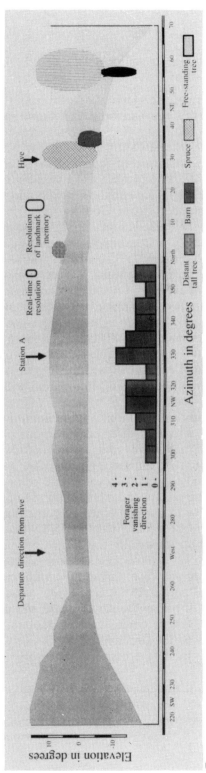

picture of the markers as seen from the food on previous visits, and generate from this comparison a directional signal that sends them closer to the goal. Even assuming the Cartwright/Collett model is correct for near-feeder orientation (the situation for which it was developed), there is no evidence to suggest that this procedure could or does work on a larger scale. One problem for both the snapshot and matching hypotheses is the very limited quality of the pictorial information stored and used in landmark mapping (von Frisch & Lindauer, 1954; Gould, 1987), or even the real-time visual resolution of bees (Seidl & Kaiser, 1982). It is difficult for members of a species with extremely fine-grained vision to realize the limitations of a 3.5° visual memory; for example, the moon, whose shape and surface features are readily made out, has a visual diameter of only 0.4°. Most of the markers we take note of are either invisible or ambiguous for insects. Another difficulty is that when a bee is displaced 60° from its line of flight, the relative position of any landmark not very close to the goal is radically altered by parallax; this creates enormous difficulties for both the snapshot and matching hypotheses. Finally, the actual release site was chosen to minimize or eliminate these potential problems, with near-goal landmarks hidden, treeline heights near the limit of visual resolution, and with clear, useful markers near the release site.

In an effort to make these limitations clear independent of actual calculations, I took a series of panoramic photographs from two release locations, Site B and Hive, and prepared drawings from them recording the treeline profile, field outline, and any other distinctive features that stand out – large, isolated trees or objects whose color contrasts with the background (Figure 6). The resolution of landmark memory – or even real-time vision – is clearly too low to use any features in the direction of Site A other than the general placement of the treeline. The landmarks that are large and distinctive enough – especially the spruce near the hive and the free-standing tree NE of Site B – are too small to be seen from Site A, and hidden by the intervening ridge in any case. Using the two distinctive trees that are visible from Site B would permit the high degree of accuracy displayed by released foragers (plotted below the panoramas), but using the treelines obviously would not. Even if bees could use the treeline, they would make systematic parallax errors on the order of 30° clockwise (departing from Site B toward the point in the treeline crossed in the course of their normal flight from the hive to

Figure 7. *(A) The view from an elevated position at Site B, with reduced resolution corresponding to real-time vision; a forager attempting to match to memory would have even less information. (B) The equivalent view from the hive.*

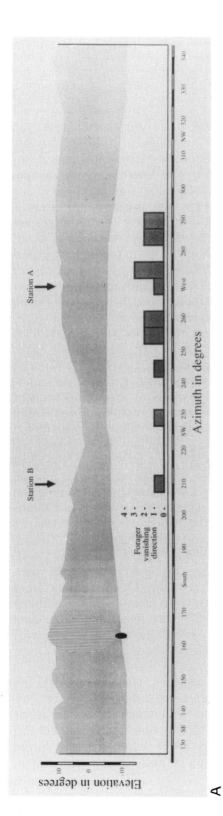

A

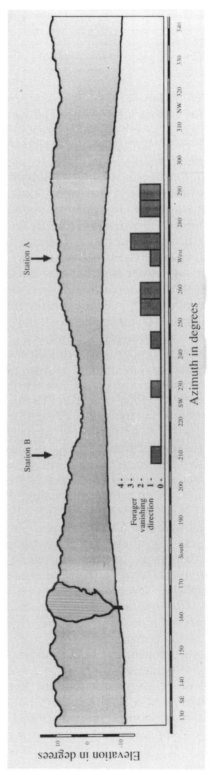

B

Site A); as the data indicate, the error in departure was only 5°, and even that was counter-clockwise. (The view as it might appear to bees from Site B and Hive have been reconstructed in an approximate way to give a flavor of the visual limitations involved (Figure 7). The lower accuracy of bees departing from the hive is a consequence of the indirect training route to Site A; different foragers adopt slightly different personal routes to the target.)

One thing these views make clear is that it is possible to choose release sites at which map information could not be used because there are no clear, unambiguous landmarks. This fact was impressed on me in preliminary experiments in which bees were released further along the treeline southwest of Site B; because the two trees the bees were likely to use were both visually smaller and closer together, the clustering (though not the accuracy (mean bearing)) of the departing foragers was considerably lower.

The most likely scenario for the map-orientation process in bees, at least in the cognitive-map experiment, begins with circling. The bee probably takes in the treeline horizon and distinctive landmarks, and may be able to judge the distance to nearby features on the basis of the degree of parallax generated by the circling motion. (Judging the range of distant treelines should be nearly impossible given the low vertical-axis visual resolution, as von Frisch and Lindauer (1954; rev. von Frisch, 1967) discovered when they attempted to reorient foragers with displaced landmarks.) Assuming the near-goal use of landmarks is similar to the strategy employed on a larger scale, the most important factor for orienting, at least where it is sufficient, is the relative azimuth of distinctive landmarks; bees will ignore discrepancies of color and shape (Gould, 1987) and absolute size and distance (Cartwright & Collett, 1983) in favor of azimuth matching, though they also remember and use the color (Cheng, Collett, & Wehner, 1986; Gould, 1985b) and shape (Gould, 1987) as well (see also the discussions of von Frisch, 1967, and Dyer, 1984). This hierarchy of cue use is analogous to the way they employ odor, then color, then shape in flower matching during foraging (Gould, 1986c). Bees seem to be selective in their use of landmarks, concentrating on the outlying markers when several are present (Gould, 1987). Taken together, these data suggest that the role of distinctive, widely spaced (or spatially extensive) landmarks is more important in judging location than the general structure of the visual horizon.

Another conclusion that emerges from the honey bee work is that the storage of landmark information is both separate and different from the storage of other visual information. Landmarks are learned on the forager's *departure* from a food source (Gould, 1988b) and stored at a (horizontal) resolution of about 3° (Gould, 1987), whereas flower shape is learned during the bee's approach and stored at a resolution of about 8° (Gould, 1985a,

1986a, 1988a). Whether other aspects of the landmark system differ as well
– the ability or inability to recognize mirror images or rotations, for instance
– remains to be determined.

It is possible that the bees' ability to use their cognitive map goes well
beyond ad hoc navigation in the field. The original basis for this suspicion
was the observation that dance attenders were not recruited by dances indicating a location in an adjacent lake, whereas simultaneous dancing to an
equally distant site along the shoreline elicited vigorous recruitment (Gould
& Gould, 1982). (In some of the tests, the same dancers were used for both
locations to control for odor and other variables, using a "redirection"
technique developed to test the reality of the dance language (Gould, 1975);

Figure 8. *Experimental layout for the preliminary lake experiment. Foragers were
trained to the shore station and made to indicate by their dancing either that
location or a boat with a feeder in the lake. Later, foragers were trained to
the boat and allowed to advertise those coordinates directly. In neither case
did any recruits visit the boat, though recruitment to the shore site was brisk.
When the boat was moved near the far shore, however, it began to get
substantial numbers of recruits.*

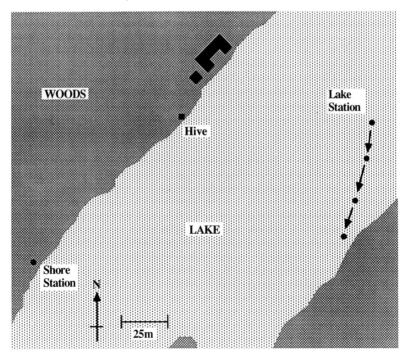

in other cases, the lake-station foragers actually collected food from a feeder in a boat on the lake.) One possible interpretation of this result is that, while still in the hive, the attenders used the direction and distance information in the dance to position the advertised site on their mental map, determined that it was in the lake and therefore implausibly located, and refused to respond. This hypothesis is consistent with the observation that when the boat was moved to within a few meters of the far shore of the lake, substantial recruitment began (Figure 8). On the other hand, perhaps there were olfactory cues (the odor of the lake, for instance, carried back on the bodies of the lake-station foragers) that were responsible for this outcome.

The first step toward a more controlled test of this interpretation has been made (Gould & Gould, 1988). A group of foragers was trained to each of two boats, one in the treelined lake and the other docked on the shoreline. After a week of training – enough time to permit the forager force to learn the locale – the hive and boats were moved overnight to the edge of a treelined field whose orientation and dimensions roughly matched those of the lake. Bees readily accept a new site as the home locale if the most prominent landmarks are roughly equivalent, and substitutions of grass for water and vice versa are not the most outrageous exchanges bees will tolerate (Dyer, 1984; von Frisch & Lindauer, 1954). Ther boats were placed at the same relative locations (Figure 9) and high-quality food offered to stimulate dancing and recruitment. If dance attenders evaluate only food quality, they should arrive at the two sites in the field in approximately equal numbers. If, on the other hand, potential recruits really do "imagine" the advertised location before flying forth, some (those that have not yet been out to note that the lake has mysteriously dried up overnight) will attend the mid-field dances and reject them; recruitment would therefore favor the field-edge site, particularly early in the test. This is just what happened (Figure 9). The essential control of beginning the experiment at the field site and then moving to the lake has yet to be performed.

Figure 9.   *Experimental layout for hive-displacement experiment. Foragers were trained to identical boats, one anchored along the shore and the other at the same distance out in the lake. Later, the hive and boats were moved overnight to a field with similar dimensions and orientation, and the boats placed at equivalent locations relative to the hive. Dancing was permitted and recruits captured as they arrived at the feeders; all were new to these stations. The edge station – corresponding to the shore station of training – garnered 83 recruits from 68 dances, but the field station received only 27 recruits from 64 dances, and most of those arrived later in the morning when the attenders might have had time to gain experience outside.*

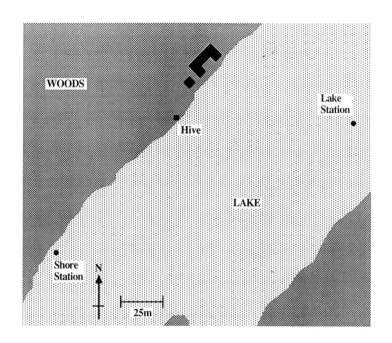

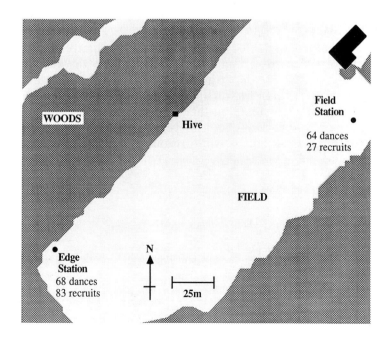

Conclusion

That honey bees have at least modest cognitive powers seems reasonably well established, though the full extent of their abilities is yet to be determined. For instance, there is some suggestion of concept formation on the basis of preliminary experiments analogous to procedures used with pigeons (Gould & Gould, 1988); an ability to generalize could be useful in forming an operational "definition" of a floral species. A more difficult question is whether the apparent ability of bees to "turn" objects in their minds, or formulate new routes after unexpected displacements, represents a series of specialized processing routines which have evolved to solve particular, predictable problems, or a reflection of some more general cleverness. In view of the highly structured and well-tailored nature of honey bee learning, the customized-cognition hypothesis seems quite plausible. It is not too difficult to imagine a program that automatically fills in an initially blank mental map, a second routine for landmark matching, and a third to set courses. All these are tasks faced by essentially every bee in the course of its life, and surely a preordained system would have been favored by evolution given the highly predictable nature of the task involved.

On the other hand, von Frisch's (1967) report that foragers can learn the pattern of regular movements of a training station as it is displaced ever further from the hive, and begin anticipating these repositionings, does not easily fit this model: there is nothing obvious in the natural behavior of flowers that could have selected for this capacity. Similarly, it is hard to see what evolutionary pressures could have led to an ability to "imagine" the site indicated by a dance before departing the hive; there is no evidence of lying by dancers, and no advantage to dissimulation in a colony of nonreproductive sisters. Of course it is possible that there is a logic to these abilities, and we have simply not been clever enough as yet to see it; alternatively, perhaps neither of these apparent talents will turn out to be real.

References

Bornstein, M.H., Gross, C.G., & Wolf, J.Z. (1979). Perceptual similarity of mirror images in infancy. *Cognition, 6*, 89–116.

Cartwright, B.A., & Collett, T.S. (1982). How honey bees use landmarks to guide their return to a food source. *Nature, 295*, 560–564.

Cartwright, B.A., & Collett, T.S. (1983). Landmark learning in bees. *Journal of Comparative Physiology, 151*, 521–543.

Cheng, K., Collett, T.S., & Wehner, R. (1986). Honey bees learn the color of landmarks. *Journal of Comparative Physiology, 159*, 69–73.

Collett, T.S. (1987). Insect maps. *Trends in Neurosciences, 10*, 139–141.

Corballis, M.C., & Beale, I.L. (1970). On telling left from right. *Psychological Review, 77*, 451–464.

Dyer, F.C. (1984). Comparative studies of the dance language and orientation of four species of honey bees. PhD dissertation, Princeton University, Princeton, NJ (1984).

Dyer, F.C., & Seeley, T.D. (1988). On the evolution of the dance language. *American Naturalist, 133*, 580–590.

Gould, J.L. (1975). Honey bee recruitment: The dance-language controversy. *Science, 189*, 685–693.

Gould, J.L. (1982). *Ethology.* New York: W.W. Norton.

Gould, J.L. (1984). Natural history of honey bee learning. In P. Marler & H.S. Terrace (Eds.), *The biology of learning* (pp. 149–180). Berlin: Springer-Verlag.

Gould, J.L. (1985a). How bees remember flower shapes. *Science, 227*, 1492–1494.

Gould, J.L. (1985b). Honey bee learning and memory. In G. Lynch, J.L. McGaugh, & N. Weinberger (Eds.), *The neurobiology of learning and memory* (pp. 193–210). New York: Academic Press.

Gould, J.L. (1986a). Pattern learning by honey bees. *Animal Behaviour, 34*, 990–997.

Gould, J.L. (1986b). The locale map of honey bees: Do insects have cognitive maps? *Science, 232*, 861–863.

Gould, J.L. (1986c). The biology of learning. *Annual Review of Psychology, 37*, 163–192.

Gould, J.L. (1987). Landmark learning by honey bees. *Animal Behaviour, 35*, 26–34.

Gould, J.L. (1988a). Resolution of pattern learning by honey bees. *Journal of Insect Behavior, 1*, 225–233.

Gould, J.L. (1988b). Timing of landmark learning by honey bees. *Journal of Insect Behavior, 1*, 373–378.

Gould, J.L. (1988c). A mirror-image ambiguity in honey bee pattern matching. *Animal Behaviour, 36*, 487–492.

Gould, J.L., & Gould, C.G. (1982). The insect mind: Physics or metaphysics? In D.R. Griffin (Ed.), *Animal mind – Human mind* (pp. 269–298). Berlin: Springer-Verlag.

Gould, J.L., & Gould, C.G. (1988). *The honey bee.* New York: W.H. Freeman.

Gould, J.L., & Marler, P. (1984). Ethology and the natural history of learning. In P. Marler & H. Terrace (Eds.), *The biology of learning* (pp. 47–74). Berlin: Springer-Verlag.

Gould, J.L., & Marler, P. (1987). Learning by instinct. *Scientific American, 255*, 74–85.

Gould, J.L., & Towne, W.F. (1983). Honey bee learning. *Advances in Insect Physiology, 20*, 55–86.

Holland, V.C., & Delius, J.D. (1983). Rotational invariance in visual pattern recognition by pigeons and humans. *Science, 218*, 804–806.

Janzen, D.H. (1971). Euglossine bees as long-distance pollinators of tropical plants. *Science, 171*, 203–205.

Romanes, G.J. (1885). Homing facility of Hymenoptera. *Nature, 32*, 630.

Seidl, R., & Kaiser, W. (1982). Visual field size, binocular domain, and the ommatidial array of the compound eyes in worker honey bees. *Journal of Comparative Physiology, 143*, 17–26.

Shepard, R.N., & Metzler, J. (1971). Mental rotation of three-dimensional objects. *Science, 171*, 701–703.

Sutherland, N.S. (1969). Shape discrimination in rat, octopus, and goldfish: A comparative study. *Journal of Comparative Psychology, 67*, 160–176.

von Frisch, K. (1967). *The dance language and orientation of bees.* Cambridge, MA: Harvard University Press.

von Frisch, K., & Lindauer, M. (1954). Himmel und Erde in Konkurrenz bei der Orientierung der Bienen. *Naturwissenschaften, 41*, 245–253.

Wehner, R. (1972). Pattern modulation and pattern detection in the visual system of Hymenoptera. In R. Wehner (Ed.), *Information processing in the visual system of arthropods* (pp. 183–194). Berlin: Springer-Verlag.

Wehner, R. (1981). Spatial vision in arthropods. In H. Autrum (Ed.), *Handbook of sensory physiology* (pp. 287–616). Berlin: Springer-Verlag.

Cognition, 37 (1990) 105–131

5

Event representation in Pavlovian conditioning: Image and action*

PETER C. HOLLAND

Duke University

Abstract

Holland, P.C., 1990. Event representation in Pavlovian conditioning: Image and action. Cognition, 37: 105–131.

In a typical Pavlovian conditioning experiment, a relatively insignificant event, the conditioned stimulus (CS), is paired with a biologically more meaningful event, the unconditioned stimulus (US). As a consequence of those pairings, the CS is thought to acquire response characteristics of the US. In this article I describe experiments with rats that suggest that under some circumstances, the CS acquires control of perceptual processing of the US, in the absence of that US itself. I present three kinds of evidence for this surrogate processing, which I liken to imagery or hallucination: (1) CSs come to control specific, sensory-evaluative responses normally evoked only by the USs; (2) CSs can substitute for USs in the establishment of new learning about those USs themselves; (3) CSs can substitute for USs in the modulation of conditioning to other events, either overshadowing (interfering) or potentiating learning, in the same manner as the USs themselves. Finally, I compare these data with evidence for conditioned sensation and imagery in humans, and suggest that imagery may be a very basic process, evolutionarily derived from perceptual and conditioning processes adapted to deal with remote or absent objects.

Introduction

To adapt to relatively short-term variations in their environments, animals must be sensitive to the flow of events around them. They must adjust to the "causal texture" (Tolman & Brunswik, 1935) of their worlds, responding to particular temporal, spatial, and predictive relations among those events. A

---

*This research was conducted at the University of Pittsburgh, with the support of grants from the National Science Foundation and the National Institute of Mental Health. Requests for reprints should be sent to Peter Holland, Department of Psychology, Duke University, Durham, NC 27706, U.S.A.

question that pervades modern conditioning theory is, "How much of this texture is represented by the organism?"

The Pavlovian conditioning procedure is an attempt to model, however simplistically, this potentially rich learning in the laboratory. In this procedure, some relation is arranged among stimuli, without regard for the subject's behavior. At some later time, we ask if the organism has been altered by exposure to that particular relation. For example, if we arrange for a rat to reliably receive food (the unconditioned stimulus or US) immediately after the presentation of a brief tone (the conditioned stimulus or CS), the rat will acquire a variety of learned behaviors (the conditioned response or CR) in the presence of the tone.

Most students of animal conditioning today agree that the more profitable subjects of inquiry are the mental events, structures, and processes that underlie conditioned behavior, and not the conditioned behavior itself. Unlike in the heavy-handed behaviorisms of the not-too-distant past, the domain of most modern conditioning theories is not one of spit and twitches, but a conceptual one: Their predictions are couched in terms of variables such as attention, associative strength, and time/rate estimates.

Currently, the display of Pavlovian CRs is almost universally described as mediated by internal representatives of the CS and US: Associations formed between those representatives endow the CS alone with the ability to activate a representative of the US. That activation is assumed to generate conditioned behavior, in some unspecified way. Far from being the object of study, the conditioned response itself is often treated more as a necessary evil, a cloudy glass for viewing represented knowledge. Indeed, a prominent theme (though by no means the only one) in cognitive analyses of conditioning has been the separation of the representation of events and relations in conditioning from the mechanisms of response production.

I find this divorce an unpleasant one, and, paradoxically, I believe it has impeded, rather than facilitated, our appreciation for the wealth of representational processes in conditioning. In this article, I describe a sampling of Pavlovian conditioning experiments, mostly from my laboratory, which used detailed analyses of conditioned behavior to illuminate the richness of the contents and functions of animals' representations of conditioning episodes. I consider a single issue: the ability of CSs to activate perceptual and other processing mechanisms characteristic of the US. I do not intend this article to be either profoundly theoretical, or (I hope) jejunely empirical.

Conditioning as substitution

In traditional theoretical accounts, Pavlovian conditioning is described as the substitution of a previously neutral stimulus into an existing reflex system, the transfer of control of an unconditioned reflex from a biologically signifi-cant US to a more prosaic CS. This view of the CS as a substitute elicitor of the unconditioned response (UR) was encouraged by early observations that the CR was a replica of the UR, and widely accepted because of its congru-ence with the then-dominant modes of thinking about conditioning, S–R or S–S associationism.

From the S–R perspective, exposure to the CS–US relation resulted in changes in the "automatic switchboard activities of the central nervous sys-tem" (Hull, 1943, chap. 3), such that the neural impulses activated by the CS came to elicit the same efferent activity as formerly elicited by the US. Thus the S–R representation of the conditioning episode was in terms of a change in the operating characteristics of the central nervous system, so that an associative connection was formed between the afferent CS-receptor impulses and the UR-effectors.

Within the S–S view (e.g., Culler, 1938; Pavlov, 1927), the CS acquired the ability to activate a much greater range of neural activity previously activated only by the US. The associative connections were formed between CS-receptor impulses and more central processing activity relating to the US. The UR-effector mechanisms were not wired directly to the CS-receptor mechanisms, but rather were intermediated by activity of a much greater portion of the US–UR reflex circuit. Thus, the S–S versus S–R distinction essentially concerned whether a site of plastic, functional convergence of the pathways used in processing CS and US was nearer sensory or motor ends of the US–UR reflex path. The combatants asked, how much of the machine-ry of the US–UR system is engaged by the CS alone after conditioning; more casually, how much of the US-experience does the animal apprehend in the presence of the CS alone?

The S–S versus S–R controversy captured the attention of the learning psychologist at several points in the history of the field (e.g., Rescorla, 1973; Rozeboom, 1958; Tolman, 1933). But the debate was often dismissed as a quarrel over a pseudoissue (e.g., Kendler, 1952). Furthermore, many inves-tigators argued that viewing Pavlovian conditioning as merely the transfer of a simple reflex is insufficient to capture the opulence of behavioral adaptation in conditioning (see Holland, 1984, for a review). Nevertheless, consideration of the S–S/S–R distinction has provided important insights for questions of event representation in conditioning, and the neurobiology of learning.

Figure 1 shows a cartoon of two reflex pathways, one of a US, say food,

Figure 1.   *Simple diagram of S–S and S–R associations between conditioned stimulus (CS) and unconditioned stimulus (US) paths. (UR = unconditioned response.)*

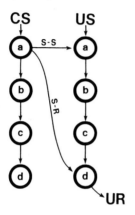

which elicits a UR, say salivation, and one of a CS, say tone, which does not elicit that response prior to conditioning. These pathways should be imagined as comprising whatever sensory, elaborative, and motor systems – neural or psychological – are necessary to produce untrained experience and behavior. Presumably, opportunity for neural convergence exists at many levels and loci along these pathways. Our question is, what is the locus of plasticity that relates these two pathways as a result of some conditioning episode? Does the CS acquire the ability to activate late portions of the US pathway, or does it act early in the US pathway?

Consider two extreme representations. The link labeled "S–S" reflects a changed potential for the CS to activate the first US-path unit. *All* of the US-path machinery is thus engaged by CS presentation alone. The rat will not only salivate when the tone is presented, but also it will taste, smell, feel, and otherwise experience food as if the food itself were present. In fact, it salivates *because* of this perceptual processing of the absent US. The tone serves as a perfect surrogate for food, invoking the same perceptual processing as food itself. In short, the rat imagines or hallucinates the absent food. On the other hand, the link labeled "S–R" reflects a changed potential of the CS to activate only the output unit that controls the UR: No other US-path machinery is engaged by the CS alone. Consequently, although the S–R rat salivates when the tone is presented, no *perceptual* processing of the absent US is engaged.

It is unlikely that any significant Pavlovian CR is generated entirely by plasticity at either one of these loci, in all but the simplest systems. Receptors and sensory neurons linked with processing of the US are unlikely to be activated by CSs, nor are final motor neurons likely to be the sole site of plasticity in conditioning. But the questions of how much US-path machinery is engaged by the CS, and under what circumstances, remain useful. Considerable evidence indicates (1) there are multiple sites of plastic convergence between CS- and US-paths, (2) the relative importance of those points of convergence is influenced greatly by the nature of the conditioning episode, and (3) in many instances, considerably more of the US-path machinery is engaged by the CS than we were previously likely to assume. Indeed, the conclusion from many of the experiments described below is that, under some circumstances, the CS does generate perceptual processing of the absent US. This is by no means a new idea (see for example, King, 1979, or Konorski, 1967), but I believe the data are now a little more compelling.

In this article, my concern is the portion of US-path activity that comes to be controlled by the CS, the "CS-activated US representative," a representative that is not a little picture in the head, but a recreation of experience and action. I defend an extreme claim, that under some circumstances, rats taste absent foods when presented with auditory cues formerly paired with those foods. Then, I distinguish between the processing of such self-generated events and of real-world events. Next, I note conditions under which such surrogate perception does and does not occur. Finally, I relate this research to issues in the study of mental imagery in humans.

Experiment 1: Mediated performance of CRs

The ability of previously conditioned CSs to elicit CRs often depends on the subject's evaluation of the US at the time of testing, not just the value of that US at the time of training. Thus, the production of CRs in those cases is apparently mediated by some updatable representative of the US. Consider an experiment performed in my laboratory. Its procedures are similar to many of those to be described in this article. First, in conditioning boxes, hungry rats received two kinds of conditioning trials, in order to establish two tone CSs as surrogates for two food USs. Tone1 was followed immediately by delivery of food1 to a clear food cup, recessed in one side wall, and tone2 was followed by food2, delivered to the same food cup. The two "tones" were a 1,500 Hz square wave and a white noise, and were 10 s long; the foods were 0.3-ml deliveries of peppermint and wintergreen-flavored sucrose solutions, which generated equal consummatory behavior and preferences (all cues were counterbalanced fully across procedures). Over the course of 16 presentations of each tone–food combination (spread over four 60-min conditioning sessions, and randomly intermixed within each session), identical

Figure 2.   *Conditioned responding during tone1 (T1) and tone2 (T2) in the four ses-*
sions of acquisition, and during the two tone test trials in Experiment 1.
(The ordinate scale is the percentage of all behavior recorded that included
contact with the food cup.)

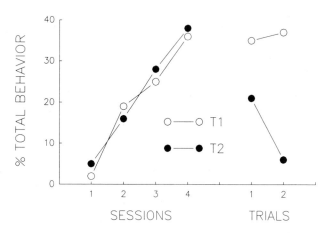

amounts of food-related conditioned behavior (contact with the food cup)
were established to the two tones (left side of Figure 2).

Then, the next day, the rats were given training designed to devalue one
of the foods, by establishing an aversion to it. In the absence of either tone,
5 min access to food2 was followed by an injection of a mild dose of the toxin,
lithium chloride. Considerable research shows that rats readily associate
flavor cues with consequent illness. To confirm these effects, a set of rats
from this experiment were given tests several days later to evaluate the effects
of food2–toxin pairings on their consumption of the two foods. Although
those rats' consumption of food1 was unaffected, their consumption of food2
was virtually eliminated. Thus, pairing food2 with the toxin can be said to
have selectively altered some component of the rats' representative of that
event.

The data of primary importance were those from other rats, who, instead
of receiving tests of their reactivity to the foods, received tests of their reactivity to the *tones*. In the first test, each of the original tone CSs was presented
twice to the rats, in the absence of the foods or toxins. Tone2, whose food2
partner had been paired with toxin, showed a substantially reduced CR, but
tone1, whose food1 associate had not been devalued, continued to display
substantial CRs (right side of Figure 2).

This outcome is consistent with the S–S view of conditioning described
above: Because tone2 activates much of the same processing as food2 itself,

Figure 3. *Diagram of possible S–S and S–R associations established in Experiment 1.*
(CS = conditioned stimulus, US = unconditioned stimulus, UR = uncon-
ditioned response, → = excitatory action, ⊣ = inhibitory action).

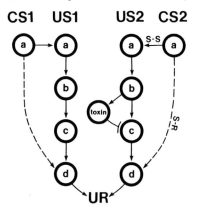

the inhibitory influence of the food2–toxin experience is also brought to bear
on the CR to tone2. For example, suppose, as Garcia, Kovner, and Green
(1970) suggested, that food2–toxin pairing alters the palatability of food2,
that is, makes it taste bad. Just as a bad-tasting food generates little consumption, activation of that bad taste by the tone will generate little conditioned
contact with the food cup.

Regardless of the nature of the toxin's influence on the US representative,
the potentiated link between tone2 and food2 pathways must be upstream
from that site (see Figure 3). If instead the tone2–food2 link was downstream
from the food2–toxin link (the S–R path, for example), then tone2 alone
would activate the output of the food pathway without involving that inhibitory influence – the rat would not experience the bad taste – and its CR would
be intact.

Perceptual nature of substitution

The information about the US coded by these CS-evoked representatives
must be quite detailed. In the experiment just described, the two foods were
delivered to the same food cup, and differed only in which flavoring was
added. Furthermore, the concentrations of the flavorings were selected so
there were no preferences for one or the other in groups of rats, or for most
individual rats. Detailed observations of the rats' consummatory behavior
indicated that they interacted with the two foods in identical ways (thus, in

Figure 3, a common UR output unit is shown). Consequently, the rats' selective reduction in conditioned responding to tone2 (but not tone1) makes it likely that the substitution of tones for foods is more easily labeled "perceptual" than "motor": Somehow, taste properties of the absent USs were involved in response production.

This conceptual distinction is made more viable by the results of two kinds of experiments. The first strategy involved slow-motion video monitoring of the form of the rats' consummatory responses, in a "taste reactivity test." The second method made use of the taste reactivity test to pit the consequences of perceptual and motor responding against each other.

Grill and Norgren (1978) described distinct patterns of responding to naturally occurring positive (e.g., sweet), negative (e.g., bitter), and neutral (e.g., water) flavors. For example, whereas infusion of sucrose solution into a rat's mouth resulted in an "ingestive" reaction, comprising rhythmic mouth movements, tongue protrusions, and paw licking, infusion of quinine produced an "aversive" reaction, including gaping, chin rubbing, head shaking, and flailing of the forelimbs. Plain water was simply swallowed, or allowed to dribble out of the mouth.

My first use of this measurement procedure to investigate the perceptual aspects of CS-activated US representatives hinged on an observation of Pelchat, Grill, Rozin, and Jacobs (1983), who paired highly palatable solutions with toxin or electric shock. They found that the two kinds of pairings both reduced consumption of the solutions, but had different effects on the *patterns* of consumption. Whereas the rats simply consumed less of the solutions when they were paired with shock, they shifted from ingestive to aversive behaviors when the flavored solutions were paired with toxin. Pelchat et al. suggested that these outcomes supported Garcia et al.'s (1970) claim that flavor–toxin pairings reduce consumption by making the flavor taste bad, but flavor–shock pairings reduce consumption less directly, by signaling an imminent aversive event. Thus, in the experiments described in the present article, taste reactivity measures will be taken to indicate perceptual, taste processing. Granted, at this point, this is an extravagant claim, but it is supported by the results of the next few experiments.

Experiment 1a: Taste reactivity measures during performance of CRs

Experiment 1a consisted of a single taste reactivity test of the rats from Experiment 1. On the day after Experiment 1's test of food cup contact CRs during the two tones, I observed the rats while they were consuming a plain sucrose solution. The solution was presented in the usual transparent food cup, under which there was a TV camera. The rats' consumption of the

Figure 4. *Results of the taste reactivity test in Experiment 1a. The left set of bars shows the frequency of ingestive responses per tape segment during the time sucrose alone (O), or sucrose plus either tone1 (T1) or tone2 (T2) was presented; the right set of bars shows aversive responses during the same periods.*

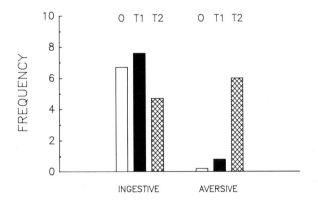

sucrose was taped in the presence of tone1, tone2, and in the absence of tones. Tapes were viewed at one-tenth the normal speed, and the number of instances of ingestive and aversive responses tabulated. During tone2, whose food2 partner had been paired with toxins, the rats showed more aversive responses (and fewer ingestive responses) than during tone1, whose food1 partner had not been devalued. Note that in the conditioning phase of Experiment 1, when the tones were paired with the flavored solutions, many ingestive and few aversive responses were likely to have occurred. Thus, if tone2 had acquired direct control of ingestive responding in the conditioning phase, it would be expected to continue controlling those ingestive responses in the taste reactivity tests. Instead (Figure 4), it controlled aversive responses, as if tone2 activated taste processing normally evoked by food 2: In the presence of tone2, the plain sucrose tasted like the now-aversive food2, and hence generated aversive responses. Conversely, tone1 controlled few aversive responses, and higher levels of ingestive responses than tone2.

Experiments 2 and 3: Stimulus compounding and taste reactivity

It could be argued that in Experiment 1, both tone2–food2 and food2–toxin pairings acted on motoric aspects of the food2 pathway (representative). That is, as a consequence of tone2–food2 pairings, tone2 came to activate the unit that generated the ingestive responses to food2. Subsequent food2–toxin pairings then may have endowed that latter unit with the power to activate a unit that controlled aversive responses. Thus, the final presentation of the tone would activate first the ingestive response unit, which in turn would activate the aversive responses. This possibility is essentially the rg–sg mechanism of Hull (1931), which permitted mediational processes without having to admit to more than S–R associations: The rat could exhibit aversive responses without tasting the absent aversive food.

Experiments 2 and 3 attempted to distinguish this S–R account from the more frankly perceptual one I proposed earlier, by pitting the perceptual (taste) and response (consummatory) consequences of the CS-evoked representatives against each other. They were designed after experiments of Rescorla, Grau, & Durlach (1985), who reported related findings in the autoshaping of pigeons. In Experiment 2, rats first received pairings of tone1 with a sucrose solution and tone2 with a salt solution in the conditioning boxes. At that time, both of those solutions generated substantial ingestive responding, and little aversive responding. Thus, any consummatory responses directly conditioned to the tone would be ingestive in form. Next, in the rats' home cages, and in the absence of the tones, the rats received pairings of a sucrose + salt compound solution with toxin, but separate presentations of the individual salt and sucrose solutions, in the absence of toxin. The rats quickly mastered this "positive patterning" discrimination, consuming either element when it was presented separately, but rejecting the compound flavor. Finally, in the conditioning boxes, the pattern of consumption of plain water was examined by itself, and in the presence of tone1, tone2, and a compound of tone1 and tone2.

If the tones' effects on consumption were mediated by consummatory responses conditioned directly to the tones, then the compound of the two tones should evoke even more ingestive responses than either of the tones individually. But if the tones generated consummatory responding by activating *perceptual* processing of the sucrose and salt USs, then the tone1 + tone2 compound would activate a compound sucrose + salt unit. Because the rats had previously learned to reject that compound flavor, they would show *fewer* ingestive responses and *more* aversive responses during the tone compound than during tone1 or tone2 alone.

The data supported the perceptual view. Although the separately presented tones increased the number of ingestive responses over the water baseline rate (plain water is typically consumed without either ingestive or aversive responses), the tone1 + tone2 compound evoked fewer ingestive and more aversive responses than did the separately presented tones (top panel of Figure 5). Thus, the tone-activated US representatives of sugar and salt appeared to interact at a perceptual level.

Experiment 3 led to a similar conclusion. Rats received pairings of tone1

Figure 5.   *Results of food consumption tests of Experiments 2 (top panel) and 3 (bottom panel). Both panels display the frequency per tape segment of ingestive and aversive consummatory responses during presentations of either tone1 (T1), tone2 (T2) or a compound of the two tones (T1 + T2). In both experiments, the frequency of ingestive and aversive responses when none of the tones was present (water only periods) was less than 1.0.*

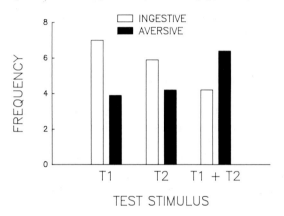

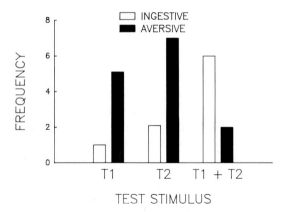

with sucrose and tone2 with salt, as in Experiment 2. In the second phase, the individual sucrose and salt elements were each paired with toxin, but their compound was presented without toxin. This "negative patterning" discrimination was also learned very rapidly (see Forbes & Holland, 1980, for other examples of rats' rapid learning of patterned discriminations in flavor aversion conditioning). In this experiment, the tone1 + tone2 compound produced an increase in baseline ingestive responses, but the tones separately generated increases in aversive responses (bottom panel of Figure 5).

It is difficult to imagine a summation rule that would permit peripheral response tendencies to combine to generate the patterns found in *both* Experiments 2 and 3. Conversely, these data are consistent with the idea that two separately activated flavor representatives combine to generate a third flavor representative, which in turn generates a CR appropriate to that flavor combination. Thus, the combination rules for CS-activated flavor representatives are similar to those for the flavors themselves.

Functional properties of CS-activated US representatives

The results of Experiments 1–3 suggest that CSs may control perceptual processing of absent USs, which ultimately results in the control of consummatory performance. In what other functions may CS-activated US representatives substitute for their referents? Is a CS's substitutability for the US limited to its response-eliciting role, or do CS-activated representatives more generally resemble activity produced by the US itself? In this section I present data that suggest that these representatives may be effective surrogates in conditioning and extinction of explicit cues, in interfering with (overshadowing) conditioning to an explicit cue, and in potentiating or catalyzing conditioning of an explicit cue.

Experiment 4: Mediated acquisition

If a tone, previously paired with a food, actually induces perception of that food's flavor, then would a rat made ill while engaging in such surrogate tasting develop an aversion to the food itself? In the first phase of Experiment 4 (reported in Holland, 1981, Experiment 3), tone1 was paired with food1 and tone2 was paired with food2, as in Experiment 1. Then, in the absence of any of the foods, one of the *tones* (tone2) was paired with toxin. Later, tests of food consumption showed that each rat acquired a more substantial aversion to food2 than to food1 (consuming 46% more of food1 than food2, on average). Apparently, receiving toxin while the food2 representative was activated by tone2 was sufficient to establish an aversion to food2 itself. In terms of Figure 3, the CS's activation of the US-path unit labeled b allowed the establishment of the food2–toxin link, just as if that unit had been activated by presentation of food2 itself.

The aversion to food2 was acquired in the absence of any evidence for aversive conditioning to tone2 itself, which was directly paired with the toxin: That tone's ability to evoke conditioned appetitive behavior was unaffected by the tone2–toxin pairing. This lack of tone–toxin learning is consonant with much other data that indicate that auditory cues are only poorly associable with illness consequences (e.g., Garcia & Koelling, 1966). Indeed, it is reasonable to suppose that the acquisition of an aversion to *food2* when tone2 was paired with toxin *depended* on auditory cues' relatively low associability with illness (and flavors' exceptionally high associability); otherwise, one might expect the physically present tone to mask or overshadow the CS-activated representative of the food flavor.

The acquisition of a food2 aversion in the absence of aversive conditioning of tone2 itself shows the independence of the CS's function as a stimulus in its own right and as a surrogate for the US. This independence is supported by the performance of other subjects in Experiment 4, who received pairings of tone2 with electric shock, rather than toxin. These rats rapidly acquired freezing behavior (characteristic of CRs based on painful USs) to tone2, and lost the previously trained appetitive CRs. However, despite acquiring a sub-stantial aversion to tone 2, these rats showed no evidence of acquiring an aversion to *food2*. This lack of an aversion to food2 is reasonable: Not only is the CS-activated flavor representative not readily associable with shock (Garcia & Koelling, 1966), but also the physically present tone, which *is* readily associable with shock, is likely to mask any conditioning to that flavor representative. All in all, the CS-activated representative of the flavor and the CS itself acted in opposite ways: The tone itself was more readily as-sociated with shock than with illness, but the flavor representative activated by that tone was more readily associated with illness than with shock. Thus, the tone's role as a surrogate flavor was differentiable from its role as a simple stimulus.

Experiment 5: Mediated extinction of an aversion

If pairing of a CS-activated flavor representation with illness can *establish* an aversion to that flavor itself, might the CS-activation of a flavor representa-tive in the *absence* of illness *extinguish* an aversion already established to that flavor? Holland & Forbes (1982) found evidence for such "mediated extinc-tion" of a flavor aversion. As in Experiment 4, two tones were first paired with two foods, presumably enabling each tone to activate a representative of its food partner. Then aversions were established to both foods, by pairing each of them (separately) with toxin. Then one of the tones (tone2) was presented repeatedly, in the absence of food or toxin. Subsequent consump-tion tests showed a reduced aversion to the food whose tone partner had been extinguished in the preceding phase: Each rat consumed more of food2 than of food1 (25% more, on average).

Apparently, nonreinforcement of a CS-evoked representative of an avoided food substance was sufficient to at least partially extinguish the aversion to that food. This mediated extinction effect is reminiscent of an often used human antiphobic treatment: Patients are taught to relax while imagining scenes associated with fear, with the hope that the replacement of fear by relaxation in the presence of imaginary surrogates for fearful situations will transfer to the real situations.

Experiment 6: Mediated overshadowing

Typically, a CS acquires less conditioned responding if it is reinforced in the presence of another CS than if it is reinforced alone. This *overshadowing* effect is found in many conditioning preparations, and has played an important role in the formulation of modern conditioning theories (e.g., Mackintosh, 1975; Pearce & Hall, 1980; Rescorla & Wagner, 1972). Holland (1983, Experiment 1) showed that toxin-based conditioning of an aversion to one food substance can be overshadowed not only by the simultaneous presentation of another food substance, but also by a CS-activated representative of another food.

In three groups of rats, a tone was first endowed with the ability to evoke a representative of a flavored food, X, by presenting several tone-X pairings; in a fourth group, Group AT−, the tone and X were not paired. In a second phase of the experiment, another flavored food, A, was paired with toxin in all four groups. In Group A, A alone was paired with toxin, in Group AX, a compound of A and X was paired with toxin, and in Groups AT+ and AT−, a compound of A and the tone was paired with toxin. Finally, consumption of A alone was examined (top panel of Figure 6). The questions of interest were, first, did the presence of flavor X itself along with A (Group AX) interfere with (overshadow) conditioning of an aversion to flavor A, and second, did the presence of a tone-evoked representative of flavor X along with A (Group AT+) overshadow conditioning to A?

The strongest aversion to A (hence the lowest consumption) was established in Group A, indicating that, in the other three groups, the presence of other cues at the time of A's pairing with toxin interfered with the establishment of the aversion to A. Most important for my present purposes is the observation of a weaker aversion (greater consumption) to A in Group AT+, in which a tone that activated a representative of flavor X accompanied A in training, than in Group AT−, in which the accompanying tone did not activate such a representative. That comparison parcels out any overshadowing effect of the tone itself. Thus, a CS-activated representative of flavor X interfered with conditioning of the real flavor, A, in Group AT+, just as flavor X itself interfered with conditioning of A in Group AX.

Figure 6. *Consumption in the test sessions of Experiments 6 (top panel), 7 (middle panel), and 8 (bottom panel). In the top panel, more consumption of flavor A indicates more overshadowing by its partner (flavor X in Group AX, a tone that also activated a representative of flavor X in Group AT+, and a tone that did not activate a representative of flavor X in Group AT−). In the middle panel, less consumption of the odor A solution indicates more potentiation by its partner (the same as in the top panel). In the bottom panel, less consumption of solutions with odors X or Y indicates more potentiation by their partner (a flavor in Group A, but a representative of that flavor, activated by odor X, in Group R).*

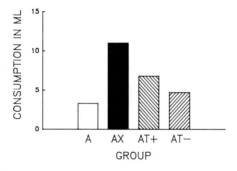

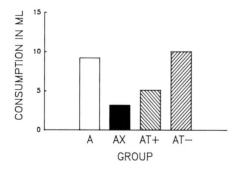

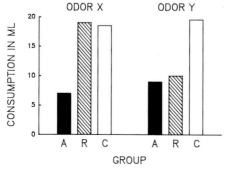

Experiment 7: Mediated potentiation

Although conditioning of an aversion to a *flavor* is overshadowed when it is compounded with another flavor, conditioning of an aversion to an *odor* is often *potentiated* when it is compounded with a flavor. That is, more conditioning of the odor is observed if it is accompanied by a flavor in conditioning than if it were conditioned alone. Holland (1983, Experiment 3) duplicated the experiment just described, but substituted an odor A for the flavor A. In that experiment, presence of the flavor X *augmented* the aversion established to the odor A (middle panel of Figure 6): There was less consumption (more conditioned aversion) of a fluid bearing odor A in Group AX (in which the odor A + flavor X compound was paired with toxin) than in Group A (in which odor A alone was paired with toxin). More critical was the performance of the rats in Group AT+, in which odor A was accompanied by a tone-evoked representative of flavor X when it was paired with toxin. In that group, the conditioned aversion to odor A was potentiated (less consumption) relative to the aversions established in both Group A and Group AT− (in which the odor had been accompanied by a tone that did not activate a representative of flavor X). Thus, the CS-activated representative of a flavor substituted for the flavor itself, serving the same function that was served by that flavor. It is especially worth noting that, in Experiments 6 and 7, the same CS-activated flavor representatives served opposite functions (over-shadowing or potentiation), depending on the function of the flavor itself.

Limits to the function of CS-activated event representatives

The results of the experiments I've described so far imply that CS-activated US representatives and their referents are interchangeable in at least four functions: (1) generation of conditioned/unconditioned behavior, (2) acquisition and extinction of conditioning, (3) interference with conditioning between other CSs and USs (overshadowing), and (4) catalyzing the formation of associations between other CSs and USs (potentiation).

It is unreasonable to imagine, however, that rats do not distinguish between events and evoked representatives of those absent events: Presumably a little reality monitoring is as adaptive for rats as for humans. In fact, several aspects of my data suggest that even the rich CS-activated representatives of events I've described here and the events themselves are not processed identically. I discuss this evidence in the section headed "Differential processing of events and their surrogates," below.

In addition, these robust CS-activated representatives may be generated only rarely. The experiments described above were carefully designed to demonstrate these effects, to assure activation by the CS of upstream portions of the US path. Many variations in the procedures and events chosen can greatly modify the mediational effects I have described; I discuss two of these in "Procedural variations and the nature of CS-activated representatives," below.

Differential processing of events and their surrogates

First, event representatives generate much smaller effects than the events themselves. The magnitudes of mediated conditioning (Experiment 4) and extinction (Experiment 5) effects were less than 25% of those generated by the events themselves, even when we made serious efforts to equate the timing and so forth of the experiences with real and surrogate events. Only mediated potentiation (Experiment 7) effects came close to being as large as the corresponding effects with actual events. Perhaps this difference reflects only an intensity difference; nevertheless, it can not be ignored.

Second, although real events affect stimuli regardless of whether or not those stimuli activate event representatives, we have evidence that event representatives do not affect the stimuli that activated them. This immunity of CSs to effects of the US-representatives they activate may be highly adaptive. Consider, for example, simple extinction. If presentation of a CS activates a representative of the US, then functional CS–US pairings would occur even if the real US was omitted. In the extreme, extinction might never occur, because of "self-reinforcement" of the CS by the US representative evoked by that CS. Immunity of the CS to the conditioning powers of its evoked representative would avoid this paradox.

Experiment 8: Mediated potentiation 2

Although the logic of the experiment is a bit convoluted, the best evidence for this immunity comes from a potentiation experiment, like Experiment 7. Suppose we first train rats so that odor X activates a representative of flavor A. Then, we pair a compound of odor X and a novel odor Y with toxin. Thus, the XY compound odor is conditioned in the presence of a representative of a flavor, activated by X. We know from Experiment 7 that such a representative may indeed potentiate conditioning of an odor aversion. The question here is, will the flavor representative (activated by X) equally potentiate X and Y? If odor X itself is immune to the effects of the flavor representative it activates, then that representative might potentiate conditioning of Y, but not conditioning of X. Three groups of rats received two pairings of an XY compound odor with toxin. In Group A, that compound was accompanied by a flavor, A, which should potentiate the conditioning of aversions to both odors X and Y. In Group R, the XY compound was not accompanied by an explicit flavor, but because the X odor had been previously paired with A, X should have activated a representative of that flavor during XY presentations. Finally, in Group C (control), the XY compound was paired with toxin in the absence of either a representative of A or A itself (X had not been previously paired with A in that group).

The bottom panel of Figure 6 shows that the conditioning of aversions to both X and Y was potentiated (less consumption) by the flavor itself (Group A), relative to the aversions established in the control group (Group C). Of critical interest is the performance of Group R, in which X presumably activated a representative of flavor A. Relative to the control group, Group R showed substantial potentiation of conditioning to odor Y, but none to odor X, which activated the flavor representative. Thus, although flavor A itself potentiated conditioning to both odors X and Y, a CS-activated representative of that flavor only potentiated conditioning to the odor (Y) that did not activate that representative. Apparently, events and their CS-activated representatives are not treated identically: The evoker of a representative is uniquely immune to modification by that representative. In some fashion, a CS's current activation of a US pathway apparently prevents further plasticity between those two paths at that time.

Procedural variations and the nature of CS-activated US representatives

I have investigated two variables that substantially alter CSs' abilities to serve as surrogate USs in many of the roles discussed earlier. The first, amount of training, was examined within conditioning procedures like those already discussed. The second, relative salience or associability of potential associates, was investigated with the aid of a different preparation, to be described later.

Experiment 10: Effects of practice on the nature of CS-activated US representatives

At least some of the mediational effects I've described vanish if the original CS–US training period is prolonged. In all of the experiments mentioned so far, only minimal training (up to 16 pairings of tones and food, and one or two pairings of odors and flavors) was used. Experiment 10 examined the effects of amount of tone–food training on the mediated conditioning of an aversion to a food (produced, as in Experiment 3, by pairing that tone with toxin). In the first phase of Experiment 10, all rats received 16 tone1–food1

Figure 7. *Consumption of food1 and food2 in the consumption tests of Experiment 10. All of the groups initially received 16 tone1–food1 pairings; the number of tone2–food2 pairings is indicated by the group label. Prior to the test, either tone1 (T1) or tone2 (T2) was paired with toxin (in separate subgroups).*

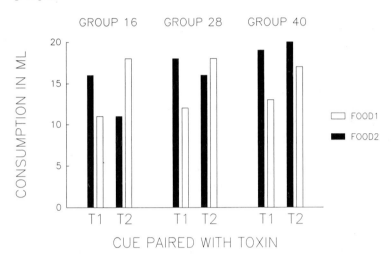

pairings, intermixed with tone2–food2 pairings. Separate groups of rats received 16, 28, or 40 tone2–food2 pairings. (To equate the groups for experience with food2, those groups received either 24, 12, or 0 light–food2 pairings as well.) Next, half of the rats in each group received tone1–toxin pairings, and half received tone2–toxin pairings. Finally, consumption of food1 and food2 was assessed (Figure 7). Consumption of food1 was reduced after tone1–toxin pairings in all three groups, but consumption of food2 was significantly reduced only in the group that had initially received 16 tone2–food2 pairings.

Thus, with extended tone2→food2 pairings, tone2 seemed to lose its ability to activate a representative that was effective as a food2 surrogate in aversion conditioning. This loss of plasticity (or gain in automaticity) with more experience has a variety of parallels in psychology (e.g., Adams, 1982; Allport, 1937; Kimble & Perlmuter, 1970; but see Colwill & Rescorla, 1985 for an opposing view) and neurobiology (e.g., Held & Hein, 1963). It implies different functional properties of newly altered and extensively altered convergent pathways: with repeated execution of the CS–UR complex, more downstream portions of the circuit seem to become more highly tuned, and come to predominate.

Effects of relative salience or associability on the nature of CS-activated US representatives

The experiments I describe briefly in this section used a somewhat different set of conditioning procedures. In most of these experiments, hungry rats received presentations of two-element serial compounds (S1→S2) of auditory and/or visual stimuli, for example, a 5-s light followed by a 5-s tone. The question of interest was how the nature of the S1-activated S2-representative could be affected. Under what conditions did S1 acquire the ability to activate perceptual processing of S2, as in Experiments 1–9 (link S–S in Figure 1), and under what conditions did it activate more "downstream," response-like portions of the S2 processing system (link S–R in Figure 1)?

In general, variables that might be expected to alter the relative salience or associability of the perceptual and response properties of S2 with S1 affected the nature of the S2 representative activated by S1. First, if S2 possessed potent response attributes at the time of its pairings with S1, there was little evidence for the mediational effects that I argued implied signal-evoked perceptual processing of the absent event (Experiments 1–10), but if S2 was relatively neutral at the time of S1–S2 pairing, those effects were evident.

For example, consider a set of "serial conditioning" experiments, in which CRs were acquired to S1 when S1→S2 serial compounds were reinforced with a food US (Holland, 1985; Holland & Ross, 1981). We asked whether S1 came to activate perceptual processing of S2 (which in turn generated the CRs), or to activate only more downstream, response-generating portions of the S2-processing pathway. We addressed these questions several ways, two of which are of special interest to the present discussion. In one case, after completion of S1→S2→food conditioning, we examined the effects of changing the value of S2 on CRs elicited by S1. (This strategy is analogous to my examining, in Experiment 1, the effects of changing the value of food on responding to the tone CSs.) If S1 generated CRs by activating perceptual features of S2, which in turn activated CR production pathways, then any functional "disconnection" of the link between those perceptual features of S2 and response production mechanisms (for example, by extinguishing or habituating S2's responses) would reduce responding to S1, just like training an aversion to the food US in Experiment 1 reduced CRs evoked by the tone CS. A second method was analogous to the strategy of Experiment 5: After S1→S2→food, conditioning, the ability of nonreinforced S1 presentations to produce the "mediated extinction" of S2–food associations was examined. If S1 came to activate a surrogate for S2, then S1 presentations in the absence of food should encourage extinction of S2 as well as of S1.

If S2 was relatively neutral (that is, if it did not elicit much responding) when S1→S2 pairings were introduced, the results of both of the test methods just described (as well as others not described here) indicated that S1 indeed came to activate a surrogate of S2: Extinction of either S1 or S2 produced the extinction of responding to the other cue (the designs used ruled out contributions of stimulus generalization). However, if S2 was accompanied by a strong CR (for example, as a result of prior S2–food pairings), then there was no evidence for such surrogate perceptual processing of S2 in the presence of S1: CRs elicited by each CS were immune to the effects of extinguishing the other CS. Thus, "S–S" associations between S1 and "upstream" portions of S2 processing systems were favored to the extent that perceptual features of S2 were salient, relative to response attributes of S2, whereas increasing the relative salience of S2's response attributes favored more downstream, S–R links. In fact, Holland (1985) produced a variety of proportions of S–R and S–S learning in serial conditioning procedures by artificially suppressing or enhancing the level of CR production during S2 at the time of learning, providing further support for this claim.

The relative associability of S1 with perceptual and response aspects of S2 also seems to affect the nature of the S2 representative activated by S1. Using pigeons, in a related "second order conditioning" procedure (in which S2 is first paired with a US, and then S1 is paired with S2, in the absence of the US), Rescorla (1989) manipulated the associability of S1 with perceptual features of S2 by varying the similarity of S1 and S2. Because S1–S2 association is enhanced by similarity of the two cues (e.g., Rescorla & Furrow, 1977), S1 would be more likely to activate perceptual features of S2 if those features were similar to S1's. Indeed, Rescorla (1980) found that S1–S2 learning was more likely to be S–S in nature if S1 and S2 were similar: Even when the experimental design eliminated effects of stimulus generalization, extinction of S2 had greater effects on responding to S1 if S1 and S2 were similar.

All of these outcomes indicate that plasticity may occur at many levels within a response system, depending on the nature of the conditioning episode. Associative elements have their own intrinsic physical properties, and probably perceptual and/or response properties acquired as a consequence of previous learning. Many of those properties may compete with each other for association, and the salience and relative associability of those attributes will influence the nature of the US representative that will be activated by a CS. Consequently, conditioned behavior may have different characteristics and sensitivities to a variety of manipulations, depending on the locus of plasticity between CS and US pathways. Although the effects of CS-activated US representatives I have described here are unlikely to be universal, and perhaps not even major contributors to behavior in many traditional conditioning paradigms, they may have important implications for our understanding of the basic mechanisms of conditioning and integration of behavior systems.

A note on the integration of behavior systems

It is essential to recognize that, in all but the simplest systems, a US pathway or representative is unlikely to be the simple linear array of units I portrayed in Figures 1 and 3. Rather, many aspects of events will be processed, in a variety of perceptual, memory, and response systems. Furthermore, the circuitries of these co-pathways are likely to be well-integrated, such that the presentation of any particular US will encourage not only processing that generates the precise response evoked by that particular event, but also more elaborate processing appropriate to a class of events, a sort of archetypal representative. Thus, CSs and USs should be viewed not only as specific events in their own right, but also as tokens for gaining access to a broader repertoire of action, higher-level behavior patterns which are undoubtedly themselves represented in the nervous system (e.g., Gallistel, 1980).

For example, feeding is a complex activity comprising many separate, sequentially organized action patterns such as foraging, investigation, predation, social approach and food sharing, food handling, and ingestion or rejection of the food. Conditioning may occur at many levels within a behavior system; the precise conditioned behaviors observed might depend on the nature of the cues used, and their resemblance to cues naturally used in the feeding situation. Experiments conducted in my laboratory (reviewed in Holland, 1984), and more extensively by Timberlake (reviewed in Timberlake, 1985) support these claims. For instance, the use of short CSs encourages behavior appropriate to imminent food, such as mouthing and search of the food cup, but longer CSs encourage behaviors normally found earlier in the food-getting sequence. Those CSs, because of their timing, tap into different portions of natural feeding sequences. The form of the CR is further tuned by other features of the cues. For example, static cues like tones and lights encourage investigatory and consummatory responses, but small moving objects as CSs encourage predatory activity, and the use of a conspecific to herald the arrival of food leads to social, food-sharing activities, prior to the actual arrival of the food. Thus, an enormous range of organized behavior can be brought within the purview of substitution, when that notion is broadly conceived. As we begin to examine the effects of less impoverished CSs and USs, we are likely to observe not only more and more complex control of behavior, but also more and more evidence of sophisticated representational systems.

Relation to investigation of mental imagery in humans

The notion that CSs can under some circumstances activate perceptual processing of an absent US has much in common with theories of imagery that
claim imagining an object leads to the activation of the same perceptual
mechanisms that are used in perceiving the object (e.g., Finke, 1980). A
CS-activated US representative with a large perceptual component is essentially an image of that absent US; the experiments I've been describing were
investigations of the functions of imaginary events. There are in fact many
parallels between the data just described and the performance of humans
involved in experiments on imagery.

The basic question is, when people are exposed to the coincidence of two
events, can the first one produce an image of the second? In fact, there is
considerable evidence that when people expect to see an object, they often
imagine seeing the object in advance, and sometimes confuse the real and
imagined objects (Finke, 1985). For example, 40 or 50 years ago there was a
literature on what was called "learned synesthesia" (Howells, 1944) or "conditioned sensation" (e.g., Leuba, 1940; even Skinner, 1953, discussed "conditioned seeing"). Simply described, after repeated pairing of a stimulus of
one sense modality with one of another modality, the second event was omitted, and evidence for perceptual processing in the modality of the absent
second event was sought.

That evidence was of several types. In the extreme, subjects sometimes
reported actually experiencing the missing event, analogous to my claims that
the rats were tasting the absent USs in some of the experiments described
above. For example, experienced subjects in Perky's (1910) experiments in
Tichener's laboratory sometimes reported seeing weak test patterns after a
ready signal, but before the patterns were actually presented. Cole (1939),
Garvey (1933), and Mowrer (1938) reported that human subjects in aversive
Pavlovian conditioning experiments sometimes reported feeling a weak shock
US after the CS even on trials in which no USs were presented. And Ellson
(1941) reported that 80% of his subjects reported hearing a tone, when, after
experience with a light + tone compound, the light alone was presented.
Similar, but even more dramatic were the reports of subjects under hypnosis
(e.g., Erickson & Erickson, 1938; Hilgard, 1977).

A second type of evidence for the perceptual processing of absent, but
imagined or CS-activated events is the observation of the image's interference
with the perception of real events, like the interference that would be produced by the image's real counterpart. For example, Howells (1944) presented subjects with pairings of one tone with light of one hue, and another
tone with light of the complementary hue. When the two lights were later

reversed, so that the "wrong" lights were presented after the tones, subjects reported that the colors took a few seconds "to clear up," the hue even "changing while they were looking at it." In fact, if the "wrong" light was presented at reduced saturation, some subjects persistently identified it as being the other light, that is, the one associated with the preceding tone. Furthermore, if one of the tone signals alone was presented while subjects were performing a simple color mixing/matching task, their judgments indicated a significant contribution of the color that had previously been paired with the tone.

Similarly, subjects who have experience viewing black horizontal and vertical bars superimposed on red and green backgrounds, later report seeing the complementary colors between bars when the bars are presented on a white background (the McCullough effect; McCullough, 1965). Indeed, the primary method of quantifying the McCullough effect is to measure the contribution of the absent, imagined color to the subject's judgment of the color of the bars' (white) background, using a color mixing/matching test similar to Howells' (1944). Furthermore, Finke & Schmidt (1977) found that subjects who only imagined bars superimposed on real red and green backgrounds reported seeing the complementary color aftereffects in testing with real bars on a white background. In a different vein, Segal & Fusella (1970) found that detection of faint auditory or visual patterns in a signal detection task was made more difficult by imagining stimuli of the same modality, but not by imagining stimuli of the other modality. This last finding might be analogous to my report of imaginary flavors interfering (overshadowing) with the conditioning of an aversion to a real flavor.

A third type of evidence involves the converse, the facilitation of perceptual processing of a real event by an imagined event, as in my observation of potentiation of odor conditioning by an imaginary flavor. For example, Freyd & Finke (1984) reported that subjects' judgments of the relative lengths of horizontal and vertical arms of a cross were easier when they first imagined a square where the cross was to be presented. Similarly, Finke (1985) reported that reaction time for identifying the presentation of horizontal or vertical bars was lower if the subject was instructed to imagine the bar with the orientation in which it was to be presented.

Of course, there are alternate explanations for each of the findings just presented. Psychologists have attributed those outcomes variously to experimenter bias, tacit knowledge about the imagined events, demand characteristics of the tasks, and peripheral responses such as eye movements (see, for example, Finke, 1985, for a discussion of these issues). These alternate explanations are perhaps less likely in the experiments with rats described here. For example, it is not clear what the rats' "tacit knowledge" about wintergreen or peppermint would be to solve problems when they are arbitrarily revalued. Experimenter bias seems less likely, as most of the experimental consumption measures were volumes or weights of solutions, taken by assistants blind to the purposes of the experiments, and the taste reactivity measures were rated by an observer blind to the cues, and the rats' and cues' experimental histories. Furthermore, it is unlikely that the rats figured out what I wanted from the instructions given or from extensive experience with the paradigm (one-trial learning procedures were frequently used). I suppose that tongue movements could be implicated, but the results of Experiments 2 and 3, in which the effects of peripheral and perceptual responding were pitted against each other, suggest otherwise.

The "imagery" described in this article is of a different sort than is usually discussed by cognitive psychologists, which tends to be fairly abstract, schematic, and lacking in more concrete and sensory aspects (e.g., Shepard, 1984): The image here is more like an incomplete "hallucination" (e.g., Konorski, 1967). Regardless, the experiments reported here support the view that imagery may be a very basic process, evolutionarily derived from relatively "simple" processes of perception and conditioning that were designed to deal with remote or even absent objects (see Rilling & Neiworth, 1987, and especially, Shepard, 1984, for extended discussions of this view). Indeed, the emergence of organisms' use of internal states and images of absent objects, rather than current external stimuli, to control behavior is an important issue in its own right, worthy of comparative, developmental, and evolutionary analysis.

References

Adams, C.D. (1982). Variations in the sensitivity of instrumental responding to reinforcer devaluation. *Quarterly Journal of Experimental Psychology, 34B*, 77–98.

Allport, G.W. (1937). *Personality: A psychological interpretation.* New York: Holt.

Cole, L.E. (1939). A comparison of the factors of practice and knowledge of experimental procedures. *Journal of General Psychology, 20*, 349–373.

Colwill, R.M., & Rescorla, R.A. (1985). Instrumental responding remains sensitive to reinforcer devaluation after extensive training. *Journal of Experimental Psychology: Animal Behavior Processes, 11*, 520–536.

Culler, E.A. (1938). Recent advances in some concepts of conditioning. *Psychological Review, 45*, 134–153.

Ellson, D.G. (1941). Hallucinations produced by sensory conditioning. *Journal of Experimental Psychology, 28*, 1–20.

Erickson, M.H., & Erickson, E.M. (1938). The hypnotic induction of hallucinatory color vision followed by pseudo negative afterimages. *Journal of Experimental Psychology, 22*, 581–588.

Finke, R.A. (1980). Levels of equivalence in imagery and perception. *Psychological Review, 87*, 113–132.

Finke, R.A. (1985). Theories relating mental imagery to perception. *Psychological Bulletin, 98*, 236–259.

Finke, R.A., & Schmidt, M.J. (1977). Orientation-specific aftereffects following imagination. *Journal of Experimental Psychology: Human Perception and Performance, 3*, 599–606.

Forbes, D.T., & Holland, P.C. (1980). Positive and negative patterning after CS preexposure in flavor aversion conditioning. *Animal Learning and Behavior, 8,* 595–600.

Freyd, J.J., & Finke, R.A. (1984). Facilitation of length discrimination using real and imagined context frames. *American Journal of Psychology, 97,* 323–341.

Gallistel, C.R. (1980). *The organization of action: A new synthesis.* Hillsdale, NJ: Erlbaum.

Garcia, J., & Koelling, R.A. (1966). Relation of cue to consequence in avoidance learning. *Psychonomic Science, 4,* 123–124.

Garcia, J., Kovner, R., & Green, K.S. (1970). Cue properties versus palatability of flavors in avoidance learning. *Psychonomic Science, 20,* 313–314.

Garvey, C.R. (1933). A study of conditioned respiratory changes. *Journal of Experimental Psychology, 16,* 471–503.

Grill, H.J., & Norgren, R. (1978). The taste reactivity test. I. Mimetic responses to gustatory stimuli in neurologically normal rats. *Brain Research, 143,* 263–279.

Held, R., & Hein, A. (1963). Movement-produced stimulation in the development of visually-guided behavior. *Journal of Comparative and Physiological Psychology, 66,* 872–876.

Hilgard, E.R. (1977). *Divided consciousness: Multiple controls in human thought and action.* New York: Wiley-Interscience.

Holland, P.C. (1981). Acquisition of representation-mediated conditioned food aversions. *Learning and Motivation, 12,* 1–18.

Holland, P.C. (1983). Representation-mediated overshadowing and potentiation of conditioned aversions. *Journal of Experimental Psychology: Animal Behavior Processes, 9,* 1–13.

Holland, P.C. (1984). The origins of Pavlovian conditioned behavior. In G. Bower (Ed.), *The psychology of learning and motivation* (Vol. 18, pp. 129–173). Englewood Cliffs, NJ: Prentice-Hall.

Holland, P.C. (1985). Element pretraining influences the content of appetitive serial compound conditioning in rats. *Journal of Experimental Psychology: Animal Behavior Processes, 11,* 367–387.

Holland, P.C., & Forbes, D.T. (1982). Representation-mediated extinction of flavor aversions. *Learning and Motivation, 13,* 454–471.

Holland, P.C., & Ross, R.T. (1981). Within-compound associations in serial compound conditioning. *Journal of Experimental Psychology: Animal Behavior Processes, 7,* 228–241.

Howells, T.H. (1944). The experimental development of color-tone synesthesia. *Journal of Experimental Psychology, 34,* 87–103.

Hull, C.L. (1931). Goal attraction and directing ideas conceived as habit phenomena. *Psychological Review, 38,* 487–506.

Hull, C.L. (1943). *Principles of behavior.* New York: Appleton-Century.

Kendler, H.H. (1952). "What-is-learned?" – a theoretical blind alley. *Psychological Review, 59,* 269–277.

Kimble, G.A., & Perlmuter, L.C. (1970). The problem of volition. *Psychological Review, 77,* 361–384.

King, D.L. (1979). *Conditioning: An image approach.* New York: Gardner.

Konorski, J. (1967). *Integrative activity of the brain.* Chicago: University of Chicago Press.

Leuba, C. (1940). Images as conditioned sensations. *Journal of Experimental Psychology, 26,* 345–351.

Mackintosh, N.J. (1975). A theory of attention: Variations in the associability of stimuli with reinforcement. *Psychological Review, 82,* 276–298.

McCullough, C. (1965). Color adaptation of edge detectors in the human visual system. *Science, 149,* 1115–1116.

Mowrer, O.H. (1938). Preparatory set (expectancy) – a determinant in motivation and learning. *Psychological Review, 45,* 62–91.

Pavlov, I.P. (1927). *Conditioned reflexes.* London: Oxford University Press.

Pearce, J.M., & Hall, G. (1980). A model for Pavlovian learning: Variations in the effectiveness of conditioned but not of unconditioned stimuli. *Psychological Review, 106,* 532–552.

Pelchat, M., Grill, H.J., Rozin, P., & Jacobs, J. (1983). Quality of acquired responses to tastes by rattus norvegicus depends on type of associated discomfort. *Comparative Psychology and Behavior, 97*, 140–153.

Perky, C.W. (1910). An experimental study of imagination. *American Journal of Psychology, 21*, 422–452.

Rescorla, R.A. (1973). Second-order conditioning: Implications for theories of learning. In F.J. McGuigan & D.B. Lumsden (Eds.), *Contemporary approaches to conditioning and learning* (pp. 127–150). Washington, DC: V.H. Winston.

Rescorla, R.A. (1980). *Second-order conditioning*. Hillsdale, NJ: Erlbaum.

Rescorla, R.A., & Furrow, D.R. (1977). Stimulus similarity as a determinant of Pavlovian conditioning. *Journal of Experimental Psychology: Animal Behavior Processes, 3*, 203–215.

Rescorla, R.A., Grau, J.W., & Durlach, P.J. (1985). Analysis of the unique cue in configural discriminations. *Journal of Experimental Psychology: Animal Behavior Processes, 11*, 356–366.

Rescorla, R.A., & Wagner, A.R. (1972). A theory of Pavlovian conditioning: Variations in the effectiveness of reinforcement and nonreinforcement. In A.H. Black & W.F. Prokasy (Eds.), *Classical conditioning II* (pp. 64–99). New York: Appleton-Century-Crofts.

Rilling, M.E., & Neiworth, J.J. (1987). Theoretical and methodological considerations for the study of imagery in animals. *Learning and Motivation, 18*, 57–79.

Rozeboom, W.W. (1958). "What is learned?": An empirical enigma. *Psychological Review, 65*, 22–33.

Segal, S.J., & Fusella, V. (1970). Influences of imaged pictures and sounds on detection of visual and auditory signals. *Journal of Experimental Psychology, 83*, 458–464.

Shepard, R.N. (1984). Ecological constraints on internal representation: Resonant kinematics of perceiving, imagining, thinking, and dreaming. *Psychological Review, 91*, 417–447.

Skinner, B.F. (1953). *Science and human behavior*. New York: Free Press.

Timberlake, W. (1985). The functional organization of appetitive behavior: behavior systems and learning. In M.D. Zeiler & P. Harzem (Eds.), *Advances in the analysis of behavior: Vol. 3. Biological factors in learning* (pp. 177–221). Chichester: Wiley.

Tolman, E.C. (1933). Sign-gestalt or conditioned reflex? *Psychological Review, 40*, 391–411.

Tolman, E.C., & Brunswik, E. (1935). The organism and the causal texture of the environment. *Psychological Review, 42*, 43–77.

Cognition, 37 (1990) 133–166

6

Levels of stimulus control: A functional approach*

R.J. HERRNSTEIN

Harvard University

Abstract

Herrnstein, R.J., 1990. Levels of stimulus control: A functional approach. Cognition 37: 133–166.

This paper surveys some illustrative experiments on categorization of visual stimuli by animals other than human. The results suggest a classification of categorical powers in five steps from simple discrimination to rote and open-ended categorization, to concepts and the use of abstract relations. Nonhuman animals evidently readily categorize up to the fourth level as here defined, which is the level of concepts. With difficulty, they can sometimes be induced to rise even to the level of abstract relations. It is at the level of abstract relations that a large gap opens up between human categorizations and categorization by other animals.

Introduction

There have been numerous efforts to systematize the stimulus control of behavior, or, as it is more often called outside the behaviorist tradition, categorization.[1] In the spirit of cognitive psychology, for example, are the contributions of Smith and Medin (1981) or the essay by Homa (1984). Pre-

*For support of the preparation of this article and some of the work described herein, Grant IST-85-11606 from the National Science Foundation to Harvard University is gratefully acknowledged. Versions were presented at the Neurosciences Institute Symposium on Signal and Sense, June, 1987; in October, 1987, at the Columbia University Seminar on the Psychobiology of Animal Cognition and Harvard University's "Pigeon Meeting," in April, 1988, to a seminar at the Center for Biological Information Processing at MIT, and in March, 1989, to a seminar at the Department of Psychology at New York University. A largely overlapping version of this article is in G.M. Edelman, W.E. Gall, and W.M. Cowan (Eds.) (in press), *Signal and sense: Local and global order in perceptual maps*, New York: Wiley, under the title "Levels of categorization." Thanks to sponsors and participants of these seminars for eliciting, then shaping, these ideas. Thanks also to M.L. Commons, C.R. Gallistel, R.D. Luce, M. Rilling, H.S. Terrace, W. Vaughan, Jr., G. Zuriff, and an anonymous reviewer, for many helpful comments and criticisms. Reprint requests should be addressed to: Dr. Richard Herrnstein, Psychology Department, Harvard University, 33 Kirkland Street, Cambridge, MA 02138, U.S.A.

[1]The review of the literature contained in this paper was intended to be illustrative, not exhaustive. It was largely completed in mid-1987, and, except for a few studies that seem to be especially relevant, I have not attemped to update it for more recent contributions.

0010-0277/90/$10.70 © 1990—Elsevier Science Publishers B.V.

mack (1986) proposes a more behavioristic framework, as adapted by him in light of modern psycholinguistic theory. Dore and Dumas (1987) apply the Piagetian theory, with its stages of cognitive development, to subhuman categorical behavior. Some approaches are informed by inferences about what nervous systems do, inferences that may shift radically depending on the level of neurological analysis chosen or on the growth and development of neuroscience – others, by the results of attempting to simulate natural categorization on computers, or to express it in formal theory. Still other approaches attempt to follow developmental pathways (e.g., Commons, Hallinan, Fong, & McCarthy, 1990). What follows below is an attempt of my own. Neither physiology, computer simulation, nor specific psychological theory, beyond the general notions of reinforcement theory, explicitly influence the scheme I propose. If the scheme has any virtue at all, it is that it seems to provide a convenient framework for thinking about behavioral data.

The present classification of stimulus control is *functional*, in the sense suggested by a consideration of an animal's stimulus problem in nature. In order to behave appropriately an animal needs a description of the stimuli in any environment that renders as invariant as feasible the predictors of psychologically significant consequences of behavior, which may be called the contingencies of reinforcement (for inherited responses no less than for learned ones – see Herrnstein, 1977). Different occasions may thus dictate different descriptions and different dimensions of invariance. The evidence suggests that natural selection has equipped animals with considerable adaptations for dealing with the categorization problem in this very sense, as will be illustrated below.

The problem gets tricky mainly for two reasons – the "occasion" an animal confronts may, first, bear a logically complex relationship to the physical events of which it is composed and, second, it is in the nature of the relevant physical events to be variable and nonrecurrent. Logical complexity arises because the consequences of behavior rarely depend on the mere presence or absence of features of objects – their precise shapes or sizes or colors or the like – but on more complex concatenations of stimulus descriptors. Similarly, even the ordinary objects in an animal's life are variable and ambiguous. Is the present stimulus an acorn, a stone, a predator's spoor? None of those ordinary objects, nor any other, presents itself to a perceiver invariantly. The incentive to identify as such acorns, stones, and so on, arises from the psychological consequences associated with them – one may eat acorns, flee predators, and ignore stones.

If the psychological consequences have been potent and stable long enough in a species' history, then, by virtue of natural selection, the relevant sensory system may have evolved so that the recognition may have innate elements in it. If not, recognition is likely to depend mostly on learning. There must be a continuum of innateness, along which an animal's identifications spread out. How they do so is a rich issue for analysis, but, for the question of categorization itself, nothing inherent seems to depend upon whether the association between stimulus and consequence is innate or must be learned. In either case, animals solve categorization problems by analyzing stimuli in ways that remain unaccounted for neurophysiologically and out of the reach of formal theory, let alone computer simulation.

For one species, acorns may themselves segregate into multiple classes; for another, they may be classed with beech nuts. Nothing about the appearance of acorns or beech nuts per se determines how they will be grouped. Categorization problems are jointly determined by physical variation in stimuli and the consequences of behavior. The recognition problem is complex or simple from the animal's standpoint depending on the relations among the stimulating objects, the consequences of action in their presence, and the perceptual machinery of the creature. That is to say, if acorns vary widely given an animal's perceptual apparatus, then the animal faces a more difficult recognition problem than if they vary little (assuming at this point that acorns set a common contingency for its behavior, no matter what they look like). Or, the contingencies may be conditional, depending not on any particular object, but, for example, on conjunctions and disjunctions of particular configurations (spatial or temporal) of objects.

The interaction between objective contingencies of reinforcement and the capacities of animals suggests five levels of categorization, roughly increasing in abstractness from 1 to 5 below. Where in this progression a given animal is operating for a given categorization problem – the operational tests for these levels of categorization – will be discussed at greater length subsequently.

(1) *Discrimination:* The allowable variation in stimuli, given the contingency of reinforcement, may be so small that categorization collapses on to mere discrimination. An animal in a psychological experiment may be reinforced for responding to a patch of light of a particular wavelength, plus some small band of error. Categorization is then merely failure to discriminate. The situation may be such that if the subject can discriminate among particular stimuli, then those stimuli have discriminable behavioral consequences; if the subject cannot discriminate, then they have essentially the same consequences. In nature, this may be a null class, but, in the contrived environments of the psychological laboratory, it has been the standard for studying stimulus control. Although there are worthy questions of discriminative fineness or coarseness involved here, little will be said about this most

elementary level of categorization, beyond noting that it sets the minimum in abstractness, as that term will be used here.

(2) *Categorization by rote:* The stimuli within a class that is implicitly defined by a contingency of reinforcement may vary substantially more than the resolving power of discrimination, but the entire class can be approximated by a relatively small number of discriminable exemplars. By a relatively small number of exemplars, I mean a set of exemplars that a subject could conceivably learn as a list (disregarding any implication of serial organization). The jacks in a deck of cards would be an example of this sort of category, except insofar as jacks resemble each other. Because they may resemble each other, the subject, when recognizing the four jacks in a given deck, may actually be drawing on a category with unlimited membership, namely the category of all jacks in all decks, whether ever seen before or not. The stops on the subway system's "Red Line" in and around Boston are a clearer example. Here, the 23 exemplars can be learned only as a list, assuming there is no underlying rule that determines membership. Given the name "Kendall," or a photograph of the station bearing this name, one either does or does not know that this is a stop on the line. This would be the pure rote level of categorization.

(3) *Open-ended categories:* The distinction just made between jacks and stations on the Red Line suggests the next step in abstractness. If the contingency of reinforcement entails open-ended or very large membership, as jacks do, then some principle beyond pure rote learning is required. Given the variation of objects in nature, and the variation in organisms' vantage points in perceiving them, the typical natural situation brings us to at least this level. Acorns vary; even a given acorn varies in the aspect it presents to a given organism. Organisms at any level of psychological development may be expected to have means at least for sorting exemplars as open-ended categories.

Perceptual similarity appears to be an evolutionary adaptation to contingencies of reinforcement that circumscribe classes with unlimited membership. No account of categorization by animals can fail to recognize the existence of some primitive ordering of perceptual distances between objects. Acorns vary, but they probably resemble each other from the standpoint of any creature that has truck with them as a class. What is, in a purely physical sense, a class with unlimited membership may become, because of similarity, a class containing one or several clusters of mutually similar members. Although these clusters must have their physical descriptions, it is often not the case that psychological proximity is captured by physical proximity along the standard physical variables.

For a creature that deals with acorns and beech nuts as a single class, it is not necessary to argue that the two sets of objects coalesce perceptually. Rather, for this hypothetical creature, the acorn–beech-nut class may comprise two subcategories, two "clusters," as that term was just used. The creature may be capable of detecting differences not only between acorns and beech nuts, but among examples of either. Similarity is not equivalent to indiscriminability. Objects said to be similar are usually discriminable. Similarity is best viewed as biological, rather than physical: an evolutionary adaptation to the open-endedness of exemplars in the reinforcement contingencies that creatures usually must contend with.

(4) *Concepts:* Level 3, by introducing similarity, converts itself to something resembling Level 2, which is pure rote. By allowing the psychological representation of exemplars some range of variation and a psychological metric of similarity, we rise from rote to open-ended categorization. Nothing has yet been said about any psychological representation of the contingency of reinforcement with respect to which the exemplars are behaviorally invariant. Any such representation would be a concept, as that term will be used here.[2] A creature that has concepts in this sense would adapt to changing contingencies more efficiently than one that did not. For example, suppose acorns became bitter. It can be argued that an animal with some sort of psychological representation for the *class* of acorns, beyond the exemplars themselves, would associate bitterness with acorns in general, not just with the previously tasted acorns or acorns that look like the previously tasted ones, more rapidly and more completely than one without it. This rapid propagation over class members signifies the concept level of categorization. As will be shown later, it is often hard to test whether an animal is sorting by a concept or by just an open-ended category based on similarity, but, in principle, concepts need involve no similarities at all.

(5) *Abstract relations:* In much of the current work on categorization, the focus is on trying to resolve the exemplars of various categories into features or attributes or values along various dimensions, or the like. It is, after all, self-evident that an acorn is not a unitary perceptual entity (for humans), but that it is somehow composed of finer elements – shape, color, size, and so forth. The elements may be complex and relational, including disjunctions, conjunctions, and conditional properties of all sorts. However, this last level

---

[2] Few terms have been used in psychological and epistemological theory in as many different senses as "concept" and its derivatives. I will make no attempt to review those senses, nor to relate them to my proposed usage. Some of this is done in Gallistel's accompanying introduction.

of categorization deals not with the exemplars themselves, but with relations between and among concepts, as defined at Level 4. A reinforcement contingency stipulating "acorns on stumps" exemplifies an abstract relation as meant here, assuming that acorns and stumps are represented as concepts. Another example would be: "color chips in stacks of the same colors." The relations are carried by "on" or "the same," respectively. The abstractness refers to the idea that it is not particular acorns or stumps or colors that are characterized, but acorns, stumps, and colors in general, which is to say, the concepts that embrace them. Creatures capable of forming concepts may be incapable of responding differentially and reliably to such relations between concepts when they are tested with new exemplars. But if they can so respond, they would be categorizing according to abstract relations.

Interest in categorization is often motivated by an interest in language, or human cognition more generally. For humans, language is the natural behavioral medium for displaying categories, particularly those beyond the lowest levels of abstraction defined above. The foregoing list stops about where psycholinguistic considerations become interesting, namely, where language embodies not just concepts and relations between concepts, but relations between relations, concepts whose exemplars are themselves abstract relations, intentions and other descriptions of a speaker's psychological state, and so on.

Those interested in categorization as part of human cognitive capacity or as part of the background for human language usually disregard animal data entirely (see, for example: Estes, 1986; Homa, 1984; Smith & Medin, 1981). Even discussions of the categorizations of preverbal infants are likely to omit any consideration of subhuman data (e.g., Younger & Cohen, 1985), as if categorization were a saltation in mental capacity. But categorization is no saltation. It has turned up at every level of the animal kingdom where it has been competently sought.

One reason for looking more carefully at lower levels of categorization is that the continuity of cognitive processes linking humans and other animals is clear and undeniable here. And, as the evidence to be summarized suggests, it is probably at the upper end of this span that animal and human cognitive capacities diverge.

Categorization by rote

Animals can obviously categorize by rote, but there is a question about how powerful a capacity this can be. Using pigeons as subjects, Vaughan and

Figure 1.   *Examples of the stimuli used by Vaughan and Green (1984) in their experiment on rote categorization by pigeons. (From Vaughan & Greene, 1984.)*

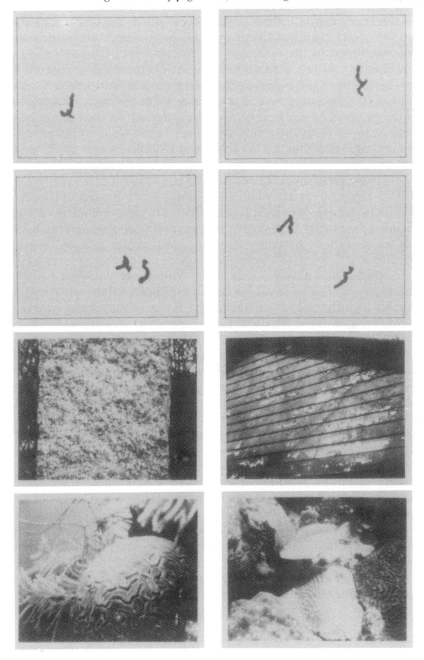

Greene (1984) hoped to examine the sheer size of an animal's storage for a rote category. The general procedure was to assign visual stimuli randomly to positive and negative categories, then to add additional exemplars as a pigeon learned what it had already been given. Pecking a response key was intermittently reinforced with food in the presence of positive stimuli, and not reinforced in the presence of negative stimuli. Stimuli were presented seriatim, for no less than about 20 s each. Further details of the procedure can be found in the original publication (and in Vaughan & Greene, 1983). It need only be noted here that the procedure trains pigeons to peck the key in the presence of exemplars from one category and not to peck in the presence of those from the other. Measures based on the rate of responding in the presence of a stimulus in procedures like this have been shown to provide sensitive and stable estimates of the subject's categorization (Herrnstein, 1979, 1984; Herrnstein, Loveland, & Cable, 1976).

Two kinds of visual stimuli were used for two groups of pigeons – photographs of natural scenes and arbitrary squiggles, examples of which are in Figure 1 – in order to assure at least a modicum of generality to the results. For each kind of stimulus, after an initial population of 10 exemplars (5 positive and 5 negative), pairs were added as the pigeon learned to discriminate what it had already been given. Stimuli were assigned to the positive and negative class by tossing a coin. No superordinate rule could, therefore, reliably identify category membership. As far as the contingency of reinforcement was concerned, this was rote categorization, pure and simple.

The results for squiggles are in Figure 2, for the four pigeons in this part of the study. The measure of discrimination is *rho* (Herrnstein et al., 1976), a nonparametric statistic estimating the probability that the average positive exemplar is ranked above the average negative exemplar, using ranked rates of pecking as the measure of performance. With perfect discrimination, *rho* is 1.0; with no discrimination, it is .5. For 40 pairs of slides, discrimination reaches a .05 level of statistical significance at a *rho* value of .62 (the larger the number of pairs, the closer to .5 is this threshold level of statistical significance). The *rhos* in Figure 2, approaching 1.0, signify high levels of discrimination, given the numbers of slide pairs. When the pigeons were sorting 40 or more pairs, the associated p values per session were usually smaller than 10^{-12}.

But what is even more notable than the height of the ordinate in Figure 2 is its general flatness. Two of the pigeons (the other two died from illness or injury) were, by the end of this experiment, sorting with high accuracy 160 exemplars of squiggles, ranking almost every positive above almost every negative. There was no lowering level of performance as the population of slides grew from 10 to 160, nor were the pigeons taking longer to learn new

Figure 2. *For four pigeons, rho, an index of discrimination, for increasing numbers of "squiggle" stimuli, which were introduced a pair at a time. The pigeons were required to sort squiggles into two arbitrary categories. (From Vaughan & Greene, 1984.)*

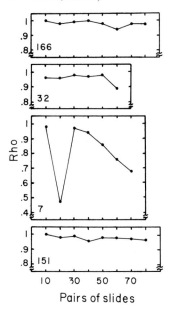

pairs as they were added. In short, it may be said that 160 squiggles do not appear to tax the pigeon's storage capacity for squiggles.

Figure 3 gives the comparable data for the three pigeons working on photographs of natural scenes. Performance is similarly high up to 80 pairs, and similarly gives no sign of taxing storage capacity. If anything, judging from the speed of learning to sort new pairs, scenes were easier to learn than squiggles, despite the much larger amount of visual information ostensibly in them. Stimulus pairs that resembled each other to human observers were harder for the pigeons to learn to sort than pairs that looked different. This simple finding suggests that the pigeons were seeing the photos much as we see them ourselves.

Two pigeons in each procedure were tested for retention of the last 40 pairs of exemplars after more than a year of not having seen them. For the squiggles, the test came 490 days after last seeing any of those particular stimuli; for the scenes, it came after an interval of 629 days. All pigeons discriminated the 80 positive and negative exemplars significantly the first

Figure 3.   *For three pigeons, rho for increasing numbers of photographs of natural scenes, which were introduced a pair at a time. The pigeons were required to sort photos into two arbitrary categories. (From Vaughan & Greene, 1984.)*

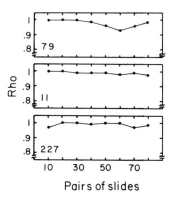

time seen after those intervals. For the very first presentation, values of *rho* were down but still highly significant – in the .7 to .8 region – but by the second viewing of the stimuli, the values of *rho* almost recovered to their original levels above .9.

Vaughan and Greene (1984) also plumbed the pigeon's rote memory capacity by introducing large numbers of slides at once, not just in pairs as described above. With another group of subjects, 40 pairs of randomly assigned scenes were presented starting with the first training session. The pigeons saw the 80 slides twice per daily session. The acquisition of discrimination is shown in Figure 4. Within 10 sessions, *rho* rose to high levels, comparable to those in the earlier experiment. At the session labeled B in Figure 4, a new set of 40 pairs was substituted for the original set. *Rho* then dropped to approximately .5, signifying no discrimination, as appropriate for a rote sorting task. But then, even more rapidly than for the original set, the pigeons learned to sort the new slides correctly. Yet another set of 40 pairs was used starting at C, and likewise at D. Each set was rapidly learned.

At this point, the pigeons had been trained to sort 320 slides into two arbitrary categories. The eight sessions starting at E show that all those discriminations were simultaneously within the pigeons' reach. On consecutive sessions, the pigeons saw slide sets 4, 3, 2, 1, 4, 3, 2, 1. The points are for the first presentations per session, so that they show retention without benefit of practice within these test sessions. The pigeons were also retested, without additional practice, more than 730 days later. Levels of *rho*, on the very first test, were above .7 for all sets of slides.

Figure 4.   *New sets of 80 natural scenes, arbitrarily divided into two categories, were introduced at A, B, C, and D. Starting at E, the sets were shown on successive sessions in the order 4, 3, 2, 1, 4, 3, 2, 1. Rising values of rho show the acquisition and maintenance of discrimination for three pigeons. (From Vaughan & Greene, 1984.)*

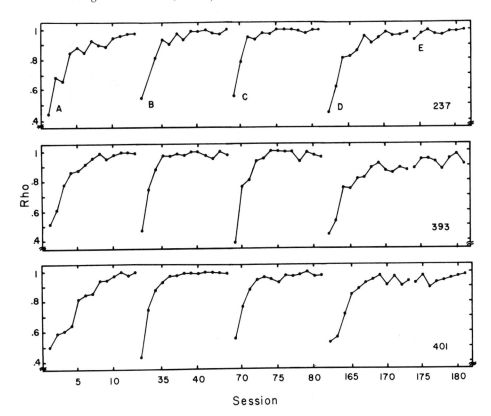

Numerous control procedures by Vaughan and Greene (1983, 1984) leave little or no plausible doubt that the pigeons were, as the data imply, learning to sort complex visual stimuli on the basis of visual appearance. The rote capacity of this subject is large enough for at least 320 photos of natural scenes or more than 160 arbitrary squiggles. But those numbers may be gross underestimates, for nothing in the learning curves betrays any strain on the pigeon's capacity to impress new exemplars on its memory. The high degree of retention is consistent with this – had Vaughan and Greene been taxing their subjects, a rapid loss of retention would open up storage capacity to new learning. But, on the contrary, pigeons recalled with high accuracy the first set of 80 slides even after being trained to sort 240 additional ones.

The pigeon's large capacity for arbitrarily classified exemplars is not unique. Shettleworth and Krebs (1986), for example, report that food-storing birds (e.g., marsh tits, black-capped chickadees, and Clark's nutcrackers) remember many more locations of hidden seeds than the number of visual scenes that pigeons have been demonstrated to retain. For estimates of remembered locations in the tens of thousands by Clark's nutcracker, see Vander Wall and Balda (1977; also see Vander Wall, 1982). Kamil's study (1978) of the Hawaiian honeycreeper uncovered evidence of a capacity to keep track visually of which among more than 1,000 flowers the bird had already visited. Human beings, of course, have comparably large capacities for rote categorization (Nickerson, 1965; Shepard, 1967). Perhaps other mammals do too, although not many are as visual as birds and people are, and it is easiest to do the necessary experiments in the visual modality.

Open-ended categories

However large the capacity for arbitrarily classified exemplars, it cannot be large enough for the ordinary demands of the natural environment. Animals usually need to recognize exemplars at levels of aggregation above the individual level. For the recognition of living forms, exemplars of a class are likely to be at the species level or something approximating it. Squirrels recognize the generic acorn, not a particular acorn; likewise cats recognizing mice and vice versa. Inanimate objects are also likely to be generic – *a*, rather than *the*, pool of water, for example. At these levels, variability is the rule, not the exception. Even when individual recognition is appropriate – for example, parents recognizing their young and vice versa, or a particular turn in a brook – the conditions of viewing impose variability. Any natural contingency of reinforcement is therefore likely to be open-ended in the present sense, comprising a virtually limitless set of exemplars from the subject's vantage point. Mere rote will not suffice, unless it also includes some principle of similarity. The inevitability of this demand, and its solution by perceptual similarity, are what suggest that similarity is an evolutionary adaptation.

The evidence is more than anecdotal. Trained, for example, with one set of photographs containing or not containing trees, pigeons generalize to new exemplars (e.g., Herrnstein, 1979). The ability to handle open-ended reinforcement contingencies has frequently been experimentally demonstrated, not just in pigeons but in other animals (e.g., cryptic moths as a category for blue jays [Pietrewicz & Kamil, 1977]; various objects for a parrot [Pepperberg, 1981] and for mynahs [Turney, 1982]; Munsell color chips for a chimpanzee [Matsuzawa, 1985a]). The results of a wide variety of experiments on many species leave no doubt of a capacity for categorizing beyond rote memorization (see review in Herrnstein, 1984).

The test of a categorization beyond rote is generalization. Figure 5 reproduces results of generalization tests for pigeons in three experiments (Herrnstein et al., 1976), in which the categories were photographs of trees, bodies of water, and a particular woman in many different settings. The pigeons had been trained by a version of the procedure already described, and they saw differing, but overlapping, sets of photographs once per daily session for several weeks, approximately half containing the relevant object and half not containing it. After this initial training, they were shown 800 new photographs only once, over 10 consecutive sessions, divided equally between exemplars and nonexemplars of the appropriate category. The values of *rho* for those generalization tests are plotted as filled points in Figure 5.

Within the cross-hatched area, values of *rho* would fall short of conventional statistical significance for discriminating between positives and negatives. Almost all of the filled points are well outside this region. The horizontal lines show medians for individual pigeons, which are all above .7 and most are above .8. The pigeons had generalized whatever it was they learned, and their generalization conformed quite well to what the experimenters considered to be the principle of categorization. The open points and x's summarize attempts to ascertain further whether human experimenters and pigeon subjects were sorting in the same way.

For the regular generalization tests, the slides were drawn at random from a large collection, but the x's came from a session in which pigeons saw 80 stimuli that the experimenters selected as being hard to discriminate. Positive slides had obscure views of trees or water or the person; negative slides had features that could be confused for those objects or were otherwise ambiguous. Nine of the eleven pigeons failed to discriminate on this session; the exceptions were two of the four pigeons in the person experiment. It seemed possible to the experimenters that we humans rely more on faces for identification than our pigeon subjects, but this has not been tested. Except for the two deviant pigeons, this special test strongly suggests that pigeons and humans view these categories similarly.

The other special test, summarized by the open points, was a session using only slides judged easy by the experimenters. Here, no clear pattern emerged. Judging from the values of *rho*, some pigeons found this set of slides easy, others found it comparable to the usual generalization test, and for two pigeons (24C and 44C), discrimination failed with these supposedly easy exemplars. The original report attempts to explain these mixed results, but

Figure 5.   *Filled points give rho values for sessions presenting 80 photographs for the first time, half containing, and half not containing, the relevant object (T = trees; W = water; P = person), for 11 pigeons. Open points for sessions presenting photos judged easy to categorize by the experimenters; x's for sessions presenting difficult photos. Inside the cross-hatched region, rho is not significantly different from .5, which would indicate no discrimination. (From Herrnstein, Loveland, & Cable, 1976.)*

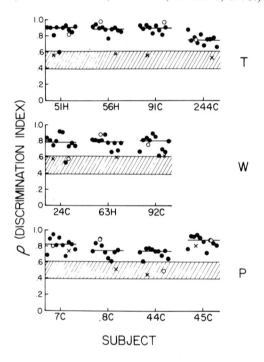

whatever the explanation, from this test, we could not be encouraged to infer complete equivalence of the categorizations of people and pigeons. Taking the two tests together, we may tentatively conclude that the experimenters and pigeons were working with overlapping, but not precisely equivalent, categories. The lack of equivalence should not be surprising, not just because humans and pigeons are different species, but because their reinforcement histories are so different with respect to the particular categories and to the reading of photographs, and because the methods used to assess the categories were so different.

It may be unwise to equate similarity with mere confusability or imprecision in perception, as is often done. The dimensions of similarity can only be inferred from behavior, but the pattern of data from many experiments makes it clear that something more dynamic than mere error in discriminative precision is afoot. There is a long tradition in formal theories of similarity (e.g., Restle, 1959; Tversky, 1977) according to which two items are similar as a decreasing function of the elements (or attributes) they do not share and as an increasing function of the elements they have in common. This insight may be formalized in many ways, as long as it expresses that similarity depends upon context. The same pair of printed capital A's in different typefaces may look similar among an assortment of different letters of the alphabet and different among a collection of varying upper-case A's. Attributes that produce similarity in the first set give way to attributes that produce difference in the second. Theories assume something like a periodic table, or alphabet, of attributes, which are then compounded or spelled into the categories at hand. Promising as this approach has been, it has insufficiently captured in any formal model yet articulated how plastic and diverse the attributes themselves appear to be.

When adequately challenged, subjects have an uncanny knack for finding surprising attributes to help them distinguish between categories. To uncover this knack, it is essential that it be profitable for the organism to resort to it. Three studies should make the point. In an experiment using blue jays as subjects, Real, Iannazzi, Kamil, and Heinrich (1984) took advantage of the differing leaf-damaging patterns made by different species of caterpillars. The authors distinguished between a particular pair of caterpillar species by saying that one damages leaves "neatly," whereas the other does so "messily." This difference itself is probably an evolutionary adaptation, inasmuch as the neat eaters are palatable and the messy ones are not. Neatness, by disguising the traces on a leaf of having been nibbled on, protects the palatable caterpillar who did the nibbling.

Blue jays were trained to behave in two different, but arbitrary, ways in the presence of silhouettes of leaves nibbled by the two species. Only one leaf of each type was used in training, yet the blue jays generalized to other exemplars readily, responding in one way to leaves attacked by one species and in the other way to those attacked by the other. The birds had, from only one example, learned to sort leaves according to the nibbling patterns of the caterpillars. Where or how much or precisely how the nibbling was distributed was so diverse that, according to the authors, "no simple rule of geometry ... could lead to correct categorization of all of the novel stimuli" (Real et al., 1984, p. 208). Whatever the geometrical algorithms that could discriminate between the classes, the blue jays proved themselves to be capable of finding just the right stimulus attributes to master an open-ended categorization based on the nibbling patterns of caterpillars.

The two other experiments to be described here seem to me to provide even stronger evidence of the adaptability of open-ended categorization. Vaughan and Greene (1984) showed that pigeons can learn to sort a set of 80 slides into two categories, but the sorting rule was conditional on mirror orientation. The 80 slides were arbitrarily divided into two classes, A and B. No single class of objects, such as trees, or any other perceptual feature, characterized either category. The pigeons learned to sort the two arbitrary categories, but then all 80 slides were mirror-reversed. With mirror reversal, all the reinforcement contingencies were also reversed: If Class A was positive in the original orientation, it was negative when mirror-reversed, and vice versa for Class B.

Initially, because pigeons readily generalize to mirror reversals, they responded inappropriately: The pigeons continued to respond to exemplars of Class A and not to those of Class B, even when reversed in orientation. But they learned the new rules within several sessions. When they were properly responding to the reversed categories, the contingencies were again reversed, along with another mirror reversal. The slides were now in their original orientation, with the original contingencies of reinforcement. Learning was more rapid, and, after it was completed, once again orientation and contingencies were reversed. This pattern of reversing orientation and contingencies continued until the pigeons learned to respond appropriately to each and every slide, depending upon its orientation. The rule that eventually came to dictate behavior was: If a slide was positive as originally oriented, then it was negative when mirror-reversed, and vice versa. Without the peculiar training of this procedure, pigeons generalize spontaneously and fully to mirror reversals, but they learned to use something arising in reversal as a cue to categorization. Orientation, or some by-product of orientation, emerged as a controlling attribute when it paid.[3]

The final experiment used pigeons who had homed either around Ithaca, NY, or Lincoln, MA, or who had not homed at all (Gray, 1987). The stimuli were aerial photographs, landscape scenes from 15 to 25 square mile regions in the vicinity of the two homing lofts, and of a comparably rural area mostly near Georgetown, NY, where none of the subjects had flown. All three regions seemed similar in topography, vegetation, and population density; Ithaca and Georgetown seemed particularly similar. The pigeons were trained to respond, in a standard laboratory procedure, in the presence of photo-

---

[3]In this experiment, in which orientation was not consistently associated with reinforcement or nonreinforcement (it was associated one way with Class A slides and the other way with Class B slides), nothing decisive could have been learned from testing the subjects with novel slides in one orientation or the other. Although the results might have raised some interesting questions, no such test was attempted.

graphs of the Ithaca and Lincoln locales, but not of the Georgetown locale. Whatever a pigeon's past history, it learned quickly and well to discriminate between scenes from Ithaca or Lincoln and Georgetown. Having homed in an area did not seem to confer any special advantage in recognizing it in photos. All pigeons also generalized successfully to photographs taken in a locale but not used in training, or not overlapping with those used in training. This finding suggests that pigeons recognize scenes from a locale as such, based solely on samples seen in photographs. To the experimenter or her associates, including the present author, who have studied those photographs, the cues to locale remain obscure.

In these three studies, we may presume visual attributes, without having anticipated them on the basis of other findings with blue jays or homing pigeons. The attributes for leaf damage, locale, or orientation may be behaviorally invisible until the contingencies of reinforcement highlight them. The results point to a large theoretical gap, not in a formula for subdividing or aggregating attribute sets, but in an account of the dynamic character of the attribute sets themselves.

Concepts

Similarity was the distinguishing element as we moved from rote to open-ended categories. The distinguishing element in the further step to concepts is harder to say or to grasp. Indeed, it may safely be assumed that some readers may be, and some will remain, unconvinced that this further step is necessary. Until I read the relevant essay by Stephen Lea (1984), I was unconvinced myself. What follows is a formulation inspired by and similar to, but, in detail and in substantiation, differing from, Lea's.

Let us start by assuming that the mythical grandmother cell (e.g., Barlow, 1972) exists. Someplace in the brain, a neuron becomes active whenever granny appears in any of her manifestations. Such a cell would be at the apex of a hierarchy of neural analyzers of increasing generality across such variables in the proximal stimulus as size, location, luminance level, color, perspective transformations, and so forth, and increasing specificity for invariance in the distal, objective world, ultimately delimited to granny herself. The grandmother cell could itself establish connections with other functional loci – sensory, motor, or motivational. The organism may find the cell's activation reinforcing or punishing. Its activation may evoke activity in the system controlling speech – for example, the utterance "granny." The point is simply that the cell operates as a functional entity in the nervous system, entering into relationships available to functional entities.

The notion of a concept is like the notion of a grandmother cell, with one vital qualification. A concept need not be mediated by a neuron or any particular set of neurons. It need not even be localized in neurons, rather than, say, in synaptic neurochemistry or in more global patterns of activity in the nervous system. As far as the *definition* of a concept within the present scheme is concerned, behavior, not neurophysiology, is central. However, if a case for concepts can be made behaviorally, then finding its neurophysiological basis becomes a proper challenge.

A concept is, to begin with, a basis for categorization, a differential response of the organism to a set of stimuli. The set may be limited or open-ended, as in the two levels of categorization already discussed. Beyond that, however, the effects of contingencies applied to members of the set propagate to other members more than can be accounted for by the similarities among members of the set. In the ideal case, they propagate to all members of the set, without regard to similarity. Because similarities for a given organism under particular circumstances can themselves only be inferred from behavior, we may expect difficulty in demonstrating concepts, as distinguished from the lower levels of categorization. It is also the case, however, that what seems to be merely open-ended categorization, may turn out to be, when appropriately tested, a case of conceptualization.

In vocabularies that have fallen into disuse, "mediated generalization" and "mediated association" resemble what is here being called a concept (see, for example, Osgood, 1953, p. 359f, and Underwood, 1966, p. 533f, respectively). The terms were used to describe transfer of conditioning across stimuli too different to be attributed to common features or attributes. The theoretical notion was that the stimuli may have had no stimulus elements in common, but, presumably because of past conditioning, they evoked overlapping responses. The overlapping responses provided the bridge for transfer. For example, imagine conditioning the eyeblink response of a human parent to the word "baby." Transfer would then be expected to the word "cradle." Baby and cradle fall into a common category, but not because of similarity as ordinarily defined, but because of a connection at some other level of aggregation.[4] Unlike the earlier writers, I make no theoretical assumptions about the bridge for the mediated generalization. The issue here is simply whether analogous examples of categorization can be convincingly shown for nonverbal animals.

For mediated generalization, the link between members of a set is presumed to be based on learning. For grandmother cells and the like, it has, at

---

[4] In words, the concept would be something like "pertaining to my baby."

least by some workers at some times, been supposed that they are substantially hard-wired (e.g., Hubel & Wiesel, 1962). The present scheme is agnostic on this point. It is assumed that concepts may be either learned or more or less hard-wired.

Suggestive evidence for concepts in pigeons can be found in an experiment already cited as showing an open-ended category (Herrnstein, 1979). Pigeons learned to sort slides containing trees from those not containing trees. The training procedure consisted of showing 40 exemplars and 40 nonexemplars once per daily session. On successive sessions in this particular experiment, the pigeons saw the same 80 stimuli in different orders. Because the same stimuli were used daily, it is possible to draw a plausible inference about whether the pigeons were sorting on the basis of exemplars or a concept.

The reinforcement schedule for responding in the presence of exemplars was so lean that as the discrimination was being formed, exemplars were associated with varying total numbers of reinforcements summing across sessions, from zero on up. Figure 6 plots, along the x-axis, the total number of reinforcements associated with given exemplars. The y-axis plots the mean rank of the exemplars with the indicated numbers of reinforcements. Mean rank is a measure of discrimination; it should "rise" from 40.5, when there is no discrimination, toward 20.5, when all 40 exemplars are ranked above all 40 nonexemplars. The figure shows sessions 2 to 6, which is when the animals were learning the sorting task.

If the pigeons were sorting open-endedly by exemplars, it would be reasonable to expect the lines in Figure 6 to have positive slope, indicating that the more reinforcement an exemplar had in its history, the better it was discriminated. Pigeon 58 had lines of positive slope up to Session 4, but this was the slowest learner of the four (see the original report for details). More reinforced exemplars were discriminated better. The other pigeons had flat lines from the start (as did Pigeon 58 after the fourth session). The level of performance rose for all exemplars, without regard to reinforcements in their history. Even exemplars with no reinforcements were rising with the set.

It is plausible to infer that, when the lines were flat down to zero on the x-axis, sorting is on the basis of something more general than exemplars and similarity to those exemplars. Were such results obtained from a human subject, we would have no hesitation in invoking the concept called "tree." On the other hand, it may be argued that the unreinforced exemplars were, by virtue of how pigeons average exemplars (assuming that is what they do), no less similar to the reinforced exemplars than the reinforced exemplars were to themselves. But this argument would be indefensible on its face, because, in this procedure, which stimuli were unreinforced was an accidental and variable outcome of the reinforcement and stimulus presentation

Figure 6.   *Photographs containing trees (i.e., positive stimuli) are grouped according to the total number of reinforcements received in their presence, counting from the beginning of the experiment to the session number indicated at the top of the figure. The mean rank of positive stimuli (r_p) is a measure of discrimination, which is at 40.5 at no discrimination and advances to lower values as discrimination forms. Four pigeons are represented. (From Herrnstein, 1979.)*

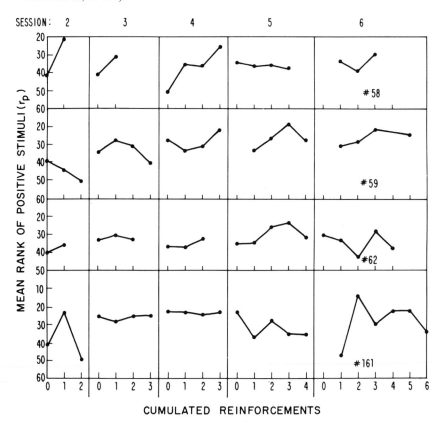

schedules and, more relevantly, differed for each subject. It is highly improbable that those differing sets of exemplars appropriate to the averaging hypothesis for each subject coincided, by chance, with the unreinforced exemplars for each subject. The effects of reinforcing a few exemplars of trees propagated with no decrement to an open-ended set of exemplars of trees, independent of the number of reinforcements per exemplar. A tree-like concept may be denied to these pigeons, but not plausibly.

In another study, pigeons were again required to discriminate between photographs containing trees and those not containing any (Vaughan & Herrnstein, 1987). Responding was reinforced in the presence of all slides, but different schedules provided reinforcements for responding in the presence of trees and nontrees. Reinforcement sometimes came at a higher rate in the presence of trees than in the presence of nontrees; at other times, vice versa. Under these conditions, subjects approximately obey the "matching law," responding to the two categories in the same ratio as of the respective rates of reinforcement (Herrnstein, 1970).

During the course of the experiment, the ratio of rates of reinforcement was changed four times, and, each time, the pigeons suitably adjusted the ratio of their rates of responding. In addition, during the course of the experiment, five sets of 80 different photographs were shown, each one including 40 containing, and 40 not containing, trees. A summary of the results is shown in Figure 7.

Figure 7. *Proportion of reinforcements received (points) and time spent (lines) in the presence of photographic slides of trees, for four pigeons. According to the matching law, points and lines should be superimposed. The initial sessions used Slide Tray 1, which was replaced as indicated by Slide Tray 2, and so on, until Slide Tray 1 was restored at the 157th session. Each slide tray contained different slides, of which just half contained trees. (From Vaughan & Herrnstein, 1987.)*

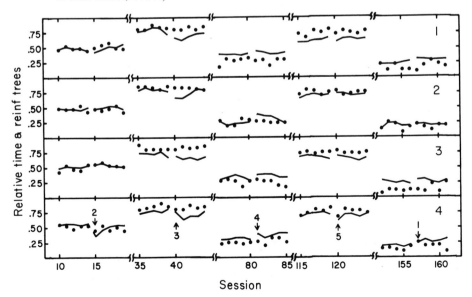

The solid lines show the proportion of time spent in the presence of the tree slides, for five consecutive sessions before and after the stimuli were changed. The subjects themselves controlled stimulus duration, so this is an appropriate measure of behavior. The points track relative rate of reinforcement. The approximate convergence of points and lines exemplifies the matching law. The numbers along the lines show where sets of slides were replaced; for example, at Session 15, Slide Tray 1 was replaced by Slide Tray 2, and so on. The replacements were at no point coincident with a change in the reinforcement schedule, and vice versa. At each change in slides, the pigeons continued responding in approximate accordance with the matching law. This continuity of behavior demonstrates generalization from one set of slides to another, a case of at least open-ended categorization and, possibly, conceptualization.

The results of the final replacement, labeled 1, suggest a concept, which is to say, something more than the sorting of particular exemplars plus extensions owing to similarity. Here, Slide Set 1 replaced Slide Set 5. Responding generalized: The approximately .25 proportion of time in the presence of trees transferred from Slide Set 5 to Slide Set 1. However, the pigeons had seen Slide Set 1 at the beginning of the experiment, when they had been spending about .5 of their time in the presence of tree slides (see Figure 7). At the final replacement, the pigeons generalized the behavior appropriate to the category of trees as a whole rather than the behavior previously conditioned to the particular exemplars in Slide Set 1. The current contingency of reinforcement had propagated to the exemplars in Slide Set 1, displacing the effects of the contingency of reinforcement in force when Slide Set 1 was last seen, which satisfies the present definition of a concept.

A different approach to concepts is exemplified in an experiment by Vaughan (1988). Pigeons were shown the same 40 tree-containing slides in each session, always in a different, random order. The slides were divided into two arbitrary categories, one positive (reinforcement in their presence), the other, negative (no reinforcement). Different divisions of the 40 slides were used for different pigeons, so as to eliminate the possibility that some unknown perceptual feature could signal category membership. After the pigeons learned to sort the slides, reinforcement contingencies were reversed – positives were now negative and vice versa. When this new task was mastered, the categories were re-reversed, restoring the original contingencies. The reversals continued until the pigeons learned to detect, from the first few slides in a session, whether the contingencies were as they were originally or reversed. The pigeons had, in effect, created a file for each category, and could tell by sampling a few slides (less than a half dozen) whether the file had a positive or negative valence on any particular session.

No principle of similarity as perceptual proximity can account for these results, since the slides in either category were no more similar to each other than to the slides in the other category. Nor does the usual notion of a conditional discrimination apply, for no additional stimulus, signalling the conditional relationship, was provided. The contingency of reinforcement at the beginning of a session was extrapolated by the pigeon to all the slides in the tray. Vaughan's experiment demonstrates an arbitrary concept, with small, rather than open-ended, membership, namely the 20 slides in each category.

The operational distinction between concepts and open-ended categorization is that something besides similarity gradients permits new exemplars to be categorized. This "something" is a representation within the organism at a more inclusive level than individual exemplars and their similarity domains. Since similarity itself can be inferred only from behavior, distinguishing between these alternatives may seem a futile undertaking or worse. However, human beings evidently conceptualize in the present sense in the very act of using language. Language is a sufficient condition to permit the inferring of concepts, but it is not also a necessary one. The evidence suggests that non-linguistic creatures conceptualize as defined here.

The difficulty of distinguishing concepts and categories cuts both ways. Some people may be disposed to argue that the examples presented here of concepts are more parsimoniously interpreted as mere categories. On the other hand, the inverse argument is also possible. What looks like simple categorization based on similarities may, if suitably analyzed, prove to be based on concepts.

Abstract relations

Concepts may stand in relation to each other. Members of Class A may be bigger, longer, faster than, above, to the right of, prior to, or just different from, members of Class B. Relations may be quantitative: Members of A may have half the area of members of B. They may be logically dependent on other conditions: There is leaking water in the Red Line stations only after it rains a certain amount. The psychological questions are whether, and to what degree, behavior can be brought under the control of a relation between concepts, what I am here calling an abstract relation. It is *abstract* because it should be generalized to all exemplars of the relevant classes, even those exemplars not previously experienced in the given context.

The prototypical laboratory demonstration of an abstract relation is a matching or oddity procedure. In their close conceptual proximity to simple category membership, matching and oddity may be considered among the most elementary abstract relations, yet they are a step beyond. A subject is reinforced for choosing, among a set of alternatives, that choice which matches, or, in the case of oddity, does not match, a standard in some respect. The subject may, for example, be choosing the color match of the standard. After training with, say, red, blue, and green standards, the subject is tested with a yellow standard. If it chooses correctly, it has given evidence of an abstract relation, one we may equate with "the same color as." In the oddity version, the subject would be required to choose the one color that differs among a set of three or more color alternatives. It would again be tested with new sets of colors, not previously used in training.

If the experiments are well constructed, then the generalization of training cannot be accounted for by anything other than an abstract relation itself – such other accounts, for example, as unwitting stimulus similarities between training and test stimuli. Even when the obvious plausible alternative explanations of the data are excluded, an inescapable ambiguity remains about the scope of the relation. From what was said above about the color experiment, it would have been just as correct, logically, to infer the abstract relation "the same as," or "the same visual stimulus as," rather than "the same color as." A narrower construction was also possible – "the same color as, except for yellow." Each such relation dictates its own implications for tests of generality.

The subject's task in an experiment on abstract relations is to draw an inductive inference. This is also the case with any categorization problem in which the subject must extrapolate to new exemplars. In testing for any such categorization, we are inexorably limited by the indeterminacy of induction. If, for example, the subject is using an abstract relation to categorize stimuli, then only the subject can, by its behavior, reveal its scope. An animal may fail our test of generality, yet still be using an abstract relation consistent with the evidence it had to go on.

Many experiments have explored matching, oddity, and other logically analogous procedures, with nonhuman subjects, since the pathbreaking work of Harry Harlow and his associates on primates (Harlow, 1949; Meyer & Harlow, 1949). Some of the research and controversy surrounding chimpanzee language verges on the question of the capacity to learn abstract relations and the degree to which that capacity is the evolutionary precursor of human linguistic ability (e.g., Premack, 1976, 1986; Ristau & Robbins, 1982; Rumbaugh & Pate, 1984; Terrace, 1979, 1985). The simple declarative sentence itself is the very embodiment of an abstract relation, with its subject and object linked by a verb. Even the most concrete example (e.g., "A dog bit a man") conforms to the paradigm – two concepts in a particular relation. So it is no surprise that here is where categorization and language converge, and where the first clear traces of differentiation among species have been observed.

In one recent experiment, Cebus monkeys learned the identity relation over sets of visual stimuli (D'Amato, Salmon, & Colombo, 1985). They were first trained to match one or the other of two simple stimuli drawn from a small collection of such stimuli – dots, triangles, vertical lines, and so forth. On any given trial, one or the other of the stimuli was the standard, and both of the pair were presented simultaneously as alternatives. Reinforcement was earned by picking the matching alternative. After learning this task, the monkey was tested with a new pair of stimuli as standards and comparisons, to see if identity as such controlled choice, or at least if learning was much more rapid than with the original pair. Of eight monkeys in the sample, four met a criterion for transfer after learning with the first pair; two, after learning the identity problem with two pairs; and the seventh, after three pairs. The eighth monkey was dropped as inept at matching early in the experiment. Of four monkeys who successfully transferred matching with steady stimuli drawn from the original set, none transferred when tested with flickering stimuli.

Pigeons in a similar experiment fell even shorter of generality in abstract matching (Holmes, 1979). Indeed, the author concluded that what little evidence of the identity relation there was in his data could be discounted as owing to a nonspecific improvement in performance, having nothing to do with matching as such. Other studies have found better evidence for abstract relations by pigeons. But they have usually also found that the abstract relation is narrow and easily disrupted, which may explain why the evidence as a whole is as mixed as it is (for some indication of the lack of consensus, see Carter & Werner, 1978; Pisacreta, Lefave, Lesneski, & Potter, 1985; Zentall & Hogan, 1978).

Pisacreta and his associates have developed procedures that guide pigeons to use the abstract relations of matching and oddity more reliably than is typical (Pisacreta et al., 1985; Pisacreta, Redwood, & Witt, 1984). In these experiments, the stimuli are usually complex – drawings or photographs of faces or animals, for example – more than two alternatives to choose among are often presented, and the alternatives are presented serially, so that the pigeon is, as it were, allowed to make its choice about alternatives one at a time. Which, if any, of these procedural innovations are responsible for the success, I cannot say. Delius and his associates have also been relatively successful in their matching and oddity experiments on pigeons (Delius & Nowak, 1982; Holland & Delius, 1982; Lombardi, Fachinelli, & Delius, 1984), using novel procedures of their own. Urcuioli has shown, in his experiments (Urcuioli, 1985), that pigeons do better with the identity relation when they are trained to behave differently for the different standard stimuli they are to match, but this procedural detail does not appear to explain the successes of Pisacreta and Delius and their associates. The point is that procedural details appear to be far more critical when pigeons are being asked to use abstract relations than when monkeys or apes are, or when pigeons are asked to categorize at a lower level.

Questions of psychological capacity are tricky (Herrnstein, 1985). It has been observed that a procedure that evokes moderately successful use of the identity relation by monkeys fails to do so with pigeons (Wright, Santiago, Urcuioli, & Sands, 1983). How shall this be interpreted? The authors of the study suggest, guardedly, that monkeys can master the abstraction, but that pigeons cannot. An even more guarded conclusion would be that, in their experiments, monkeys did and pigeons did not. The existential question of capability, a negative answer to which verges on the assertion of a universal negative, should not be answered hastily. Pisacreta's, Delius's, and Urcuioli's data, among others, illustrate why it is prudent to be so guarded about questions of capacity, for they show pigeons to be capable of categorizing according to an abstract relation. The capacity may be fragile, but it is not wholly absent.

A similar conclusion is suggested by the results of an experiment testing whether pigeons can learn to use the abstract relation of "inside–outside" (Herrnstein, Vaughan, Mumford, & Kosslyn, 1989). Inspired by Ullman's discussion of "visual routines" (Ullman, 1984), we tested pigeons with stimuli consisting of a closed curve and a dot, which the pigeons were required to sort according to whether the dot was inside or outside the curve. The stimuli were constructed so as to permit no local cues to insideness: In the vicinity of the dot, the curve could be either convex or concave, whether the dot was inside or outside. Several of the stimuli are shown in Figure 8. Human observers find the discrimination trivially easy. But the pigeons failed to learn to categorize even a set of 40 dot-inside and 40 dot-outside slides, shown repeatedly in a changing random order, let alone to generalize to other exemplars.

The pigeons were then subjected to a "tutorial" for inside–outside. The insides of the white closed curves were made bright red, while the backgrounds were black. Now the task no longer relied on an abstract relation. The pigeon could sort according to whether the white dot was on a red or black field, a task easily learned. Next, the red was darkened – still discriminably different, to the experimenters and presumably also to the pigeons, from the black background. The pigeons continued to categorize accurately. Then the dark red was replaced by the same black as the background, so the

Figure 8.   *Four typical stimuli used in an experiment with pigeons, requiring categorization according to the abstract relation of insideness. (From Herrnstein, Vaughan, Mumford, & Kosslyn, 1989.)*

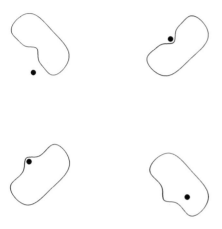

task was, once again, a matter of the abstract relation of inside versus outside. The pigeons now sorted accurately. They also transferred categorization to new exemplars, so long as the new closed curves were not too radically different from what they were familiar with and did not have invaginations or protuberances that were extreme. An abstract relation, of limited scope, was being used for categorization.

Abstract relations and their derivatives may increase in complexity without bound. A step up the ladder of complexity are the cardinal numbers. All sets of, say, five objects are in the relation of identity for number. The number itself is the concept whose members are sets of objects of the given cardinality, five in this case. With considerable effort and ingenuity, Pepperberg trained a parrot to utter the correct number for sets of two to six objects (1987). Alex, the parrot, generalized to new sets of objects, and even to heterogeneous collections of objects. Two chimpanzees were similarly trained by Rumbaugh, Savage-Rumbaugh, and Hegel to "sum" (albeit not vocally) across objects in an experiment involving the abstract relation, greater-than (Rumbaugh, Savage-Rumbaugh, & Hegel, 1987). There are many reports of counting in animals, but the famous tale of Hans, the clever but noncounting horse, dictates caution (Pfungst, 1911). These experiments are, however, convincing, and so is a similar one by Matsuzawa, using a single chimpanzee (1985b).

Yet even Alex, the parrot, and the various chimps fall far short of displaying a set of numerical concepts robust yet flexible enough to be woven into the logical structures of arithmetic and mathematics. No one has yet, to my knowledge, even attempted to train an animal to solve a linear equation in one variable. Even suggesting the possibility seems fatuous. Where the abstract relations among concepts are themselves concatenated into more highly derived conceptual structures, human capacities diverge sharply from the animal precursors. From this perspective, the difference between our closest primate relatives and many other animals, including birds as well as mammals, seems far smaller than the difference between our species and all others.

Conclusions

Some, but not all, of this story of levels of stimulus control, as well as some of its gaps, are illustrated in Figure 9. The arrows point to what may be called the loci of stimulus control, corresponding to the five levels of categorization, from discrimination to abstract relations. The arrows indicate how the objects to be categorized are linked to, or are in control of, behavior. Filled circles are exemplars previously experienced, which is to say, exemplars confirmed by past consequences of behavior; open circles, exemplars to which generalization appropriately takes place, given the contingencies of reinforcement. At the two lowest levels – discrimination and rote categorization – the loci of control comprise descriptions of the familiar exemplars themselves, and there is only as much generalization as would be allowed by psychophysical indiscriminability.

At the next level, open-ended categorization, the exemplars still constitute the loci of control, but now generalization extends further from those points, owing to similarity. A category approximates a continuous region in what may be called the animal's subjective quality space, rather than a finite set of points, because of the spread of similarity. The spread is probabilistic, in the sense that near exemplars are more likely to be reached by generalization than remote ones.

Earlier, I noted that animals are remarkably good at finding whatever attributes of a set of stimuli serve their purposes in relation to the contingencies of reinforcement. The spread surrounding exemplars is thus not fixed in the animal's perceptual apparatus, but an adaptation to a given set of reinforced exemplars. The adaptability must, however, be limited: first, by the information provided by the animal's sensory receptors, and, second, by any inherent similarity gradients or other organismic predispositions ("prepared" associations and the like, see Herrnstein, 1977; Shettleworth, 1972). An animal cannot, for example, make use of potentially useful information from regions of the electromagnetic spectrum where it is blind, even if this information could predict reinforcement. Likewise, similarities or associative biases built into the organism may, in some circumstances, impede adaptation, as useful as they are in other circumstances.

Figure 9.   *Levels of categorization. Arrows point to the loci of stimulus control; filled circles to confirmed exemplars; open circles to exemplars to which generalization is appropriate, given the contingencies of reinforcement, and x's to exemplars to which generalization is not appropriate.*

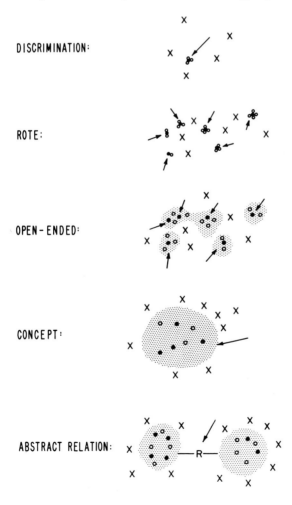

At the concept level, the locus of control no longer resides with the exemplars, but at a more inclusive level, the conceptual grandmother cell discussed earlier. The concept is inferred from, or merely activated by, experienced exemplars. Other exemplars, beyond, or orthogonal to, those directly linked by gradients of similarity, are then responded to appropriately. The category has become truly a region in a subjective space, but probably not a sharply defined one and not one of which the dimensions need be constrained by similarity. The concept's "perimeter" may be probabilistic, as human concepts, with their prototypes and peripheral exemplars, have been shown to be (Rosch, 1973; Smith & Medin, 1981). Robins are better examples of birds than penguins, for example. Similar structures within concepts may be inferred from data on nonverbal categorizers (e.g., see Herrnstein & de Villiers, 1980, for what constitutes good and bad examples of fish for pigeons). As Vaughan's experiment (1988) on arbitrary concepts shows, a concept may comprise members not linked by similarity or anything else, except their common membership. Next to nothing general is known about how the perimeter of a concept is set, but we may guess that it depends on interaction between contingencies of reinforcement as they have been experienced or on perceptual or motivational predispositions.

The fifth level of categorization, abstract relations, covers a multitude of complexity. At its lowest level, it is a simple relationship between concepts, such as identity or difference in some respect. Were this article going on to consider human behavior per se, especially language, this level would demand further elaboration. However, even for the most elementary abstract relations (oddity, identity, and the like), the evidence reveals substantial interspecies variation and also a large gap between humans and the closest primates.

We may surmise that the survival demands on animal life account for the ubiquity of at least the first three levels, up to open-ended categorization. Objects in nature, set into the classes that are behaviorally relevant in the life of animals, vary. Sometimes a perceptual system evolves to counteract the natural variation. Ticks need mammalian blood to survive, so they must be able to recognize exemplars of this class, which is so diverse from our point of view. Mammals are not diverse for ticks, which, trading perceptual richness for efficiency, have evolved to detect their hosts by their warmth and by a volatile compound emanating from all mammalian flesh (von Uexkull, 1934, see Herrnstein, 1982). But if the natural variation of objects is echoed in a perceptual system, then open-ended categorization is required.

The next level, concepts, is a less irreversible approach to efficiency than the tick's. The economy of concepts is illustrated in Figure 9 by the shift from many loci of control at Level 3 to just one at Level 4. Concepts are especially adaptive for creatures that learn, for it enables the implications of a change in the consequences of behavior, or in the class of stimuli with which the consequences are associated, to be rapidly propagated across the members of the class. The rapid propagation is economical, but may sometimes be wrong. As noted earlier, any categorization that extrapolates from past experience is heir to the risks of inductive inference.

Efficiency is promoted further by the step up to abstract relations, for a small amount of logic can displace a large amount of description. Each abstract relation can be considered a substitute for a new concept, of which the exemplars would be the related sets of objects in the abstract relation. Instead of the abstract relation, "this chip is the same color as that chip," a concept could constitute the class of pairs of color chips of the same color. The classes of triplets or quadruplets of like-colored chips, and so on, would each require a concept of their own. But describing pairs, or triplets, or quadruplets, of chips of the same color, per se, is needless mental work if the organism can use the abstract identity relation applied to the concept of a chip, taken in sets of any size.

It may be needless in another sense as well. Abstract relations often express transient states of the animal's environment. The contingency of reinforcement may be the identity of the colors on one occasion, but a difference in color on another. The relation, "acorn on a stump," may be of less enduring interest to a squirrel than the concepts of either acorn or stump. To the extent that abstract relations spare organisms the effort of constructing concepts they are unlikely to resort to thereafter, they are a clear benefit.

Beneficial as they are, abstract relations differentiate most sharply among animals. It has been noted that we see the largest gaps in comparative performance at the level of abstract relations. This observation is well grounded in the comparative data sampled here, but not just there. Charles Spearman, a major figure in the history of human intelligence testing, defined general intelligence as the ability to "educe relations" (Spearman, 1927), an insight into human intellectual variation that has been massively confirmed by decades of testing.

It may not be surprising that the means for dealing with just the transient contingencies of reinforcement has had lower evolutionary priority than the means for the enduring ones represented by concepts or by open-ended categories. But once an evolving species has a foothold at the level of abstract relations, the possibilities are unbounded. What then lies ahead are systematic descriptions, not just of transient contingencies of reinforcement, but of conditional ones. Language, logic, and mathematics, are the forms of abstract relations; knowledge itself is the substance.

References

Barlow, H.B. (1972). Single units and sensation: A neuron doctrine for perceptual psychology? *Perception*, *1*, 371–394.

Carter, D.E., & Werner, T.J. (1978). Complex learning and information processing by pigeons: A critical analysis. *Journal of the Experimental Analysis of Behavior, 29*, 565–601.

Commons, M.L., & Hallinan, P.W., with Fong, W., & McCarthy, K. (1990). Intelligent pattern recognition: Hierarchical organization of concepts. In M.L. Commons, R.J. Herrnstein, S.M. Kosslyn, & D.B. Mumford (Eds.), *Quantitative analyses of behavior: Computational and clinical approaches to pattern recognition and concept formation* (Vol. IX, pp. 127–153). Hillsdale, NJ: Erlbaum.

D'Amato, M.R., Salmon, D.P., & Colombo, M. (1985). Extent and limits of the matching concept in monkeys (*Cebus apella*). *Journal of Experimental Psychology: Animal Behavior Processes*, 11, 35–51.

Delius, J.D., & Nowak, B. (1982). Visual symmetry recognition by pigeons. *Psychological Research, 44*, 199–212.

Dore, F.Y., & Dumas, C. (1987). Psychology of animal cognition: Piagetian studies. *Psychological Bulletin, 102*, 219–233.

Estes, W.K. (1986). Array models for category learning. *Cognitive Psychology, 18*, 500–549.

Gray, E.M. (1987). *Visual recognition of landmarks by the homing pigeon.* Unpublished undergraduate honors' thesis, Harvard University.

Harlow, H.F. (1949). The formation of learning sets. *Psychological Review*, 56, 51–65.

Herrnstein, R.J. (1970). On the law of effect. *Journal of the Experimental Analysis of Behavior, 13*, 243–266.

Herrnstein, R.J. (1977). The evolution of behaviorism. *American Psychologist, 32*, 593–603.

Herrnstein, R.J. (1979). Acquisition, generalization, and discrimination reversal of a natural concept. *Journal of Experimental Psychology: Animal Behavior Processes, 5*, 118–129.

Herrnstein, R.J. (1982). Stimuli and the texture of experience. *Neuroscience & Biobehavioral Reviews, 6*, 105–117.

Herrnstein, R.J. (1984). Objects, categories, and discriminative stimuli. H.L. Roitblat, T.G. Bever, & H.S. Terrace (Eds.), *Animal cognition* (pp. 233–261). Hillsdale, NJ: Erlbaum.

Herrnstein, R.J. (1985). Riddles of natural categorization. *Philosophical Transactions of the Royal Academy, London, B 308*, 129–144.

Herrnstein, R.J., & de Villiers, P.A. (1980). Fish as a natural category for people and pigeons. In G.H. Bower (Ed.), *The psychology of learning and motivation* (Vol. 14, pp. 59–95). New York: Academic Press.

Herrnstein, R.J., Loveland, D.H., & Cable, C. (1976). Natural concepts in pigeons. *Journal of Experimental Psychology: Animal Behavior Processes, 2*, 285–311.

Herrnstein, R.J., Vaughan, W., Jr., Mumford, D.B., & Kosslyn, S.M. (1989). Teaching pigeons an abstract relational rule: Insideness. *Perception & Psychophyics, 46*, 56–64.

Hollard, V.D., & Delius, J.D. (1982). Rotational invariance in visual pattern recognition by pigeons and humans. *Science, 218*, 804–806.

Holmes, P.W. (1979). Transfer of matching performance in pigeons. *Journal of the Experimental Analysis of Behavior, 31*, 103–114.

Homa, D. (1984). On the nature of categories. In G.H. Bower (Ed.), *The psychology of learning and motivation* (Vol. 18, pp. 49–94). New York: Academic Press.

Hubel, D.H., & Wiesel, T.N. (1962). Receptive fields, binocular interaction and functional architecture in the cat's visual cortex. *Journal of Physiology, 160*, 106–154.

Kamil, A.C. (1978). Systematic foraging by a nectar-feeding bird, the Amakihi (*Loxops virens*). *Journal of Comparative and Physiological Psychology, 92*, 388–396.

Lea, S.E.G. (1984). In what sense do pigeons learn concepts? In H.L. Roitblat, T.G. Bever, & H.S. Terrace (Eds.), *Animal cognition* (pp. 263–276). Hillsdale, NJ: Erlbaum.

Lombardi, C.M., Fachinelli, C.G., & Delius, J.D. (1984). Oddity of visual patterns conceptualized by pigeons. *Animal Learning and Behavior, 12*, 2–6.

Matsuzawa, T. (1985a). Colour naming and classification in a chimpanzee (*Pan troglodytes*). *Journal of Human Evolution, 14*, 283–291.

Matsuzawa, T. (1985b). Use of numbers by a chimpanzee. *Nature, 315*, 57–59.

Meyer, D.R., & Harlow, H.F. (1949). The development of transfer of response to patterning by monkeys. *Journal of Comparative and Physiological Psychology, 42*, 454–462.

Nickerson, R.S. (1965). Short-term memory for complex meaningful visual configurations: A demonstration of capacity. *Canadian Journal of Psychology, 19*, 155–160.

Osgood, C.E. (1953). *Method and theory in experimental psychology*. New York: Oxford University Press.

Pepperberg, I.M. (1981). Functional vocalizations of an African grey parrot (*Psitticus erithacus*). *Zeitschrift für Tierpsychologie, 55*, 139–151.

Pepperberg, I.M. (1987). Evidence for conceptual quantitative abilities in the African parrot: Labeling of cardinal sets. *Ethology, 75*, 37–61.

Pfungst, O. (1911, reprinted in 1965). *Clever Hans (the horse of Mr. von Osten)* (C.L. Rahn, Trans.). New York: Holt, Rinehart and Winston.

Pietrewicz, A.T., & Kamil, A.C. (1977). Visual detection of cryptic prey by blue jays (*Cyanocitta cristata*). *Science, 195*, 580–582.

Pisacreta, R., Lefave, P., Lesneski, T., & Potter, C. (1985). Transfer of oddity learning in the pigeon. *Animal Learning and Behavior, 13*, 403–414.

Pisacreta, R., Redwood, E., & Witt, K. (1984). Transfer of matching-to-figure samples in the pigeon. *Journal of the Experimental Analysis of Behavior, 42*, 223–237.

Premack, D. (1976). *Intelligence in ape and man*. Hillsdale, NJ: Erlbaum.

Premack, D. (1986). *Gavagai! Or the future history of the animal language controversy*. Cambridge, MA: MIT Press.

Real, P.G., Iannazzi, R., Kamil, A.C., & Heinrich, B. (1984). Discrimination and generalization of leaf damage by blue jays (*Cyanocitta cristata*). *Animal Learning and Behavior, 12*, 202–208.

Restle, F. (1959). A metric and an ordering on sets. *Psychometrika, 24*, 207–220.

Ristau, C.A., & Robbins, D. (1982). Language in the great apes: A critical review. *Advances in the Study of Behavior, 12*, 141–225.

Rosch, E.H. (1973). Natural categories. *Cognitive Psychology, 4*, 328–350.

Rumbaugh, D.M., & Pate, J.L. (1984). The evolution of cognition in primates: A comparative perspective. In H.L. Roitblat, T.G. Bever, & H.S. Terrace (Eds.), *Animal cognition* (pp. 569–587). Hillsdale, NJ: Erlbaum.

Rumbaugh, D.M., Savage-Rumbaugh, S., & Hegel, M.T. (1987). Summation in the chimpanzee (*Pan troglodytes*). *Journal of Experimental Psychology: Animal Behavior Processes, 13*, 107–115.

Shepard, R.N. (1967). Recognition memory for words, sentences, and pictures. *Journal of Verbal Learning and Verbal Behavior, 6*, 156–163.

Shettleworth, S.J. (1972). Constraints on learning. In D.S. Lehrman, R.A. Hinde, & E. Shaw (Eds.), *Advances in the study of behavior* (Vol. 4, pp. 1–68). New York: Academic Press.

Shettleworth, S.J., & Krebs, J.R. (1986). Stored and encountered seeds: A comparison of two spatial memory tasks in marsh tits and chickadees. *Journal of Experimental Psychology: Animal Behavior Processes, 12*, 248–257.

Smith, E.E., & Medin, D.L. (1981). *Categories and concepts*. Cambridge, MA: Harvard University Press.

Spearman, C. (1927). *The abilities of man: Their nature and measurement*. New York: Macmillan.

Terrace, H.S. (1979). *Nim*. New York: Knopf.

Terrace, H.S. (1985). In the beginning was the "name." *American Psychologist, 40*, 1011–1028.

Turney, T.H. (1982). The association of visual concepts and imitative vocalizations in the mynah (*Gracula religiosa*). *Bulletin of the Psychonomic Society, 19*, 59–62.

Tversky, A. (1977). Features of similarity. *Psychological Review, 84*, 327–352.

Ullman, S. (1984). Visual routines. *Cognition, 18*, 97–159.

Underwood, B.J. (1966). *Experimental psychology* (2nd ed.). New York: Meredith.

Urcuioli, P.J. (1985). On the role of differential sample behaviors in matching-to-sample. *Journal of Experimental Psychology: Animal Behavior Processes, 11*, 502–519.

Vander Wall, S.B. (1982). An experimental analysis of cache recovery in Clark's nutcracker. *Animal Behavior, 30*, 84–94.

Vander Wall, S.B., & Balda, R.P. (1977). Coadaptations of the Clark's nutcracker and the pinon pine for efficient seed harvest and dispersal. *Ecology Monographs, 47*, 89–111.

Vaughan, W., Jr. (1988). Formation of equivalence sets in pigeons. *Journal of Experimental Psychology: Animal Behavior Processes, 14*, 36–42.

Vaughan, W., Jr., & Greene, S.L. (1983). Acquisition of absolute discriminations in pigeons. In M.L. Commons, R.J. Herrnstein, & A.R. Wagner (Eds.), *Quantitative analyses of behavior: Discrimination processes* (Vol. IV, pp. 231–238). Cambridge, MA: Ballinger.

Vaughan, W., Jr., & Greene, S.L. (1984). Pigeon visual memory capacity. *Journal of Experimental Psychology: Animal Behavior Processes, 10*, 256–271.

Vaughan, W., Jr., & Herrnstein, R.J. (1987). Choosing among natural stimuli. *Journal of the Experimental Analysis of Behavior, 47*, 5–16.

von Uexkull, J. (1934). *Streifzüge durch die Umwelten von Tieren und Menschen*. Berlin: Springer. Translated by Claire H. Schiller as "A stroll through the worlds of animals and men", in C.H. Schiller (ed.) (1957). Instinctive behavior: The development of a modern concept (pp. 5–80). New York: International Universities Press.

Wright, A.A., Santiago, H.C., Urcuioli, P.J., & Sands, S.F. (1983). Monkey and pigeon acquisition of same/different concept using pictorial stimuli. In M.L. Commons, R.J. Herrnstein, & A.R. Wagner (Eds.), *Quantitative analyses of behavior: Discrimination processes* (Vol. IV, pp. 295–317). Cambridge, MA: Ballinger.

Younger, B.A., & Cohen, L.B. (1985). How infants form categories. In G.H. Bower (Ed.), *The psychology of learning and motivation* (Vol. 19, pp. 211–247). New York: Academic Press.

Zentall, T.R., & Hogan, D.E. (1978). Same/different concept learning in the pigeon: The effect of negative instances and prior adaptation to transfer stimuli. *Journal of the Experimental Analysis of Behavior, 30*, 177–186.

Cognition, 37 (1990) 167–196

7

The representation of social relations by monkeys*

DOROTHY L. CHENEY
ROBERT M. SEYFARTH
University of Pennsylvania

Abstract

Cheney, D.L., and Seyfarth, R.M., 1990. The representation of social relations by monkeys. Cognition, 37: 167–196.

Monkeys recognize the social relations that exist among others in their group. They know who associates with whom, for example, and other animals' relative dominance ranks. In addition, monkeys appear to compare types of social relations and make same/different judgments about them. In captivity, longtailed macaques (Macaca fascicularis) *trained to recognize the relation between one adult female and her offspring can identify the same relation among other mother–offspring pairs, and distinguish this relation from bonds between individuals who are related in a different way. In the wild, if a vervet monkey* (Cercopithecus aethiops) *has seen a fight between a member of its own family and a member of Family X, this increases the likelihood that it will act aggressively toward another member of Family X. Vervets act as if they recognize some similarity between their own close associates and the close associates of others. To make such comparisons the monkeys must have some way of representing the properties of social relationships. We discuss the adaptive value of such representations, the information they contain, their structure, and their limitations.*

Introduction

The vervet monkeys had moved out of their sleeping trees to forage on the ground. While the adults fed, the juveniles played in a nearby bush. Macauley, the son of a low-ranking female, wrestled Carlyle, the juvenile

*Research supported by NSF Grant BNS 85-21147 and NIH Grant 19826. We thank Susan Abrams, Jeffrey Cynx, Verena Dasser, Daniel Dennett, Lynn Fairbanks, Randy Gallistel, Lila Gleitman, Sandy Harcourt, Robert Hinde, Peter Marler, Barbara Smuts, Kelly Stewart and three anonymous reviewers for comments on earlier drafts. Requests for reprints should be sent to Dorothy L. Cheney, Department of Anthropology, University of Pennsylvania, Philadelphia, PA 19104, U.S.A.

daughter of the highest-ranking female, to the ground. Carlyle screamed, chased Macauley away, and then went to forage next to her mother. Apparently, however, the fight had been noticed by others, because twenty minutes later Shelley, Carlyle's sister, approached Austen, Macauley's sister, and without provocation bit her on the tail.

This anecdote sets the stage for what is by now the familiar sort of popular article on nonhuman primates. Read any description of a longterm study of monkeys and apes and you will find an account of complex kinship networks, friendships, struggles for dominance, and shifting alliances. In fact, one of the fascinations of studying monkeys and apes is that their social structure often seems as rich and complex as our own. Like the Montagues and the Capulets, monkeys apparently recognize that the relations within their own families are similar to relations in other families, and they use this knowledge to retaliate against their opponents.

But still a nagging question remains: How much do the monkeys really know about what they are doing? Do they actually make use of concepts like "kinship" or "closely bonded," or are they simply responding on the basis of associations that they have formed between other group members?

Mental representations in animals are usually considered in terms of how different species store information about their physical environment: what pigeons know about trees (Herrnstein, 1990, this issue; Herrnstein & Loveland, 1964); what ducks and fish know about the rate of return at different feeding sites (Gallistel, 1989), or what rats know about time (e.g., Church & Broadbent, 1990, this issue; Gibbon & Church, 1990, this issue). For many animals, however, the most complicated problems in survival and reproduction concern members of their own species. Nonhuman primates, for instance, live in highly social groups where animals both compete with each other for access to scarce resources and cooperate to defend a home range against other groups. As a result, an individual must maintain relations with others that are delicately balanced between competition and cooperation. Further complicating matters, within each group some individuals are close genetic relatives while others are not, some are dominant while others are subordinate, and competition frequently takes the form of temporary alliances in which two animals join together to defeat a third. Because of alliances, one individual interacting with another must predict not only what the other is likely to do but also which third parties are likely to come to his opponent's aid. In short, monkeys and apes must assess each others' social relationships. Moreover, the demands placed on individuals by life in a social group may have favored the evolution of complex cognitive processes. This paper examines what nonhuman primates know about each other, and considers the extent to which monkeys and apes might be said to form "mental representations" of their own and other animals' social relationships.

Research on animal intelligence frequently attempts to distinguish between "knowing how" and "knowing that," a distinction first drawn by the philosopher Gilbert Ryle (1949; see also Dickinson, 1980; Whiten & Byrne, 1988a). "Knowing how" refers to the ability to perform a specific, procedural task based on recognition of a particular stimulus. Ants, for example, remove the carcasses of dead conspecifics from their nest. The function of this behavior is to rid the nest of bacteria, but ants certainly are not aware of the relation between corpses and disease; they are simply responding to the presence of oleic acid on the decaying corpse. Ants will remove anything that smells of oleic acid, regardless of whether it is dead or infected (Wilson, 1971). Even a live ant dabbed with oleic acid will be dragged, struggling, out of the nest. Similarly, a monkey mother's response to her offspring's scream might be relatively unmodifiable; she might simply run to her offspring's aid whenever she heard a vocalization with a particular set of acoustic properties.

By contrast, "knowing that" refers to "declarative representations or knowledge" (Dickinson, 1980), and implies an ability to make causal inferences about the world. Rather than simply running whenever her offspring screams, for example, the monkey mother might understand enough about the relation between dominance rank and kinship to recognize that discretion is often the greater part of valor, and that she should only intervene on her offspring's behalf when the offspring is fighting with a member of a lower-ranking matriline. In other words, because it refers to more general knowledge about things and can be divorced from a particular response, "knowing that" allows greater flexibility in behavior depending upon changes in the social and physical environment (Whiten & Byrne, 1988a).

In analyzing primate social knowledge, therefore, we must distinguish between knowledge that can be used in only a limited set of circumstances and knowledge that can be applied more broadly. A monkey may have formed an association between two members of the same matriline because the two animals are often encountered together. As a result, the monkey knows that whenever she approaches one individual she is also likely to be near the other. Such knowledge, however, might be limited to these two individuals, or to a small set of animals within the monkey's own group. It would prepare the monkey for some (indeed, many) sorts of interactions, but not for those that depended on the recognition of more differentiated relationships – for example, the difference between a relative and a "friend."

Alternatively, the monkey might have interacted with many different kin pairs and she might have inferred, on the basis of her experiences and observations, that such relationships share similar properties regardless of the particular individuals involved. The monkey might even have labels, like "closely bonded" or "enemies," that help order relationships into types. In this case the monkey's knowledge would be less constrained by particular stimuli, more general, and more abstract. It could also be applied in a much wider variety of circumstances.

There is now a variety of evidence suggesting that monkeys' and apes' knowledge of their social environment – that is, their knowledge of each other – is declarative rather than procedural. Among baboons, macaques, and vervet monkeys, for example, adult females compete with each other to interact with the members of high-ranking families. In so doing, they act as if they recognize that some animals are useful allies, and that bonds with these individuals can potentially help to maintain or even improve their own status. But is this really so? Can we actually provide evidence that the monkeys assess each others' relationships and classify them into types? Or are the animals just responding to a relatively narrow set of stimuli? To answer these questions we must examine more closely what monkeys actually know about social relationships and how such knowledge affects their behavior. That is the purpose of this paper.

Probing into the minds of monkeys, however, is not easy. Unlike anthropologists studying humans, or even psychologists working on captive apes, we cannot simply interview our subjects and ask them what they think about each other. Instead, we must rely on a variety of indirect methods, including observations, anecdotes and experiments, each focusing on situations in which the monkeys reveal, by their behavior, some of what they know about the principles that govern their interactions. By using different methods and drawing on data from a number of different species, we hope that conceptual or methodological weaknesses in one area can be wholly or partially overcome by work in another. As readers will quickly become aware, no single set of experiments or observations can ever provide the kind of ringing, definitive proof one would like. Instead we circle the problem, trying, from as many different angles as possible, to understand a perspective on social life that is different from our own.

Recognizing the relationships of others: Kinship, friendship and dominance rank

Knowledge about other animals' companions

In order to understand a dominance hierarchy, or to predict which individuals are likely to form alliances with each other, a monkey must step outside its own sphere of interactions and recognize the relations that exist among others. Such knowledge can only be obtained by observing interactions in which one is not involved and making the appropriate inferences. There is, in fact, growing evidence that monkeys do possess knowledge of other animals' social relationships, and that such knowledge affects their behavior.

Studies of hamadryas baboons (*Papio cynocephalus hamadryas*) in Ethiopia were the first to show that nonhuman primates assess the relationships that exist among others. Under natural conditions, hamadryas baboons are organized into one-male units, each of which contains one fully adult male and two to nine adult females (Kummer, 1968; Sigg, Stolba, Abegglen, & Dasser, 1982; reviewed in Stammbach, 1987). One-male units frequently come into contact with single, unattached males, and a male unit leader must constantly defend himself against attempts by other males to take over his females. Experiments using captive hamadryas have shown that "rival" males assess the strength of an owner's relationship with his females before competing to acquire them. Rival males do not attempt to take over a female if they have previously seen her interact with her owner. Such "respect of possession" holds even when the rival is dominant to the owner in other contexts (Kummer, Goetz, & Angst, 1974). This phenomenon seems to be widespread. Among both geladas in Ethiopia and savanna baboons in Kenya, challenges from a rival are less likely to occur if a male has strong grooming relations with a female, and more likely to occur if grooming relations are weak (Dunbar, 1983; Smuts, 1985).

To test the hypothesis that rivals make judgments about the strength of bonds between a male and his females, Bachmann and Kummer (1980) studied six adult males and six adult females, using choice tests to determine how strongly each male preferred each female and how strongly each female preferred each male. A male–female pair was then placed in a large outdoor enclosure and allowed to interact freely. Different "rival" males were allowed to watch the pair and then given an opportunity to challenge the owner. Bachmann and Kummer found that the probability of a challenge was not correlated with either the rival's or the owner's preference for a particular female. The female's preference, however, did make a difference: If a female was with an owner she strongly preferred, this inhibited challenges from middle- and low-ranking rivals. The two highest-ranking males challenged all owners regardless of how strongly females preferred them. Although Bachmann and Kummer could not rule out the possibility that rival males were simply responding to the females' actions rather than their relationships, the experiments suggested that the males might have been able to assess the strength of the attraction between an owner and his female and to avoid challenging owners when the pair's relationship was close. This seems an adaptive strategy because aggressive challenges, which involve potential injury, may be too costly if the contested female prefers to remain with her current mate.

Further evidence that monkeys recognize relations among others comes from playback experiments on vervet monkeys. In many primate species, mothers will run to their offsprings' aid when the offspring scream during a fight, suggesting that females can distinguish among the calls of different individuals. To test this hypothesis, we played the scream of a 2-year-old juvenile from a concealed loudspeaker to its mother and two control females who also had offspring in the group. We found that mothers consistently either looked toward or approached the speaker for longer durations than did control females, indicating that they recognized the voice of their offspring (Cheney & Seyfarth, 1980). This result was entirely expected, given the many studies that had already shown individual recognition by voice in primates (e.g., Hansen, 1976; Kaplan, Winship-Ball, & Sim, 1978; Waser, 1977) as well as birds and other mammals (e.g., Brooks & Falls, 1975; Emlen, 1971; Kroodsma, 1976; Petrinovich, 1974).

More interesting, however, was the behavior of control females. When the responses of control females were compared with their behavior before the scream was played, we found that playbacks significantly increased the likelihood that control females would look at the mother. By contrast, there was no change in the likelihood that control females would look at each other (Cheney & Seyfarth, 1980, 1982b). The females appeared to be able to associate particular screams with particular juveniles, and these juveniles with particular adult females. They behaved as if they recognized the kin relationships that existed among other group members.

At this point, it is important to emphasize that, whenever we speak of kin recognition in primates, we define the term operationally, as the recognition of a close social bond. The ability to recognize other animals' kin does not imply that monkeys have a concept of "kinship" or "genetic relatedness," but simply that they recognize the close associates of other group members. In most cases close associates are also kin, and this "rule of thumb" appears to be the primary mechanism underlying kin recognition in nonhuman primates (for reviews see Gouzoules, 1984; Gouzoules & Gouzoules, 1987; Waldman, Frumhoff, & Sherman, 1987). There is at present no evidence that monkeys differentiate among kin relationships that are characterized by similar rates of interaction – for example, sister as opposed to daughter – simply because the relevant tests have not yet been conducted.

Monkeys seem not only to distinguish among the screams of different juveniles, but also to differentiate among different types of aggressive interactions. In a study of maternal intervention in the semi-free-ranging population of rhesus macaques (*Macaca mulatta*) on Cayo Santiago, Puerto Rico,

Gouzoules, Gouzoules, and Marler (1984) noticed that the screams of juveniles varied systematically in their acoustic features, that different types of screams were given in different types of conflicts, and that mothers responded differently to different scream types. Mothers reacted most strongly to the screams given to higher-ranking opponents, next most strongly to screams given to lower-ranking opponents, and least strongly to screams given to relatives. Through its screams, in other words, a juvenile effectively classifies its opponents according to kinship and dominance. By her selective responses, an adult female reveals knowledge of both her offspring's voice and her offspring's network of social relationships.

For additional evidence that monkeys recognize the kin relationships (or close associates) of other group members, consider the phenomenon of redirected aggression. In many primate species, an animal that has been involved in a fight will "redirect" aggression and threaten a third, previously uninvolved individual. In rhesus macaques (Judge, 1982) and vervet monkeys (Cheney & Seyfarth, 1986, 1990a) such redirected aggression is not distributed randomly but is directed toward a close relative of the prior opponent. Vervets in Amboseli were significantly more likely to threaten unrelated individuals following a fight with those animals' close kin than during matched control periods (Cheney & Seyfarth, 1986, 1990a). This was not because fights caused a general increase in aggression toward unrelated animals. Instead, aggression seemed to be directed specifically toward the kin of prior opponents.

Similar kin-biased patterns of interaction were evident in a behavior that is the mirror image of redirected aggression, reconciliation. In many species of monkeys and apes, including vervet monkeys, animals sometimes reconcile after fights by approaching their former opponents and touching, hugging, or grooming them (e.g., longtailed macaques: Cords, 1988; rhesus macaques: de Waal & Yoshihara, 1983; stumptail macaques: de Waal & Ren, 1988; patas monkeys: York & Rowell, 1988; chimpanzees: de Waal & Roosmalen, 1979). It is not only the primary antagonists who reconcile, however. Monkeys will also reconcile with the kin of their former opponents. Studying reconciliation among captive patas monkeys (*Erythrocebus patas*), York and Rowell (1988) found that unrelated animals contacted the kin of their former opponents almost twice as often following a fight than during matched control periods. Similarly, vervet monkeys were significantly more likely to groom or initiate a friendly interaction with an unrelated animal following a fight with that animal's kin than in the absence of such a fight (Cheney & Seyfarth, 1990a).

Interestingly, however, reconciliation among related vervet monkeys differed in two respects from reconciliation among unrelated opponents. First, unrelated animals were more likely to reconcile with their opponents' kin than with their opponents themselves. Related animals were more likely to reconcile directly with their opponents. Second, reconciliation appeared to be a more important context for affinitive interactions among nonkin than among kin. Nonkin were significantly more likely to initiate friendly interactions both directly with their opponents and with their opponents' kin following a fight than during control periods (see also York & Rowell, 1988). In contrast, related vervet monkeys were as likely to interact with their opponents and their opponents' kin (who were also their own kin) during control periods as they were following a fight. Apparently, the generally high rates of grooming and friendly interactions among kin swamped the effect of affinitive interaction in the context of reconciliation. This result is similar to that reported by Cords (1988), who found that juvenile male longtailed macaques also reconciled at higher rates with nonkin than with kin. Relationships among unrelated animals are typically less predictable and stable than those among relatives, and Cords has suggested that post-conflict affinitive interactions may function as a repair mechanism for relationships among nonkin. Such reconciliatory interactions may be less important for kin, who interact at high rates in any case.

The fact that unrelated vervets reconciled with their opponents' kin as well as (indeed, more than) with their opponents themselves suggest that conflict resolution extends beyond individual opponents to their entire families. There is a good reason for this. Over 20% of all aggressive interactions among female vervets involved alliances by two individuals against a third, and vervets formed approximately 65% of their alliances with family members (Cheney & Seyfarth, 1987). Since an aggressive interaction with a particular individual is likely to expand to include other members of that individual's matriline, it may be as important to reconcile with the opponent's family as with the opponent herself (Judge, 1983), particularly if the opponent is a member of a higher-ranking matriline. Reconciliation with an opponent's relatives may have the added advantage of establishing affinitive contact with a relevant, yet uninvolved, individual while nevertheless avoiding the opponent (see also de Waal, 1989).

Knowledge about other animals' relationships is not limited to the recognition of matrilineal kin. Consider, for example, the pattern of redirected aggression among pairs of male–female "friends" in savanna baboons (*Papio cynocephalus anubis*, Smuts, 1983, 1985). Baboon males and females sometimes form longterm pair bonds, or "friendships," in which proximity and cooperative behavior are maintained throughout the female's reproductive cycle (e.g., Altmann, 1980; Kaufmann, 1965; Seyfarth, 1978). In some baboon groups, friendships persist for years at a time (Smuts, 1983, 1985;

Strum, 1984). In the most well documented study of friendships, Smuts (1985) found that females and males often redirected aggression against their opponents' friends. Following a fight with another male, for example, a male frequently appeared to seek out his rival's female friend and chase her. The baboons, in other words, seemed to recognize friendships.

In sum, monkeys in many different species appear to observe interactions in which they are not involved and recognize the relationships that exist among others. In this respect, monkeys make good primatologists. A male considers how strongly a female prefers her partner before he attempts to take her away; juveniles and adult females take note of their opponents' kin as they plot retaliation or reconciliation; and adult females, upon hearing a juvenile's cry for help, learn to expect a response from the mother.

Knowledge about other animal's ranks

Dominance relations in vervets and many other primates are transitive. This allows a human observer to assemble, from data on interactions in pairs of individuals, a rank hierarchy that orders the behavior of a large number of animals. The fact that we can derive such hierarchies does not, however, prove that they also exist in the minds of monkeys. It is certainly possible that monkeys attend to each others' dominance interactions and that they recognize rank orders (and transitive relations) among others in their group (e.g., Kummer, 1982). Alternatively, each monkey may simply know who is dominant and who is subordinate to itself, having derived this knowledge from personal experience. In the latter case, a dominance hierarchy would occur as an incidental outcome of paired interactions (e.g., Altmann, 1981).

A variety of observational data suggests that monkeys recognize the dominance ranks of others. When competing over grooming partners, for example, both female vervets and female baboons supplant each other, on average, most often for access to the highest-ranking individual, next most often for access to the second-highest-ranking individual, third most often for access to the third-highest-ranking individual, and so on (Seyfarth, 1976, 1980). This pattern does not occur simply because high-ranking females spend more time grooming and are therefore more likely to be available as objects of competition; females of different ranks spend roughly equal amounts of time in grooming interactions. The observed pattern, moreover, is consistent across many different individuals (Seyfarth, 1976, 1980). In other words, adult females seem not only to rank one another but also to "agree" on their ranking of the most preferred grooming partners. Similarly, in both pigtail macaques (Gouzoules, 1975) and savanna baboons (Scott, 1984) the intensity of male–male competition for mates is directly related to the rank of the female involved.

Additional hints that monkeys are able to judge the ranks of others emerge when we consider the details of social behavior when adult female vervet monkeys compete for access to grooming partners. Competition over access to a grooming partner occurs whenever one female approaches two that are grooming, supplants one of them, and then grooms or is groomed by the remaining individual. In a small proportion of all cases such competition takes a form that is especially interesting for our present purpose: A high-ranking female (ranked 2, for example, in a group of six adult females) approaches two groomers who are both lower-ranking than she is (say, females ranked 4 and 5). Though Females 4 and 5 are both subordinate to Female 2, they are not equally likely to depart. During one 8-month period in 1985–86, in 29 out of 30 interactions that took this form, the higher-ranking female (Female 4 in our generic example) did nothing, while the lower-ranking female (Female 5) moved away. This result was independent of kin relations among the individuals involved.

It is Female 4, of course, whose behavior is most interesting. She acts as if she has recognized that, even though she is subordinate to Female 2, Female 5 is more subordinate than she is. Female 4's behavior, in other words, suggests that she recognizes the ranking:

Female 2 > Female 4 > Female 5.

To do so she must not only know her own status relative to Females 2 and 5 but also their status relative to each other. In other words, she must recognize a rank hierarchy.

An alternative explanation might argue that Female 2's approach simply has a greater effect on Female 5 than it does on Female 4. If the probability of a supplant depends on the magnitude of the difference between two individuals' ranks, the result could be explained without positing that individuals know the ranks of others. Data gathered in 1985–86, however, do not support this view. For example, when dominant females approached others who ranked two, three or four steps beneath them in the hierarchy, the subordinate was supplanted in 61%, 54% and 63% of all cases, respectively ($N = 101$, 61 and 48 approaches).

It is also possible that Female 4 gave some subtle glance or shrug in Female 5's direction as Female 2 approached that was not noticeable to the human observer. Such behavior would explain the observation without requiring any knowledge of ranking on the monkeys' part. Clearly, we will never be able to exclude this possibility entirely. If these gestures do occur, however, they are extremely subtle, and do not resemble any other form of threats or supplants.

Nonhuman primates may not be the only species that rank each other.

Linear, transitive, dominance hierarchies are common, for example, in wild dogs, hyaenas, and a variety of birds (e.g., Dufty, 1986; Frame, Malcolm, Frame, & van Lawick, 1979; Frank, 1986; Rowher, 1982; Yasukawa, 1979). Studying captive goldfinches, Popp (1987) observed competitive interactions among individuals at a feeding site that contained two perches. He found that when a dominant bird flew into a site that was already occupied by two subordinate animals, it usually approached and supplanted the more subordinate of the two, as if it recognized the birds' relative ranks. As with monkeys, however, simpler explanations are possible. In this instance, rather than recognizing the other birds' relative ranks, the dominant bird may simply have distinguished individuals whose latency to fly off in past interactions was different. The subordinate birds' behavior might reveal more about goldfinches' understanding of dominance hierarchies. Did the bird that flew away recognize that it was more subordinate than the one that stayed?

In the absence of experiments designed specifically to test for animals' understanding of dominance hierarchies, no one set of data can ever prove decisively that monkeys recognize each others' ranks. For the moment, we can only conclude that a variety of data from a number of different species suggest that monkeys can rank one another. We turn now to the question of how they might do it.

Consider first some experiments by Michael D'Amato and his colleagues (D'Amato & Colombo, 1988; see also D'Amato & Salmon, 1984; D'Amato, Salmon, Loukas, & Tomie, 1985). In these tests, captive cebus monkeys were trained to respond to five stimuli (a circle, a plus sign, a dot, a vertical line and an hourglass – hereafter A,B,C,D and E) in a specified order: first AB, then ABC, then ABCD, and finally ABCDE. To test the animals' knowledge of the sequential position of each item, subjects were given pairwise tests (for example, BC or DA) and rewarded for responding only to pairs that appeared in the correct sequential order. The monkeys performed well. In addition, their latency to respond was shortest when the first item in the test series was A, longer when it was B, longer still when it was C, and so on. Their latency was also shortest when the two items in the test series were adjacently ranked, longer when they were separated by one item, and longer still when they were separated by two items. D'Amato and Colombo believe that these results demonstrate "an internal representation of the sequential order of the five items" (see also D'Amato & Colombo, in press).

D'Amato and colleagues argue that the representation of rank order in cebus monkeys is based on "associative transitivity," which they contrast with "transitive inference." In associative transitivity no inference is involved because there is nothing in the initial conditional discrimination that demands a particular pairing of stimuli on the test trials. There is no underlying rule, in other words, that is common to the pairs AB and BC. As a result, in the absence of prior association, the subject has no way of inferring that in the test trials A should be linked with C. In many respects, the experiments test only whether monkeys are capable of ordering stimuli sequentially.

By contrast, experiments that test for transitivity in children (Bryant & Trabasso, 1971), squirrel monkeys (McGonigle & Chalmers, 1977) and chimpanzees (Gillan, 1981) have all involved identification of a relation between the training stimuli: for example, A is longer than B, B is longer than C, and so on. This may have allowed transitivity to be inferred on subsequent tests (D'Amato & Salmon, 1984). Gillan, for example, taught chimpanzees that stimulus E had more food than stimulus D, D had more food than C, C more than B and B more than A. He then tested individuals on novel nonadjacent pairs like BD, BE and CE. The animals consistently chose the stimulus in each pair that was associated with the greater amount of food. In this and other tests, subjects may have inferred the relation "greater than" and solved test problems according to this relational rule rather than according to the prior association of particular stimuli (for alternative explanations see Breslow, 1981; D'Amato & Salmon, 1984; McGonigle & Chalmers, 1977).

While socially living monkeys seem to recognize the dominance ranks of others, we know very little about how these ranks are learned, or how ranks are represented in the animals' minds. One means by which a monkey might acquire information about other animals' ranks is simply through "brute force," a method similar to D'Amato's "associative transitivity." Here a monkey simply observes and remembers all possible dyadic interactions until it is able to conclude that A is dominant to everyone, B is dominant to everyone but A, C is dominant to everyone but A and B, and so on. The brute force method does not require the ability to make transitive inferences, but it does demand that a monkey observe at least one interaction between all pairs of group members before constructing a dominance hierarchy.

In contrast, a monkey who could make transitive inferences about rank relations among other group members could construct a linear dominance hierarchy on the basis of partial information, without having to observe interactions among all pairs of individuals.

At present there are no data that allow us to choose between these alternatives, though tests on captive squirrel monkeys (McGonigle & Chalmers, 1977) and chimpanzees (Gillan, 1981) suggest that transitive inference is at least possible. In some cases, it is difficult to explain the behavior of monkeys in large groups without assuming that the animals are using the more efficient method of transitive inference. Although vervet monkeys typically live in groups of fewer than 30 individuals, many macaque and baboon groups commonly exceed 100 members. Observers often report spending months with a group without ever seeing some individuals interact. Yet when data on social interactions within such groups are analyzed (e.g., Scott, 1984) there is still evidence that the animals construct rank orders of their fellow group members. Since these rank orders include individuals who interact only rarely, it seems probable that their places have been calculated by animals who observe a subset of dyadic interactions and make the additional assumption that all rank relations are transitive.

The representation of social relationships

Nonhuman primates classify other individuals according to their patterns of association and seem to recognize the bonds and enmities that exist among individuals other than themselves. Humans, though, go several steps further, to classify different types of relationships into superordinate categories that are independent of the particular individuals involved. If a friend mentions a sister, an uncle, or a husband, we immediately have some idea of the nature of her relationship with the other person, even if we have never met the individual in question. And if the friend tells us that her uncle wrecked her new car and her husband closed her bank account and left town, we are shocked at least in part because their behavior is at variance with what we typically expect of people in these categories. In fact, it could easily be argued that humans are overly eager to classify relationships. "The friend of my enemy is also my enemy" is, cognitively speaking, a delightfully complex concept, redolent of all sorts of inference, transitivity, and classification. It can, however, lead to awkward overgeneralizations and less than adaptive behavior. Is there any evidence that monkeys, too, classify social bonds into higher order units that allow relationships to be compared independent of the individuals involved?

Judgments about relations

Many animals appear to classify objects according to "concepts" – relatively abstract criteria that are not based on any single perceptual feature (Lea, 1984). For example, tests that demand cross-modal transfer of performance from lights to tones or the classification of objects according to relative size, hue, or shape demonstrate that animals as diverse as pigeons, parrots, sea lions, and monkeys are capable of forming abstract concepts and using them to classify objects in the external world (e.g., pigeons: Herrnstein, 1990, this issue; Herrnstein & Loveland, 1964; African grey parrot: Pepperberg, 1983; sea lions; Schusterman, 1988; squirrel monkeys: Roberts & Mazmanian,

1988; stumptail macaques: Schrier, Angarella, & Povar, 1984; rhesus macaques: Sands, Lincoln, & Wright, 1982; Schrier & Brady, 1987; see also Premack, 1986). The precise nature of these mental representations remains elusive. It seems clear, however, that the animals are not simply responding according to perceptual similarities, since in many studies no single set of perceptual criteria was either necessary or sufficient to account for the subjects' behavior. The critical features used by pigeons and monkeys to identify animal pictures remain unknown (Medin & Smith, 1984). D'Amato and van Sant (1988) argue that such features cannot help but remain elusive, and that further efforts to identify concepts in animals through photograph discrimination may be futile.

In addition to classifying stimuli according to relatively abstract features, monkeys can readily be taught to solve problems that require recognition of a relation between objects rather than a specific physical attribute. In oddity tests, for instance, a subject is presented with three objects, two of which are the same and one of which is different. It receives a reward only if it chooses the different object. Many monkey species achieve scores of 80% to 90% correct even when new stimuli are used for each problem and each set of stimuli is presented for only one trial (e.g., Davis, Leary, Stevens, & Thompson, 1967; Strong & Hedges, 1966). Such performance suggests that animals are using an abstract hypothesis, "pick the odd object." The hypothesis is called abstract because "odd" does not refer to any specific stimulus dimension, as does "red" or "square." Instead, oddity is a concept that specifies a relation between objects independent of their specific stimulus attributes (Essock-Vitale & Seyfarth, 1987; Roitblat, 1987).

Although judgments based on relations among items have been demonstrated more often in nonhuman primates than in other taxa, there is no a priori reason to expect that this ability should be restricted to primates. Pepperberg (1987), for example, has taught an African grey parrot to make same/different judgments about the color, shape, and material of objects. Similarly, the fact that not only chimpanzees (Boysen & Berntson, 1989; Matsuzawa, 1985) but also rats (Capaldi & Miller, 1988; Church & Meck, 1984) are able to generalize numerical discriminations from training sets to novel sets composed of entirely different items suggests that many species may have a concept of numerosity that is based on relatively abstract criteria (see also discussion by Gallistel, 1989).

Premack (1983, 1986) contends that tasks like oddity tests require only judgments about relations between elements, not relations between relations. By contrast, judgments about relations between relations are involved in tasks like analogical reasoning. They are less fundamental and universal than judgments about relations between elements, and they have thus far been demonstrated only in language-trained chimpanzees.

In his study of analogical reasoning in chimpanzees, Premack (1976, 1983) trained Sarah to make same/different judgments between pairs of stimuli. Once Sarah could use these words correctly even when confronted with entirely new stimuli, she was shown two pairs of items arranged in the form A/A' and B/B'. Her task was to judge whether the relation shown on the left was the same or different from the relation shown on the right. Alternatively, Sarah was given an incomplete analogy like A/A' *same as* B/? Her task then was to complete the analogy in a way that satisfied this relation.

In the most complex test, the objects shared no obvious physical similarity. For example, Sarah was asked "lock is to key as closed paint can is to __," with the options for completing the analogy being a can opener and a paint brush. Here the identity between two such relations is not based on physical similarity (in fact they look quite different), but on the underlying relation *opening*, which both cases instantiate. Hence it is not the stimuli themselves but this relation that must be represented in the subject's mind. To solve an analogy the chimpanzee must infer the appropriate relation for each stimulus pair and then compare these two relations to see if they are the same (Gillan, Premack, & Woodruff, 1981; Premack, 1983). In other words, she must somehow form a representation of the concept instantiated by each pair, and then compare these representations.

Premack (1983) contends that the ability to form such abstract representations is enhanced by, and may require, language training. His claim is not that chimpanzees naturally lack the ability to reason abstractly. Instead, he believes that all primates possess the potential for such skills but only chimpanzees subject to language training are able to realize this potential.

The assessment of social relationships

Premack's tests prompt one to ask whether group-living primates might use abstract criteria to make same/different judgments about social relationships. A comparable problem in the social domain might concern the judgment of relations within different kin groups: Is the relation Mother A/Infant A the same as or different from the relation Mother B/Infant B (Cheney & Seyfarth, 1982c)? Premack's analogy tests therefore bring us back to the central question of this section: Is there any evidence that primates, in their assessment of each others' behavior, ever classify relationships using criteria that are independent of the particular individuals involved?

Verena Dasser (1988a) studied social knowledge in longtailed macaques who were members of a group of 40 individuals living in a large, outdoor enclosure. After considerable effort, Dasser trained three adult females so that they could be temporarily removed from the group and placed in a small test room to view slides of other group members. In one test that used a simultaneous discrimination procedure, the subject saw two slides. One showed a mother and her offspring, the other showed an unrelated pair of group members. The subject was rewarded for pressing a response button below the mother–offspring slide. Having been trained to respond to one mother–offspring pair (five different slides of the same mother and her juvenile daughter), the subject was tested using 14 novel slides of different mothers and offspring paired with 14 novel unrelated alternatives. The mother–offspring pairs varied widely in their physical characteristics. Some slides showed mothers and infant daughters, others showed mothers and juvenile sons or mothers and adult daughters. Nonetheless, in all 14 tests the subject correctly selected the mother–offspring pair.

In a second test that used a match-to-sample procedure, the mother was represented as the sample on a center screen, while one of her offspring and another stimulus animal of the same age and sex as the offspring were given as positive and negative alternatives, respectively. Having learned to select the offspring during training, the subject was presented with 22 novel combinations of mother, offspring, and unrelated individual. She chose correctly on 20 of 22 tests.

Finally, to test whether monkeys could recognize other categories of social affiliation, Dasser (1988b) trained a subject to identify a pair of siblings and then tested the subject's ability to distinguish novel sibling pairs from (a) mother–offspring pairs, (b) pairs of otherwise related group members, like aunts and nieces, and (c) pairs of unrelated group members. The subject correctly identified the sibling pair in 70% of tests. Seven of the eight errors occurred when she was asked to compare siblings with a mother–offspring pair; one occurred when she compared siblings with two less closely related members of the same matriline.

Data on redirected aggression and reconciliation in vervet monkeys provide additional evidence that animals classify social relationships into types, independent of the particular individuals involved. Recall that in some monkey species redirected aggression and reconciliation are kin-biased, such that animals often interact with the kin of their prior opponents. In vervet monkeys, moreover, redirected aggression and reconciliation can extend even to the previously uninvolved kin of prior opponents. Data gathered in two social groups over two different time periods showed that an animal was more likely to threaten another individual if one of its own close relatives and one of its opponent's close relatives had recently been involved in a fight (Cheney & Seyfarth, 1986, 1990a). The same was true of reconciliation. Two unrelated individuals were more likely to engage in an affinitive interaction following a fight between their close kin than during matched control periods. So, in the example given at the beginning of this paper, the fight between Macauley and Carlyle apparently caused Shelley, Carlyle's sister, to attack Austen, Macauley's sister. Of course, the parallel is not exact: If the prior opponents were both adult females this did not necessarily mean that the subsequent opponents would both be their daughters. Vervet families are simply too small for these perfectly balanced analogies even to arise.

Bearing in mind the preliminary nature of these results, these more complex forms of redirected aggression and reconciliation support Dasser's experiments in suggesting that monkeys recognize that certain types of social relationships share similar characteristics. When a vervet monkey (say, A2) threatens an unrelated animal (B2) following a fight between one of her own relatives (A1) and one of her opponent's relatives (B1), A2 acts as if she recognizes that the relationship between B2 and B1 is in some way similar to her own relationship with A1. In other words, we may think of A2 as having been presented with a natural problem in analogical reasoning:

A1/B1 *same as* A2/?

A2 correctly completes the analogy by directing aggression to another member of the B family.

Definitive proof that monkeys are indeed capable of solving social analogies, and that language training is not a necessary prerequisite, can only come from laboratory tests. We can imagine, for example, an experiment in which a monkey is asked the following question about its fellow group members: Mother A is to Infant A as Mother B is to (i) Infant B, (ii) Juvenile B, or (iii) Infant C? Dasser's results and our less rigorous observational data suggest that monkeys would solve this problem with ease. The relevant tests, however, have not yet been attempted.

We have no idea how monkeys might complete these analogies, much less how they might represent social relationships in their minds. One possibility is that they use physical resemblance as a cue, since members of the same matriline often (but not always) look alike. Note, however, that vervets and longtailed macaques treat bonds between kin as similar even when they involve pairs of animals whose within-family resemblances, at least to a human observer, are markedly different. In Dasser's study, for example, subjects generalized to a diverse array of mother–offspring pairs (mothers and young black infants; mothers and juvenile sons; mothers and adult daughters) even though they had been trained with only one example from this category (Dasser, 1988a). Similarly, male and female baboon "friends" do not resemble each other, yet other baboons nevertheless recognize that certain males and females associate at high rates.

There is no hard evidence that vervets or any other monkey species recognize kinship in any sense other than a close association between two individuals (e.g., Frederickson & Sackett, 1984). However, association rates do not entirely explain differential treatment of kin and nonkin, because kin do not always interact at higher rates than nonkin. Even the same types of kinship bonds are not always characterized by similar kinds and rates of interactions. Some mother–offspring pairs, for example, are close and interact at high rates, while others are more distant (e.g., Altmann, 1980; Hinde, 1974). All, however, were classified by Dasser's subjects as falling within the same category. Similarly, while bonds within matrilineal kin groups can be extremely variable (depending, for example, on the ages and sex of family members), monkeys nevertheless treat competitive interactions as pitting one family against another (Cheney & Seyfarth, 1986, 1990b; Dunbar, 1983; Walters, 1987).

In sum, monkeys seem to use a metric to classify social relationships that cannot be explained simply in terms of physical features or the number and type of interactions. Instead, their classification seems based on an abstraction that includes all of these. Results raise the possibility that monkeys recognize a distinction between members of their own matriline and members of other, unrelated families that cannot be explained entirely in terms of close behavioral association.

In addition to recognizing the difference between bonds within their own matriline and bonds in other families, monkeys also seem to recognize the similarity among kinship bonds across different families. To recognize that certain sorts of bonds share similar characteristics independent of the particular individuals involved, monkeys must compare animals not according to physical features or a specific type of interaction, but according to an underlying relation that has been abstracted from a series of interactions over time. Monkeys take note of the elements that make up a relationship (grooming, alliances and so on). They then make judgments of similarity or difference not by comparing specific elements but by comparing the different relationships that these elements instantiate.

Representing the meaning of vocalizations

The hypothesis that monkeys classify relationships into relatively abstract categories receives additional support from experiments suggesting that vervets also classify their vocalizations into referential categories. Vervets give acoustically different alarm calls to at least five different predators, including leopards, eagles, and snakes. Each alarm call elicits a different response from other monkeys nearby, suggesting that the calls have different referents

(Seyfarth, Cheney, & Marler, 1980). By contrast, other calls in the vervets' repertoire, though acoustically distinct, have broadly similar referents. For example, vervets give two acoustically distinct calls – "wrrs" and "chutters" – at the approach of a neighboring group. Wrrs are usually given when another group has first been spotted, while chutters occur primarily when groups come together and the encounter escalates to include aggressive threats, chases, or even physical contact (Cheney & Seyfarth, 1988). Though wrrs and chutters are given under slightly different circumstances, therefore, they both occur only in the general context of an intergroup interaction.

To test the hypothesis that vervet monkeys classify vocalizations according to their referents rather than simply their acoustic properties, we repeatedly played subjects a call (for example, an intergroup wrr or a leopard alarm call) given by a specific individual in their group. Subjects rapidly habituated, and soon ceased responding to this vocalization. We then played subjects either a call with the same referent but different acoustic properties (an intergroup chutter, for example) or a call with a different referent and different acoustic properties (an eagle alarm call, for example).

Results provided clear evidence that vervet monkeys compare different calls on the basis of their referents, and not just their acoustic properties. If an animal had habituated to Individual X's intergroup wrr, she transferred habituation and also ceased responding to X's intergroup chutter. In contrast, subjects who had habituated to repeated playback of, for example, X's leopard alarm call did not transfer habituation to X's eagle alarm call (Cheney & Seyfarth, 1988).

In sum, when presented with two different vocalizations that have different acoustic properties, vervet monkeys judge them to be similar if the calls have similar referents and are given by the same individual. Just as they seem to classify social relationships into types independent of the particular animals involved, the monkeys make same/different judgments about vocalizations according to the things for which they stand, not just their acoustic properties. To make such comparisons, individuals must be able to represent, in their minds, the objects and events denoted by a vocalization, and then compare calls on the basis of these representations.

Discussion

Representing social relationships

Nonhuman primates make good primatologists. On the basis of their observations, they not only recognize the relations that exist among others but also compare *types* of social relationships and make same/different judgments about them. Longtailed macaques trained to recognize the relation between one adult female and her offspring can identify the same relation among other mother–offspring pairs, and distinguish this relation from bonds between individuals who are related in a different way. If a vervet monkey has seen a fight between a member of its own family and a member of Family X, this increases the likelihood that it will act aggressively toward another member of Family X. Vervets act as if they recognize some similarity between their own close associates and the close associates of others. In both cases, the monkeys' judgments depend not on the particular individuals involved but on the *relationships* that exist between them. Mother–offspring pairs are judged to be similar regardless of whether the offspring are old or young, male or female; relations within families are judged to be similar regardless of whether the animals in question are sisters, brothers or parents and offspring.

To make such comparisons the monkeys must have some way of representing the properties of social relationships. This representation is not explicit: We have no evidence, for example, that monkeys have labels to describe mothers and offspring or closely bonded individuals. Nevertheless, it seems clear that the social complexity of nonhuman primate groups is based, at least in part, on processes that go beyond the formation of associations between individuals. Monkeys observe who associates with whom and then infer distinct types of relationships. These relationships may be relatively independent of the individuals that instantiate them.

Why monkeys need mental representations

Throughout this paper we have adopted a functional, evolutionary approach to the study of primate intelligence. If representations of certain aspects of the world exist in the minds of monkeys, we assume that they do so because they confer a selective advantage on those who make use of them. We also assume that what is represented, as well as the structure of information contained within a representation, will be determined by the relative utility of one sort of mental operation as opposed to another.

Groups of monkeys and apes are composed of many shifting alliances among related and unrelated animals. In order to gain a social (and reproductive) advantage over others, an individual must be able not only to predict other animals' behavior, but also to assess other animals' relationships. It is not enough to know who is dominant or subordinate to oneself; one must also know who is allied to whom and who is likely to come to an opponent's aid. For this reason, we should expect knowledge of other animals' relationships to appear in any animal society where alliances are common (Harcourt, 1988).

The notion that monkeys might need representations of social relationships is buttressed by the experience of those who study them. Primatologists have long recognized that in order to explain and predict the behavior of their subjects, they cannot simply describe or list who does what to whom and how often. Instead, they must step back from the minutiae of social behavior and identify, at a more abstract level, social relationships and the general principles that underlie them. Hinde (1976, 1983), for example, defines a relationship "in terms of the content, quality and patterning of interactions" between two individuals over time. By this definition, a relationship cannot be described by any single interaction, nor is it enough simply to list what two individuals did with one another during a particular period (for example, that they groomed three times, hugged each other once, fought once and spent 23% of observation time together). What matters – and what defines a relationship – is not simply the behaviors themselves but also the temporal relations among behaviors and the way each activity is carried out. Some pairs of animals groom whenever they are together, others groom only briefly; some separate after a fight, others reconcile; for some a hug is perfunctory while for others it is a lengthy embrace. The point is: If either we (as observers) or the monkeys (as participants) want to explain or predict social behavior, we must change our unit of analysis from a set of interactions that is simple and concrete to a relationship that is more complex and abstract.

The ability to represent social relationships may have evolved because it offers the most accurate means of predicting the behavior of others (see also Humphrey, 1976, 1980; Whiten & Byrne, 1988b). There are also other advantages. Because relationships conceived in this way are abstractions, they can be more parsimonious and simpler than absolute judgments, which require learning the characteristics of every interaction (Allen, 1989; Dasser, 1985; Kummer, 1982; Premack, 1983). If a monkey can assess the relationships of others – rather than having to observe and remember all their interactions – he may be able to predict what opponents will do next even when he has seen them interact only once or twice. In other words, a monkey would be a much better social strategist if he had some way of representing different types of social relationship.

The content of representations, and their limitations

When we talk of monkeys recognizing a close association between two other animals, it is important to distinguish between "association" as referring strictly to an observable fact – that two animals are often together – and "association" as referring to a more structured and differentiated representation of a social relationship. Monkeys are undoubtedly capable of recognizing that certain other individuals interact at high rates, and their comparison of different relationships are probably often based on differences in rates of interaction. However, an association that is based solely on interaction rates cannot incorporate any other qualities of a relationship. If a monkey learns to associate other animals solely on the basis of the rate at which they interact, he will be unable to distinguish between two different types of relationship when both involve similar rates of interaction. There will be no way for him to distinguish, for example, a female's relationship with a juvenile male (her son) and the same female's relationship with an adult male (her "friend" or longterm mate).

It seems probable, however, that monkeys are sensitive to more than just interaction rates when assessing other animals' social relationships. They also appear to attend to subtler distinctions, including the types and quality of interactions, the age and sex of the participants, their dominance ranks, their past history of behavior, and so on (see, for example, Hinde, 1983). Recall, for example, that Dasser's (1988a) longtailed macaques correctly identified numerous mother–offspring pairs despite marked variation in the ages, sex, and interaction rates of the individuals involved. Similarly, vervet monkeys reconciled primarily with their opponents' kin following fights with unrelated animals, but with their opponents themselves following fights with members of their own matriline. This suggests that vervets distinguished their own close associates from the close associates of others, despite similarly high rates of interaction within all matrilineal kin groups. To give one final example, numerous studies of baboons, macaques, and vervets have shown that high-ranking females ar more attractive grooming and alliance partners than low-ranking females, regardless of the rate at which they reciprocate (reviewed in Walters & Seyfarth, 1987). This observation suggests that females assess the benefits of social relationships not just in terms of the frequency of interactions, but also according to the potential benefits that different individuals can offer.

We may hypothesize, therefore, that the primate mind is predisposed to organize data on social behavior according to both the individuals involved and the content, quality and pattern of their interactions, since information about all of these features must be incorporated if an individual is to predict other animals' behavior. The resulting representation has an abstract component because it is more than the sum of its parts. A social relationship cannot be described simply in terms of the participants' physical resemblance, identities, or any single measure of activity like time spent grooming or the proportion of fights followed by a reconciliation. Instead, it must incorporate information on all of these features.

If future investigations support the hypothesis that monkeys' representations of social relationships are not based solely on association rates, two further related issues will deserve particular attention. First, how many kinds of relationships are recognized? Is "mother" different from "sister"; is a "friend" of the same sex different from a "friend" of the opposite sex? At the moment, no empirical data address this issue, because no studies have examined whether monkeys can discriminate among relationships in which interaction rates are similar. Second, what are the consequences of having different representations for different types of relationships? How might they give one individual a selective advantage over others?

Even if monkeys do distinguish among different types of social relationships, however, it remains possible that their ability to assess these relationships is relatively inflexible and limited to circumstances in which the individuals involved are familiar. In all of the studies described to date, subjects have of necessity been tested only with the social companions that make up their group. As a result, we cannot state conclusively that a monkey confronted with an entirely new set of individuals – a young male transferring into a new group, for example – would be predisposed to look for close bonds among matrilineal kin, linear dominance relations, and so on. More to the point, how long would it take for a vervet or baboon to learn that not all primate species have the same patterns of social interaction? If a vervet male transferred into a gorilla group, where females are seldom closely related (Stewart & Harcourt, 1987), how long would it take for the male to cease expecting the females to interact at high rates? Would he ever?

There is no doubt that monkeys can learn to adjust to novel patterns of behavior, as Kummer, Goetz, and Angst (1970) demonstrated when they experimentally transferred females between groups of hamadryas and savannah baboons in Ethiopia. Unlike savannah baboons, who live in large, multimale groups, hamadryas baboons form small, relatively stable one-male units. The spatial integrity of these units is strictly enforced by the males who lead them, and male unit leaders herd and threaten their females whenever the females stray from their units (Kummer, 1968). When Kummer and his colleagues artificially introduced female savannah baboons into hamadryas groups, the females learned within an hour to follow the specific males who had chosen them as their own. In particular, the females learned to approach males who threatened them, rather than to flee from them as they normally would have done in a savannah baboon group. Similarly, female hamadryas baboons who were introduced into a savannah baboon group soon learned to cease following males and formed no particular attachments with any individuals.

Interestingly, males who were transferred from one species to another failed to modify their behavior. Male savannah baboons who were introduced into hamadryas groups, for example, never learned to herd females as hamadryas males did.

Did the females' ability to adjust to their adopted groups involve any hypothesis about the nature of social structure and relationships in these groups? Was their rapid learning due entirely to the experience of being attacked or did it also involve observation and deduction? We simply do not know the mechanisms that underlie a monkey's understanding of its social environment. While a monkey's conception of social relationships may be abstract and independent of the particular individuals involved, it may also be relatively stimulus-bound and limited to the general types of bonds to which the monkey has been exposed (see also D'Amato, Salmon, & Colombo, 1985). It remains possible, in short, that monkeys are primatologists who have spent too much time studying a single species, or living in the same group.

Monkeys' representations of social relationships may be limited in at least two other respects. First, while the animals may be able to represent social relationships in their minds, we do not know if they ever make use of such representations in reasoning or computation. Consider, for instance, the different ways in which human primatologists on the one hand and monkeys on the other deal with the simultaneous existence of close bonds among kin and the attractiveness of high rank. Humans can readily see that these two principles will be additive for high-ranking families and counteractive for low-ranking families. We deduce, therefore, that high-ranking families will be more cohesive than low-ranking families, a prediction that is borne out by data (Cheney & Seyfarth, 1990b; Seyfarth, 1980). At present, however, we have no evidence that the monkeys themselves recognize this difference: no evidence, for example, that a middle-ranking female distinguishes the relations that exist in high-ranking matrilines from the relations that exist in low-ranking matrilines. More important, even if such data were to emerge, it would be essential to distinguish between information that the middle-ranking female had acquired through observation and experience (high-ranking mothers, for instance, support their offspring in alliances at higher rates than do low-ranking mothers) and information that the middle-ranking female had acquired through deduction. Indeed, with the exception of data on the recognition of other animals' dominance ranks, we presently have no evidence that computation plays a major role either in the monkeys' representations of social relationships or in their representations of word meaning. In this respect, representations of social phenomena may differ fundamentally from the representations of rate, time, and space used by birds and other animals when computing and comparing feeding returns at alternative food patches (see also Gallistel, 1990 for reviews).

Second, as noted earlier, we have no evidence that monkeys can label social relationships or give names to the criteria they use in classifying them. While certain primate vocalizations do function in a manner that effectively labels different predators (Seyfarth, Cheney, & Marler, 1980) or different classes of conspecifics (e.g., Cheney & Seyfarth, 1982a; Gouzoules, Gouzoules, & Marler, 1984), monkeys apparently have no calls referring to "close partners," "friends," "enemies" or "strangers" that could be used to classify relationships. Whether they could learn such terms under the appropriate conditions remains an open question: None of the ape language studies has ever asked subjects about each others' relationships.

Among adult humans, accurate use of a word like "friend" implies that we recognize the necessary and sufficient characteristics for membership in this category, and hence that we can apply the category's label correctly in novel situations. If the presence or absence of a label is some measure of an individual's awareness of classes and of relations between classes, then the ability of monkeys to compare relationships and generalize to novel situations may be severely limited.

The apparent lack of vocalizations to describe different types of relationships may be symptomatic of a larger problem: The monkeys are unaware of their own knowledge. In Paul Rozin's (1976) terms, a monkey's knowledge of social relationships or word meaning may be "inaccessible." While the monkey can classify familiar relationships into types and even compare social relationships involving different individuals, he may not be able to examine his own knowledge, label it, apply it to new stimuli, or use it to deduce new knowledge. In addition, perhaps because the monkey cannot reflect on what he knows about others, he may be unable to attribute motives and hence understand why some relationships are alike and others are quite different.

We have argued that in order to succeed socially monkeys must be able to predict the behavior of others. To do this well they cannot rely on memorizing single interactions but must instead deal in abstractions, comparing the relationships that exist among others. For humans, the quest to predict behavior prompts us to search still further, for the factors that cause some relations to be different from others. A monkey that can compare social relationships is better able to predict the behavior of others than one who simply memorizes all the interactions he has observed. Vastly more powerful abilities to interpret other animals' behavior accrue to the individual who can attribute motives to others and classify relationships on the basis of these motives (Humphrey, 1980; Whiten & Byrne, 1988a, 1988b).

There are hints that nonhuman primates might occasionally attribute motives to one another (e.g., Byrne & Whiten, 1988; de Waal, 1982; Kummer, 1982; Premack & Woodruff, 1978). Most examples, however, are anecdotal, and they are largely restricted to chimpanzees. Whether monkeys ever attribute states of mind to each other and whether they recognize that different states of mind are the cause of different social relationships, is an open question. In most cases, it is as easy to explain the behavior of monkeys in terms of learned behavioral contingencies as in terms of the attribution of mental states (see Cheney & Seyfarth, 1990b for a review). We have good evidence that monkeys are adept at understanding each others' behavior and relationships; what remains to be determined is whether they are also adept at understanding each others' *minds*.

References

Allen, C. (1989). *Philosophical issues in cognitive ethology.* Unpublished Ph.D. thesis, University of California, Los Angeles.

Altmann, J. (1980). *Baboon mothers and infants.* Cambridge, MA: Harvard University Press.

Altmann, S.A. (1981). Dominance relationships: The Cheshire cat's grin? *Behavioral Brain Sciences, 4,* 430–431.

Bachmann, C., & Kummer, H. (1980). Male assessment of female choice in hamadryas baboons. *Behavioral Ecology and Sociobiology, 6,* 315–321.

Boysen, S.T., & Berntson, G.G. (1989). Numerical competence in a chimpanzee (*Pan troglodytes*). *Journal of Comparative Psychology, 103,* 23–31.

Breslow, L. (1981). Reevaluation of the literature on the development of transitive inferences. *Psychological Bulletin, 89,* 325–351.

Brooks, R.J., & Falls, J.B. (1975). Individual recognition by song in white-throated sparrows, III. Song features used in individual recognition. *Canadian Journal of Zoology, 53,* 1749–1761.

Bryant, P.E., & Trabasso, T. (1971). Transitive inferences and memory in young children. *Nature, 240,* 456–458.

Byrne, R., & Whiten, A. (Eds.). (1988). *Machiavellian intelligence.* Oxford: Oxford University Press.

Capaldi, E.J., & Miller, D.J. (1988). Counting in rats: Its functional significance and the independent cognitive processes which comprise it. *Journal of Experimental Psychology: Animal Behavior Processes, 14,* 3–17.

Cheney, D.L., & Seyfarth, R.M. (1980). Vocal recognition in vervet monkeys. *Animal Behavior, 28,* 362–367.

Cheney, D.L., & Seyfarth, R.M. (1982a). How vervet monkeys perceive their grunts: Field playback experiments. *Animal Behavior, 30,* 739–751.

Cheney, D.L., & Seyfarth, R.M. (1982b). Recognition of individuals within and across groups of free-ranging vervet monkeys. *American Zoology, 22,* 519–529.

Cheney, D.L., & Seyfarth, R.M. (1982c). Social knowledge in nonhuman primates. Paper presented at the bi-annual meeting of the International Primatological Society, Atlanta, GA.

Cheney, D.L., & Seyfarth, R.M. (1986). The recognition of social alliances among vervet monkeys. *Animal Behavior, 34,* 1722–1731.

Cheney, D.L., & Seyfarth, R.M. (1987). The influence of intergroup competition on the survival and reproduction of female vervet monkeys. *Behavioral Ecology and Sociobiology, 21,* 375–386.

Cheney, D.L., & Seyfarth, R.M. (1988). Assessment of meaning and the detection of unreliable signals by vervet monkeys. *Animal Behaviour, 36,* 477–486.

Cheney, D.L., & Seyfarth, R.M. (1990a). Reconciliation and redirected aggression in vervet monkeys (*Cercopithecus aethiops*). *Behaviour, 110*, 258–275.

Cheney, D.L., & Seyfarth, R.M. (1990b). *How monkeys see the world: Inside the mind of another species*. Chicago: University of Chicago Press.

Church, R.M., & Broadbent, H.A. (1990). Alternative representations of time, number, and rate. *Cognition, 37*, this issue.

Church, R.M., & Meck, W.H. (1984). The numerical attribute of stimuli. In H.L. Roitblat, T.G. Bever, & H.S. Terrace (Eds.), *Animal cognition*. Hillsdale, NJ: Erlbaum.

Cords, M. (1988). Resolution of aggressive conflicts by immature long-tail macaques. (*Macaca fascicularis*). *Animal Behavior, 36*, 1124–1136.

D'Amato, M., & Colombo, M. (1988). Representation of serial order in monkeys (*Cebus apella*). *Journal of Experimental Psychology: Animal Behavior Processes, 14*, 131–139.

D'Amato, M., & Colombo, M. (in press). The symbolic distance effect in monkeys (*Cebus apella*). *Animal Learning and Behavior*.

D'Amato, M., & Salmon, D.P. (1984). Cognitive processes in *Cebus* monkeys. In H. Roitblat, T.G. Bever, & H.S. Terrace (Eds.), *Animal cognition*. Hillsdale, NJ: Erlbaum.

D'Amato, M., Salmon, D.P., & Colombo, M. (1985). Extent and limits of the matching concept in monkeys (*Cebus apella*). *Journal of Experimental Psychology: Animal Behavior Processes, 11*, 35–51.

D'Amato, M., Salmon, D.P., Loukas, E., & Tomie, A. (1985). Symmetry and transitivity of conditional relations in monkeys (*Cebus apella*) and pigeons (*Columba livia*). *Journal of the Experimental Analysis of Behavior, 44*, 35–47.

D'Amato, M., & van Sant, P. (1988). The person concept in monkeys (*Cebus apella*). *Journal of Experimental Psychology: Animal Behavior Processes, 14*, 43–55.

Dasser, V. (1985). Cognitive complexity in primate social relationships. In R.A. Hinde, A. Perret-Clermont, & J. Stevenson-Hinde (Eds.), *Social relationships and cognitive development* (pp. 9–22). Oxford: Oxford University Press.

Dasser, V. (1988a). A social concept in Java monkeys. *Animal Behavior, 36*, 225–230.

Dasser, V. (1988b). Mapping social concepts in monkeys. In R.W. Byrne & A. Whiten (Eds.), *Machiavellian intelligence* (pp. 85–93). Oxford: Oxford University Press.

Davis, R.T., Leary, R.W., Stevens, D.A., & Thompson, R.F. (1967). Learning and perception of oddity problems by lemurs and seven species of monkey. *Primates, 8*, 311–322.

de Waal, F. (1982). *Chimpanzee politics*. New York: Harper & Row.

de Waal, F. (1989). *Peacemaking among primates*. Cambridge: Harvard University Press.

de Waal, F., & Ren, R.M. (1988). Comparison of the reconciliation behavior of stumptail and rhesus macaques. *Ethology, 78*, 129–142.

de Waal, F., & Roosmalen, A. van (1979). Reconciliation and consolation among chimpanzees. *Behavior, Ecology aand Sociobiology, 5*, 55–66.

de Waal, F., & Yoshihara, D. (1983). Reconciliation and redirected aggression in rhesus monkeys. *Behaviour, 85*, 224–241.

Dickinson, A. (1980). *Contemporary animal learning theory*. Cambridge: Cambridge University Press.

Dufty, A.M. (1986). Singing and the establishment and maintenance of dominance hierarchies in captive brown-headed cowbirds. *Behavioral Ecology and Sociobiology, 19*, 49–55.

Dunbar, R.I.M. (1983). Structure of gelada baboon reproductive units, 3: The male's relationships with his females. *Animal Behavior, 31*, 565–575.

Emlen, S.T. (1971). The role of song in individual recognition in the indigo bunting. *Zeitschrift für Tierpsychologie, 28*, 241–246.

Essock-Vitale, S., & Seyfarth, R.M. (1987). Intelligence and social cognition. In B. Smuts, D.L. Cheney, R.M. Seyfarth, R.W. Wrangham, & T. Struhsaker (Eds.), *Primate societies* (pp. 452–461). Chicago: University of Chicago Press.

Frame, L.H., Malcolm, J.R., Frame, G.W., & van Lawick, H. (1979). Social organization of African wild dogs (*Lycaon pictus*) on the Serengeti plains, Tanzania, 1967–1978. *Zeitschrift für Tierpsychologie, 50*, 225–249.

Frank, L. (1986). Social organization of the spotted hyaena (*Crocuta crocuta*), II. Dominance and reproduction. *Animal Behavior, 34*, 1510–1527.

Frederickson, W.T., & Sackett, G.P. (1984). Kin preferences in primates (*Macaca nemestrina*): Relatedness or familiarity? *Journal of Comparative Psychology, 98*, 29–34.

Gallistel, C.R. (1989). Animal cognition: The representation of space, time, and number. *Annual Review of Psychology, 40*, 155–189.

Gallistel, C.R. (1990). *The organization of learning*. Cambridge, MA: Bradford Books/MIT Press.

Gibbon, J., & Church, R.M. (1990). Representation of time. *Cognition, 37*, this issue.

Gillan, D. (1981). Reasoning in the chimpanzee, II. Transitive inference. *Journal of Experimental Psychology: Animal Behavior Processes, 7*, 150–164.

Gillan, D., Premack, D., & Woodruff, G. (1981). Reasoning in the chimpanzee, I. Analogical reasoning. *Journal of Experimental Psychology: Animal Behavior Processes, 7*, 1–17.

Gouzoules, H. (1975). Maternal rank and early social interactions of infant stumptail macaques (*Macaca arctoides*). *Primates, 16*, 405–418.

Gouzoules, S. (1984). Primate mating systems, kin associations, and cooperative behavior: Evidence for kin recognition? *Yearbook of Physiological Anthropology, 27*, 99–134.

Gouzoules, S., & Gouzoules, H. (1987). Kinship. In B. Smuts, D.L. Cheney, R.M. Seyfarth, R.W. Wrangham, & T. Struhsaker (Eds.), *Primate societies* (pp. 299–305). Chicago: University of Chicago Press.

Gouzoules, S., Gouzoules, H., & Marler, P. (1984). Rhesus monkeys' screams: Representational communication in the recruitment of agonistic aid. *Animal Behavior, 32*, 182–193.

Hansen, E.W. (1976). Selective responding by recently separated juvenile rhesus monkeys to the calls of their mothers. *Developmental Psychobiology, 9*, 83–88.

Harcourt, A. (1988). Alliances in contests and social intelligence. In R. Byrne & A. Whiten (Eds.), *Machiavellian intelligence: Social expertise and the evolution of intellect in monkeys, apes, and humans* (pp. 132–152). Oxford: Oxford University Press.

Herrnstein, R.J. (1990). Levels of stimulus control: A functional approach. *Cognition, 37*, this issue.

Herrnstein, R., & Loveland, D.H. (1964). Complex visual concept in the pigeon. *Science, 146*, 549–551.

Hinde, R.A. (1974). *Biological bases of human social behavior*. New York: McGraw-Hill.

Hinde, R.A. (1976). Interactions, relationships, and social structure. *Man, 11*, 1–17.

Hinde, R.A. (1983). A conceptual framework. In R.A. Hinde (Ed.), *Primate social relationships: An integrated approach* (pp. 1–7). Oxford: Blackwell.

Humphrey, N.K. (1976). The social function of intellect. In P.P.G. Bateson & R.A. Hinde (Eds.), *Growing points in ethology* (pp. 303–318). Cambridge: Cambridge University Press.

Humphrey, N.K. (1980). Nature's psychologists. In B. Josephson & V. Ramachandran (Eds.), *Consciousness and the physical world*. London: Pergamon.

Judge, P. (1982). Redirection of aggression based on kinship in a captive group of pigtail macaques (abstract). *American Journal of Primatology, 3*, 301.

Judge, P. (1983). Reconciliation based on kinship in a captive group of pigtail macaques (abstract). *American Journal of Primatology, 4*, 346.

Kaplan, J.N., Winship-Ball, A., & Sim, L. (1978). Maternal discrimination of infant vocalizations in squirrel monkeys. *Primates, 19*, 187–193.

Kaufmann, J.H. (1965). A three-year study of mating behavior in a free-ranging band of rhesus monkeys. *Ecology, 46*, 500–512.

Kroodsma, D. (1976). The effect of large song repertoires on neighbor "recognition" in male song sparrows. *Condor, 78*, 97–99.

Kummer, H. (1968). *Social organization of hamadryas baboons*. Chicago: University of Chicago Press.

Kummer, H. (1982). Social knowledge in free-ranging primates. In D.R. Griffin (Ed.), *Animal mind – human mind* (pp. 113–130). New York: Springer-Verlag.

Kummer, H., Goetz, W., & Angst, W. (1970). Cross-species modification of social behavior in baboons. In J.R. Napier & P.H. Napier (Eds.), *Old world monkeys: Evolution, systematics and behavior* (pp. 351–364). New York: Academic Press.

Kummer, H., Goetz, W., & Angst, W. (1974). Triadic differentiation: An inhibitory process protecting pair bonds in baboons. *Behaviour, 49*, 62–87.

Lea, S. (1984). In what sense do pigeons learn concepts? In H.L. Roitblat, T.G. Bever, & H.S. Terrace (Eds.), *Animal cognition*. Hillsdale, NJ: Erlbaum.

Matsuzawa, T. (1985). Use of numbers by a chimpanzee. *Nature, 315*, 57–59.

McGonigle, B.O., & Chalmers, M. (1977). Are monkeys logical? *Nature, 267*, 694–696.

Medin, D.L., & Smith, E.E. (1984). Concepts and concept formation. *Annual Review of Psychology, 35*, 113–138.

Pepperberg, I.M. (1983). Cognition in the African grey parrot: Preliminary evidence for auditor/vocal comprehension of the class concept. *Animal Learning and Behavior, 11*, 179–185.

Pepperberg, I.M. (1987). Acquisition of the same/different concept by an African grey parrot (*Psittacus erithacus*): Learning with respect to categories of color, shape, and material. *Animal Learning and Behavior, 15*, 423–432.

Petrinovich, L. (1974). Individual recognition of pup vocalizations by northern elephant seal mothers. *Zeitschrift für Tierpsychologie, 34*, 308–312.

Popp, J.W. (1987). Choice of opponents during competition for food among American goldfinches. *Ethology, 75*, 31–36.

Premack, D. (1976). *Intelligence in ape and man*. Hillsdale, NJ: Erlbaum.

Premack, D. (1983). The codes of man and beast. *Behavioral Brain Sciences, 6*, 125–167.

Premack, D. (1986). *Gavagai! or the future history of the animal language controversy*. Cambridge: MIT Press.

Premack, D., & Woodruff, G. (1978). Does the chimpanzee have a theory of mind? *Behavioral and Brain Sciences, 1*, 515–526.

Rescorla, R.A. (1988). Pavlovian conditioning: It's not what you think it is. *American Psychology, 43*, 151–160.

Roberts, W.A., & Mazmanian, D.S. (1988). Concept learning at different levels of abstraction by pigeons, monkeys, and people. *Journal of Experimental Psychology: Animal Behavior Processes, 14*, 247–260.

Roitblat, H. (1987). *Introduction to comparative cognition*. New York: W.H. Freeman.

Rowher, S. (1982). The evolution of reliable and unreliable badges of fighting ability. *American Zoology, 22*, 531–546.

Rozin, P. (1976). The evolution of intelligence and access to the cognitive unconscious. In J.M. Sprague & A.N. Epstein (Eds.), *Progress in psychobiology and physiological psychology* (Vol. 6, pp. 245–280). New York: Academic Press.

Ryle, G. (1949). *The concept of mind*. London: Hutchinson.

Sands, S.F., Lincoln, C.E., & Wright, A.A. (1982). Pictorial similarity judgments and the organization of visual memory in the rhesus monkey. *Journal of Experimental Psychology: General, 111*, 369–389.

Schrier, A.M., Angarella, R., & Povar, M.L. (1984). Studies of concept formation by stumptail monkeys: Concepts, humans, monkeys, and the letter A. *Journal of Experimental Psychology: Animal Behavior Processes, 10*, 564–584.

Schrier, A.M., & Brady, P.M. (1987). Categorization of natural stimuli by monkeys (*Macaca mulatta*): Effects of stimulus set size and modification of exemplars. *Journal of Experimental Psychology: Animal Behavior Processes, 13*, 136–143.

Schusterman, R.J. (1988). Animal language research: Marine mammals re-enter the controversy. In H.J. Jerison & I. Jerison (Eds.), *Evolutionary biology and intelligence* (pp. 319–349). Heidelberg: Springer-Verlag.

Scott, L. (1984). Reproductive behavior of adolescent female baboons (*Papio anubis*) in Kenya. In M. Small (Ed.), *Female primates: Studies by women primatologists* (pp. 77–102). New York: Alan R. Liss.

Seyfarth, R.M. (1976). Social relationships among adult female baboons. *Animal Behavior, 24*, 917–938.

Seyfarth, R.M. (1978). Social relationships among adult male and female baboons. II. Behaviour throughout the female reproductive cycle. *Behaviour, 64*, 227–247.

Seyfarth, R.M. (1980). The distribution of grooming and related behaviors among adult female vervet monkeys. *Animal Behavior, 28*, 798–813.

Seyfarth, R.M., Cheney, D.L., & Marler, P. (1980). Vervet monkey alarm calls: Semantic communication in a free-ranging primate. *Animal Behavior, 28*, 1070–1094.

Sigg, H., Stolba, A.A., Abegglen, H., & Dasser, V. (1982). Life history of hamadryas baboons: Physical development, infant mortality, reproductive parameters, and family relationships. *Primates, 23*, 473–487.

Smuts, B.B. (1983). Dynamics of "special relationships" between adult male and female olive baboons. In R.A. Hinde (Ed.), *Primate social relationships: An integrated approach* (pp. 262–266). Oxford: Blackwell.

Smuts, B.B. (1985). *Sex and friendship in baboons.* Hawthorne, NY: Aldine.

Stammbach, E. (1987). Desert, forest, and montane baboons: Multilevel societies. In B. Smuts, D.L. Cheney, R.M. Seyfarth, R.W. Wrangham, & T. Struhsaker (Eds.), *Primate societies* (pp. 112–120). Chicago: University of Chicago Press.

Stewart, K.J., & Harcourt, A.H. (1987). Gorillas: Variation in female relationships. In B. Smuts, D.L. Cheney, R.M. Seyfarth, R.W. Wrangham, & T. Struhsaker (Eds.), *Primate societies* (pp. 155–164). Chicago: University of Chicago Press.

Strong, P.N., & Hedges, M. (1966). Comparative studies in simple oddity learning, 1: Cats, raccoons, monkeys, and chimpanzees. *Psychonomic Sciences, 5*, 13–14.

Strum, S.C. (1984). Why males use infants. In D.M. Taub (Ed.), *Primate paternalism* (pp. 146–185). New York: Van Nostrand Rheinhold.

Waldman, B., Frumhoff, P., & Sherman, P. (1987). Problems of kin recognition. *Trends in Ecological Evolution, 3*, 8–13.

Walters, J.R. (1987). Transition to adulthood. In B. Smuts, D.L. Cheney, R.M. Seyfarth, R.W. Wrangham, & T. Struhsaker (Eds.), *Primate societies* (pp. 358–369). Chicago: University of Chicago Press.

Walters, J.R., & Seyfarth, R.M. (1987). Conflict and cooperation. In B. Smuts, D.L. Cheney, R.M. Seyfarth, R.W. Wrangham, & T.T. Struhsaker (Eds.), *Primate societies* (pp. 306–317). Chicago: University of Chicago Press.

Waser, P. (1977). Individual recognition, intragroup cohesion, and intergroup spacing: Evidence from sound playback to forest monkeys. *Behaviour, 60*, 28–74.

Whiten, A., & Byrne, R.W. (1988a). Taking (Machiavellian) intelligence apart: Editorial. In R.W. Byrne & A. Whiten (Eds.), *Machiavellian intelligence* (pp. 50–66). Oxford: Oxford University Press.

Whiten, A., & Byrne, R.W. (1988b). The Machiavellian intelligence hypothesis: Editorial. In R.W. Byrne & A. Whiten (Eds.), *Machiavellian intelligence* (pp. 1–10). Oxford: Oxford University Press.

Wilson, E.O. (1971). *The insect societies.* Cambridge: Harvard University Press.

Yasukawa, K. (1979). A fair advantage in animal confrontations. *New Science, 84*, 366–368.

York, A.D., & Rowell, T.E. (1988). Reconciliation following aggression in patas monkeys (*Erythrocebus patas*). *Animal Behavior, 36*, 502–509.

Index

Note: Pages in italics indicate illustrations.